WENSLEY CLARKSON

HELL HATH NO FURY LIKE A WOMAN SCORNED

BLAKE

Published by Blake Publishing Ltd,
3, Bramber Court, 2 Bramber Road,
London W14 9PB, England

First published in 2003

ISBN 185782556X

British Library Cataloguing-in-Publication Data:

A catalogue record for this book is available from the British Library.

Design by www.envydesign.co.uk

Printed in Great Britain by CPD (Wales)

1 3 5 7 9 10 8 6 4 2

Papers used by Blake Publishing are natural, recyclable products made from wood
grown in sustainable forests. The manufacturing processes conform to the
environmental regulations of the country of origin.

Every attempt has been made to contact the relevant copyright-holders, but some
were unobtainable. We would be grateful if the appropriate people could contact us.

To all the victims…
they will never be forgotten.

CONTENTS

1

THE LESBIAN
VAMPIRE KILLERS

The sound of cricket-song mingled with the gentle lapping of the river. Every now and again passing cars lit up the roadside as they weaved their way home. The lights from nearby houses went out as their owners retired to bed.

Suddenly, a metallic green saloon span out of the darkness and screeched to a halt in the dusty car park of the Lew-Mors nightclub. The ten-year-old Holden Commodore had definitely seen better days. An entirely functional car, it was often described as the Vauxhall Viva of Australia. It's shape designed with common sense — and absolutely no style — in mind.

But that didn't worry Bobby. She was a tough, brutal, masculine woman. More concerned with sex, drink and drugs than the remotest thoughts of family responsibilities or any of the standard domestic concerns.

She stumbled into the Lew-Mors with three girlfriends. She was already drunk from having consumed at least ten beers in a tiny bar just half a mile away. As she entered the club, she passed through the tatty lobby and caught a glimpse of herself in a mirror and grimaced. She hated mirrors. They were a sad reflection of her inner self. Then she felt a strange pain in her head. And it wasn't caused by the loud music blaring out from the dance floor.

This was a pain from within. Bobby was fighting something — but she did not know what.

Once inside the club, Bobby's notoriously promiscuous temperament

1

took over. She had spotted an attractive woman sitting with a friend in a corner of the club traditionally reserved for those seeking a new partner.

The girl was in her early twenties and had medium length brown hair. It was difficult to tell what her figure was like but her bizarre outfit was arousing a lot of attention. Precisely what was intended. She wore a long black coat, stockings, high-heeled shoes and a white tuxedo-style shirt with a black bow tie. She seemed almost satanic. That really appealed to Bobby.

Their eyes met instantly. They both knew what the other was thinking. Bobby's pals were at the bar buying drinks. She loved to tease and flirt first — it was always much more fun. As her friends brought over the beers, Bobby turned her back to the girl in the corner. Every now and again she would sneak a glimpse of her.

The three friends supped greedily at their drinks. But Bobby's mind was on that girl, her vivid imagination working overtime. She was seeing her partly clothed on a bed. Vulnerable, excited, desperate. She wanted her. She would have her.

Bobby's sexual drive knew few boundaries. After all, here she was preparing for her next conquest, just a few hours after making brutal love to the girl she lived with. They had both arrived home early from college and neither of their two other flatmates were around. Bobby had grabbed her from behind in the kitchen and smothered her neck in kisses. At first her friend resisted, but Bobby was forceful and strong. Soon she was holding her down as she ground into her body. It was all over in minutes but that sexual drive was satisfied — at least for a while.

Back in the club, one of Bobby's friends was telling a crude joke. But they were all well aware that Bobby wasn't listening.

'She's all yours. Stop fantasising. Just get over there and pull her.'

This was a Friday night in Brisbane, Australia. The whole town was out to enjoy the weekend. In these sunny climes, it was an excuse to commit a multitude of sins.

That was all the prompting Bobby needed. She could already feel her heart beat faster with excitement. A sexual thrill was rushing through her body, even though she hadn't spoken to the girl yet.

With black trousers and black tee shirt, hobnail boots and an ever present pair of wire rimmed sunglasses, Bobby hardly exuded glamour. But, in a club like the Lew-Mors, no one exactly dressed up for dinner.

The place was full of hard cases — all hoping to find a passion partner to share their bodies with. The dance floor was poorly lit. Soul music throbbed out of the loud speakers as couples gyrated together.

2

Bobby turned to face her admirer once more and their eyes met again. This time she did not hesitate. As she strode confidently over to the table, the girl squirmed expectantly in her seat. Lisa knew she was about to be swept off her feet.

The two talked a while. But deep, meaningful conversation was not exactly high on their list of priorities. They both knew what the other wanted.

That night was Friday the thirteenth of October, 1989.

Unlucky for some …

Lisa Ptaschinski curled up beside her sleeping lover. They had met just a few hours earlier, but she felt as if they had known each other for most of their life. On both her wrists were two tiny fresh scabs. Lisa looked at them and once more felt a rush to her brain as she remembered the sexual thrill she had experienced less than an hour before.

Within seconds of getting back to the apartment, these two strangers were exploring every inch of each other's bodies. After their first climax, both wanted more not less.

It was then that Lisa discovered her partner liked to play a game that even she had never tried before. As the two lovers lay back to recover from that first crescendo, they started to talk about blood. The taste of it. The smell of it. Even the colour of it. The more they talked about blood, the more excited Bobby became.

She was disarmingly frank: 'I think I'm a vampire. I can't resist blood. Its taste. Even its texture. Something inside me craves for it.'

For a moment Lisa stopped and stared at Bobby. Then she felt really good. Her brand new lover was already revealing her innermost thoughts to her. She wanted to please Bobby in every way.

Then, without a word, Lisa got up out of bed. A look of disappointment came over her lover's face. She presumed that she was getting up to go. But within moments Lisa had returned. Armed with a pointed kitchen knife she said simply, 'Surprise …'

The tiny droplets of blood had to be literally coaxed out of Lisa's veins at first. But as her lover sucked harder, she felt a slight, but pleasurable pain from her wrist. Then the sucking got even stronger and she could feel the excitement building up inside. As a gesture of her passion, Lisa then stabbed gently at the vein on her other wrist and watched as her lover's face looked up at her, a tiny drip of blood dribbling down the side of the mouth as it curled into a smile of satisfaction, just like a cat who's got the cream.

Every now and again, Bobby kissed the tender flesh near Lisa's wrist, as if to assure her that she wasn't just into blood. But it was purely a token gesture for, within seconds, she would return to her favoured feast. She was captivated by Lisa's flawless complexion. Her skin really was as perfect as it looked. And it felt as smooth as syrup.

Lisa's legs were ever so slightly parted as Bobby sucked deeper and deeper into her. She could feel her breath speeding up. This was as exciting as those first days of sexual experimentation she had carried out at her convent school in Sydney. Lisa loved to feel she could constantly supply pleasure. It was almost more important to her than receiving satisfaction.

Now Bobby was gently moaning to herself – the excitement carrying a throaty noise that she emitted from within. It was a strange noise – sometimes high pitched, sometimes deep. A struggling noise.

Now the groans of pleasure were becoming louder as Lisa and Bobby moaned in unison. Bobby's sounds were sheer enjoyment. Lisa's were an extraordinary combination of pain and pleasure. The pain from the sucking, the pleasure came from giving.

As the pewter light of dawn shone through the opened window, the lovers continued, oblivious to the outside world. Locked in a dangerous, erotic world from which neither wanted to escape.

The Observer looked in at the scene. One lover lay on her back with her wrists flat on the bed as her partner feasted on the blood.

Neither of them noticed that a third party had entered the room. They were so wrapped up in the passion and the pain that they were oblivious to their surroundings.

'This is sick,' muttered the Observer to herself, disgusted by the scene before her. Appalled. Yet fascinated. So she stayed in the room as the two lovers writhed, explored … and drank.

She wanted to stop them but something prevented her. Something made her stay there and witness this degradation. But she did not know what. And she did not know why …

Next morning, the two lovers held hands tightly at every available opportunity. With each squeezing motion, Lisa felt a slight twinge of pain in the scabs on her wrists. But it was a bearable pain. A sacrifice worth making for the one she adored.

As Bobby made breakfast, eight-year-old Tracey Wigginton appeared. She was a regular visitor to the flat. A child whose very presence was difficult to ever explain.

'What are you doing?' she asked in the blunt manner that only a child can

4

get away with. 'Are you in love?' Bobby looked embarrassed. After all how could she explain her actions to an eight-year-old? Love is something that children have an instinct for – and they are usually right.

Little Tracey was desperate for love. She was brought up by her grandparents. But actually they were not really her mother's parents. To make matters worse, her step-grandfather abused her. Verbally by day and sexually by night. She had never forgotten how he used to get in her bed. Her life was messed up and she longed for security. That's why she often came into Bobby's life.

She missed out on real, normal emotions and could only relate to the harsh reality of a miserable, tortured environment. Now she was trying to make up for lost time … She soon disappeared from the apartment as quickly as she had arrived …

In less than twenty-four hours, Bobby and Lisa became close – close enough that Bobby decided to introduce Lisa to her great friends Tracey Waugh and Kim Jervis. Lisa was reluctant at first. After all, why should Bobby want her to meet two of her other women friends? They were probably lovers as well. She already felt pangs of jealousy. But Bobby was very forceful about it. 'You'll love them. We can all have a good time together.'

Lisa knew there was no way out – and maybe Bobby was right. When she wanted her own way, she usually got it.

As it happened, the foursome got on famously. Lisa's fears were unfounded. She started to not even care if Bobby had slept with any of them.

Tracey was twenty-four, an unemployed secretary. Dressed in a more feminine sort of way than her friends she seemed altogether a softer sort of character. Kim, the same age, was the only member of the group with a full-time job – as a photo processor. An attention grabbing kind of girl, she lapped up every word uttered by Bobby. Appreciative of the friendship and all that could lead to.

As they all drank their ice cool beer and swapped tales of life, Lisa happily acknowledged to herself that she was being swept up by Bobby and her friends. She'd always wanted a close circle of companions. Now she had found one.

Then Kim cracked a joke about blood. The table went silent. Bobby breathed – sharply. If they had been in a restaurant or bar, perhaps the atmosphere would have swept the conversation forward and everyone would have simply ignored the remark. But this scene was being played out in Kim's spotless suburban apartment in the Clayfield area of Brisbane. The atmosphere already bordered on the intimate. Now there was a chance to take it a stage further.

Bobby dimmed the lights and returned to the table where they were all sitting. She obviously had something important to contribute. Turning to her self-appointed protégé, Kim, she said coolly, 'I want to scare you.'

The other three sat in total silence.

Bobby removed her sunglasses and stared straight into their eyes, each in turn.

'She wanted to use her mind to make us compatible,' explained Kim later. Quite simply, Bobby wanted to mind control her friends. She wanted to have the power over them that she lusted for constantly.

But first, she wanted to make Kim her 'destroyer'. That role meant Kim would become her disciple. Her messenger of all things.

The atmosphere was tightening by the second. Only Tracey remained somewhat sceptical but, as she was later to recall, 'I was powerless to do anything. She had us in the palm of her hand.'

Bobby was getting tough. 'I have satanic powers and you will all become my disciples in time.'

Lisa was fascinated. This sort of experience was what she had been looking for all her life. She was vulnerable. She desperately needed to be led – and Bobby was providing that lead.

Bobby got up from the table and picked a thick photo album out of a drawer in a nearby cupboard. She then spread the pictures across the table – about fifteen in all. They were all shots of headstones from nearby Harrisville Cemetery.

Bobby was convinced that each of the featured graves belonged to the devil. She talked of how they would come out at night and drive people to commit evil crimes.

'This is the way of the devil. You must realise this,' she said, her strange voice veering from low, deep tones to a high, almost falsetto, shrill.

At no stage did any of the women even so much as question her claims – only Tracey had any doubts and she knew that now was not the time to air them.

It was only later that Tracey realised the significance of the fact that all the curtains in the apartment were closed, even though it was still daylight outside. The only explanation at the time was that Bobby was sensitive to sunlight. They had always been aware that she hated to go out in the day.

But Bobby was now concerned with bringing the conversation around to vampires.

'They do exist. I know. I am one,' she insisted. 'I need blood. I must have it.'

The women watched in silence as Bobby went up to the fridge and took out a white butcher's plastic bag filled with blood. She devoured the entire contents, carelessly, or perhaps thirstily, spilling drops on her tee shirt.

At that moment Tracey spotted the tiny scabs on Lisa's wrists and smiled a knowing smile. They were all becoming Bobby's disciples.

'I hunger for blood all the time. I need it in me,' continued Bobby. No one sitting there was in the slightest bit surprised.

Bobby openly revealed she had feasted on the blood of virtually every type of livestock animal. She was a regular at a handful of butchers' shops in the area near her home. They learned not to raise an eyebrow at her bizarre requests for vast quantities of pig's blood. It had become a necessity as well as an obsession. Each day, she said, she had to drink blood.

But, animal blood did not really satisfy the appetite within her.

There was another, deeper need. And she wanted to feed it, to nurture it until it consumed her. Every other person at that table had, at one time or other, given into Bobby's demands. They all had the telltale scabs on their wrists.

Bobby wanted more than just an ounce or two of blood this time. She wanted pints of the stuff. Human blood. And it had to be fresh because 'that way it is cleaner and smoother and tastier.'

She added chillingly, 'By the time our man hits the ground his throat will be cut and he'll be dead.' Then she put a proposition to her friends. 'Help me find a victim.'

Ted Baldock was in a pretty good mood. It was Friday afternoon and soon he would be finished work for the weekend. A weekend that would no doubt include the two extremes of his life as a father-of-five – drunkenness and domesticity.

The weather was swelteringly hot. About ninety-five degrees in the shade. Brisbane in October was like a July day in New York. Sweat dripped off his lean shoulders.

For Ted it was harder than most. No air-conditioned office for him to sit back in. His workplace was the roads of the city and his 'typewriter' was a pneumatic drill that throbbed and hammered into the sun-baked tarmac.

Ted had struggled hard for nearly thirty years to support his huge family. He and wife Elaine had found it pretty difficult at times. But they had survived all the ups and downs that married life could throw at them. Ted had a thick skin that proved ideal for a lifelong marriage. Now, at forty-seven, he was starting to look forward to retirement, a pension and the blissful relaxation after years of providing. Maybe a bit of fishing, probably a fair deal of boozing. But no pressures. No demands.

His body ached with exhaustion from the hard week he had endured. Ted was not your macho-muscle man like many of his colleagues on the road repair squad for Brisbane City Council. He was a modest sort of fellow. Not prone to even taking his shirt off in public – let alone flaunting his biceps. Elaine and many of his friends at home in the West End district of Brisbane were always telling Ted not to overdo it.

As he jerked the drill into place for the last time on the roadside, his thoughts were rapidly wandering to the weekend. If he'd known what lay ahead, he'd have stopped thinking there and then ...

The Holden Commodore came to a halt outside Lisa's home in Leichardt. She heard her lover sound the horn twice. As the pretty brown haired girl looked out of the window of the tiny box-built house, their eyes locked. It was almost the same feeling as that first time they had met and seduced each other just seven days earlier.

Landlady Wendy Sugden was curious. She felt a great deal of responsibility for Lisa since the day, just five weeks earlier, they had met at Ipswich General Hospital. Lisa was the patient, and Wendy her nurse had taken her under her wing. They struck up a real friendship.

Lisa looked upon Wendy as a mother figure. Always there when she was needed. Providing a vital support to lean on. Wendy and her husband Wayne had an ordinary little house, but it was clean and tidy and the nearest thing to home that Lisa had ever known. When she told Wendy about Bobby, the nurse frowned. She sounded like trouble but then Lisa was always going to be a problem person.

As Lisa skipped out of the front door to her waiting admirer, she thought back to that first night of outrageous passion. Then, as if to reassure herself, she scratched the top of the tiny scab on her left wrist – just to make sure that every moment of lust they shared had actually happened.

The two lovers kissed deeply within moments of Lisa getting in the car. Lisa could feel the body heat oozing off her partner. If it hadn't still been daylight they might have made love there and then.

Wendy watched everything from a ground floor window, saddened by the inevitability that it would all end in tears ... or worse. She'd seen it all before. Lisa's life revolved around disastrous relationships.

Lisa looked at her lover for a moment as they untangled themselves. A new, darker midnight black hairstyle made the features far more severe than when they last met. She was looking more and more like the vampire she had convinced herself she was.

Lisa did not notice the bulge in Bobby's black jacket pocket. She could only think forward to another night of sex. She knew there was going to be a real 'treat' in store for Bobby this time.

It was a thirty minute drive to the other girls' homes. During that time, Bobby kept saying how hungry she was. How she was looking forward to feasting. Her appetite for blood had definitely increased.

Her thirst would soon be quenched.

But first, they had to pick up Kim and Tracey from their apartments in Clayfield.

Kim and Tracey jumped into the car, chatting rapidly, eager expectation etched on their faces. Once again, Lisa failed to notice another bulge – this time in Kim's pocket.

If she had looked inside that pocket, she would have seen a ninja butterfly pocket knife with a 10 cm blade. Kim had bought it in the nearby Fortitude Valley army disposal shop after they'd discussed their plans …

Ted Baldock was back at the council changing rooms stripping off his filthy work clothes before showering in preparation for a Friday night on the town. Like millions of manual workers the world over, Ted took a great pride in dressing up whenever he went out. It was as if he longed for the clean cut life of an office worker. Wearing a smart pair of slacks and a newly starched shirt was a real pleasure.

For him, the grass was always greener on the other side. There were many things he longed for in life. As he washed himself under a piping hot cascade of water, he felt the energy returning to those tired bones. Ted was looking forward with relish to the first glass of beer of the day. He felt he deserved to treat himself.

For the previous six Fridays, Ted, sometimes with Elaine in tow, had become a regular of the Caledonian Club at Kangaroo Point. It was a rough and ready joint but Ted liked the atmosphere and no one stopped you drinking however much you wanted. You could sup to your heart's content, and no one gave a damn. So long as you didn't puke on the floor, that is.

He'd discovered the place after being taken there by a workmate. It was a great escape from the tedium of a week spent working on the roads and watching mindless TV at his West End home.

As he strolled the short distance from the council changing rooms to the Caledonian, he could literally smell the beer in his nostrils. It was a good feeling. He was going to have a great time tonight. He could feel it in his blood.

The girls had all agreed that the Lew-Mors was the perfect place to start their night out, to savour the anticipation. But Bobby was anxious now. Counting the minutes. It had to be midnight before they could strike. It was no use before then. It had to be just like the Dracula books she used to read so avidly when she was at school.

Instead of beers and spirits, the four friends ordered champagne. This evening was special. Soon they would have something extraordinary to celebrate.

The club manageress was astounded. 'They were buzzing with excitement,' she said when she looked back on that fateful night. And some of the regulars thought the weird foursome were planning an orgy.

As they sat at a table just by the DJs booth, the girls drank a toast … to blood. The blood of a human who still had no idea he was to become their victim.

Ted had spent hours indulging in his favourite game – darts. After a few beers, he was taking on everyone and losing. But no one minded, Ted was a good loser. Always good for a laugh.

He ended the evening holding up the bar. Or perhaps the bar was holding up him. Either way the two inanimate objects were getting along just fine. This sort of vast beer consumption was nothing new for Ted and the barmen were happy to keep on feeding him alcohol because he wasn't making a pest of himself.

Every now and again he would talk to an acquaintance about the meaning of life. But it would only be a passing gesture – nothing of a seriously friendly nature. No one in the bar that evening was a great friend of Ted Baldock.

It was getting towards midnight and that meant it was time for all the Teds of Brisbane to get on their merry way home. As last orders were called, he persuaded a barman to give him one last refill. He downed it quickly, stumbled out into the balmy night, and concentrated, in vain, on finding his way home.

He knew that Elaine – while a loving, caring and patient wife – would not tolerate his non appearance, whatever the excuse.

Across town, Bobby, Lisa, Kim and Tracey were finishing off their second bottle of bubbly.

'What are you celebrating? Love and marriage?' asked one hostess.

The four giggled in expectation. Bobby admired the girl's shapely legs.

'Wouldn't you like to know sweetheart,' she cooed seductively.

Lisa felt a twinge of jealousy. Bobby had the sort of eyes that probed everywhere. Every time a pretty girl passed by, she could sense Bobby's eyes upon their body, sizing up the sex content. She consoled herself by remembering she was hers — even if Bobby did fantasise about the size of the waitress' breasts.

The champagne was now really having an effect and all four felt the headiness unique to France's favourite drink. They felt sensuous, carefree, daring. There was a buzz in the air. Bobby kept talking about her hunger. Her appetite. Her obsession. Blood.

She was the one person at that table who really knew what lay ahead …

Outside the Lew-Mors, the hunt was about to begin. It was dead on midnight. Everything was perfect. Bobby had the expectant look of someone about to win a huge prize.

'I'll drive. Then you can pick one,' said Lisa as they got into Bobby's car. At first, Bobby was reluctant to allow Lisa to drive. She was the 'man' in their relationship and it was her car. But then she saw the sense in what Lisa was saying. No one else could choose the victim except Bobby.

To begin with, they drove at a steady 30 mph towards the Botanic Gardens district of the city. It was a lively night-time area — perfect for what they had in mind. For ten minutes they drove around the streets hovering outside the nightclubs and pubs, but there was no suitable prey.

Then they headed for the New Farm Park area and they soon spotted a lonely figure staggering in a zig-zag along the pavement. The Commodore slowed down. This was what they were looking for.

The man turned and faced straight into the car's headlights. He looked perfect.

But then another man appeared from an alleyway. Two was too many. Too difficult to handle. They had to be patient.

They drove on, disappointed.

Bobby did not feel like being patient. She was hungry. She couldn't wait. It was past midnight. Feeding time.

Then they decided to head for Kangaroo Point. A last resort. There had to be someone around.

The night sounded empty and strangely quiet. It was almost as if a massive storm had passed and left in its wake an eerie, dead calm. A thin, motionless fog hung near the water's edge, catching the silver light of the moon.

Sprawled face down on the pavement lay Ted Baldock. He wasn't actually out cold. But he was definitely suffering. He blinked and waited in the hope that things would come back into focus. He inhaled deep breaths of air to try to compose himself. He had to make it home to Elaine and the children.

Gradually his vision began to clear and he hauled himself up from the ground grasping on to a lamp-post for support. As he clambered to his feet, the headlights of an approaching car shone fiercely in his eyes.

All he could see was a blur of light. He wasn't even sure if it was moving at first. It was only when the vehicle got closer that he could make out a car. For a moment, Ted forgot where he was or how he had got there. He tried to concentrate and was pleasantly surprised. It wasn't that hard after all. That brief 'rest' on the sidewalk had definitely helped recover his senses.

The car was getting closer. Ted was trying to get his mind around what all this meant. Maybe he could thumb a lift or maybe it was a taxi. He felt in his pockets. He had some money. He tried to flag it down. In the pitch black, Ted couldn't begin to even guess the size and shape of the occupants – it was all too much for his addled brain to cope with. But being a friendly drunk leaning against a lamp-post, he could not imagine their intentions were anything other than honourable.

'You want a ride?' a woman's voice beckoned. Kim and Bobby had got out of the car. They felt they should guide him to the vehicle.

Ted did not hesitate.

He hauled himself off the lamp-post and headed, unsteadily, in the direction of the car. One step at a time at first. Then, as his confidence grew, he began to walk more steadily. The couple opened the passenger door and another female voice beckoned.

'Come on in.'

Then one of them helped Ted in. He found himself hemmed between two attractive looking long haired women in their early twenties – and he wasn't complaining. The whole thing seemed so unreal.

He could only just make out the hair of one woman in front and the short back and sides of the female driver.

Ted was sobering up now. These girls were out for some fun. He couldn't believe his luck. They stroked his body through his clothes, kissed his ear and nibbled his neck. He felt himself harden at the prospect of all these girls. Who knows? Maybe he'd get a ride home as part of the bargain?

'You want to have some real fun?' asked one girl. Ted didn't even need to bother replying. There was only one real answer. He had money. But he wasn't even sure if they wanted it. They just seemed to want him.

The car stopped just near the prestigious South Brisbane Yacht Club. But it was way past those yachtsmen's bedtimes and the place was silent and locked up for the night.

Midnight had come and gone and Bobby was hungry. Very hungry.

She told a dazed Ted to go down to the river's edge with her to sort out the money and then the girls would join him. This really was turning out to be Ted's lucky night.

It was the first time he had tried to walk since struggling to the car just a few minutes earlier. Yet, now he had a fresh motive and, although still very drunk, he had purpose in his walk. He knew where he was going and he thought he knew precisely what he was about to get from these girls.

As Ted approached the river's edge, Bobby went back to the car. What little light there was disappeared from view. There had been a streetlight some half a mile away but now it was gone.

Splinters of wood that had been blown off the trees by recent gales crackled beneath his feet.

Back in the Holden Commodore, Kim and Tracey were scared.

'Let's just leave him there,' they both pleaded. But Lisa and Bobby had other plans.

Just moments before, they had all watched the pathetic figure of Ted walking down to the riverside to prepare for his night of passion. But they all knew that he was there only to provide the thrills for them.

Bobby was angry with Kim and Tracey. After all, they had all agreed on this 'celebration'. Now there was a break down of discipline in the ranks. But the two mutineers refused to budge.

In an act of defiance Kim flung her knife on to the front arm rest of the car. Bobby scowled at her, then grabbed it and stormed off.

On the riverbank, Ted stripped off completely. Despite all the drink he had consumed he had the good sense to put his wallet and keys in one of his shoes. The last thing he wanted was to lose anything valuable.

Then he sat – a slightly ludicrous figure – naked on the bank and waited for his women to appear.

It was pitch black and the only sound was the river lapping gently on the bank. Every now and again there would be a plop in the water as an insect hit the surface.

A voice then told Ted to move to a clearer strip of river bank just a few yards upstream. It was Bobby's voice – but it had become high pitched and difficult to distinguish. Also, it was said with such command that anyone would have felt obliged to obey it.

Ted turned to see who it was but there was no one there. He just presumed that the order was a guarantee of what was to come. He readily obeyed – convinced that his happy moment was fast approaching.

As he walked the short distance, he spotted what he thought was his credit card. In the poor light, Ted did not even check to see if it was actually his.

Instead, he just dropped it into one of his shoes for safekeeping. He neatly laid out his clothes in a pile. It seemed as sensible a place as any to put your valuables when you are about to indulge in some casual sex with girls you have never met before.

'He's going to be too strong for just me.' Bobby turned to Lisa. 'You've got to come.'

Lisa hesitated for a moment and then looked into those piercing eyes and felt obliged to aid her lover. She knew exactly what was intended. She had encouraged it because she wanted Bobby to be satisfied. She could not retreat now. They were lovers and you always do whatever your lover wants.

The two girls in the back looked stunned, but they kept their thoughts to themselves. They were now shivering with fright, holding each other for comfort. Desperate to escape from this nightmare and return to reality.

Bobby grasped Lisa's hand. That slight pain from the scab on her vein returned as if to remind her of what was to come. They walked gingerly around the back of the yacht club to where Ted was waiting patiently.

They were systematically holding their breath and then releasing short bursts of air, so as not to make much noise. Lisa's hand was hot and clammy. Bobby's was cool, almost ice cool, considering the heat of the night. They both realised one thing – the element of surprise was essential …

Ted was getting irritated. He wanted sex and it was not forthcoming. He was fed up with sitting on that riverbank. Although his vision was adapting well to the poor light, he failed to see the two figures approaching him from behind.

Bobby and Lisa could now clearly see Ted's back in the moonlight. He had that slightly loose skin that many men get as they approach their fifties. He was crouching, awkwardly swinging from side to side. Occasionally, Ted would shake his head to force himself awake after nodding off to sleep.

Each time he fell into a slumber, he would begin to dream vivid visions – only to snap himself awake. He was waiting for an orgy to begin and those dreams were becoming so daunting.

Bobby had a shiny object in each hand and Lisa could see in her eyes that same look that came over her whenever they were about to make love.

They stopped some yards short of Ted and quietly removed their clothes. They wanted to guarantee that Ted would not struggle until they were ready to feast. The sight of two lithe, female bodies in the dark would leave him in no doubt of their intent.

Ted shifted his position slightly as the two lovers approached. He looked behind and could just make out their naked bodies. He glanced at them before looking out to the river once more. He could not believe his luck – two nubile, young girls. Wait till he told his mates at work about this. He was happy to wait for them to come to him – after all he was going to pay. If he had stared a little harder he would have seen, rather than felt, the first frenzy of knife stabs that were soon to rain down on him from Bobby's hands.

Bobby was shaking with need. She needed blood. Here she was, about to kill as she stood in the dark on the river bank. Something inside was urging her to murder an innocent man.

She was going to kill. There was nothing she could do to stop it. The more she thought of her own cruel upbringing, the more she failed to shame herself about committing murder. She could not control her hunger.

Many people thought that murder was a sin. Bobby reckoned she knew otherwise. Some were born with a taste for blood. Others had it instilled in them. Bobby always claimed she drank the blood of live goats when she ran away from her cruel 'grandparents' at the age of just fifteen.

But God had made each man as he was and Bobby had been chosen to kill. It was all part of the masterplan. In Bobby's eyes, the only sin was to kill when your lover did not approve of the victim. But they had all chosen this victim together. They all knew what Bobby wanted. That gave her the licence to kill …

Standing there, watching by the river's edge was The Observer. She was shocked. How could Bobby kill? She should be ashamed by her terrible actions. Surely it was not too late to stop? But the beast within Bobby would always ignore the truth. And The Observer knew that really. She was powerless to stop the onslaught. It was out of her control.

As Bobby got closer, the dead calm returned. Like beasts prowling in the night, they slowed down as they approached their victim. Then they paused momentarily, waiting for the perfect moment.

The Observer was now pleading, begging Bobby to stop. Stop now.

Bobby knew what she was being told. She knew that what she was doing was wrong. But the urge from within was still too strong to resist.

'Stop. Stop. Stop.' The Observer screamed. 'This is crazy. Insane. Get ahold of yourself …' But the words were soon lost in the wind. Never to return.

Bobby let out one long pent up breath. Her family had never really taught her that killing was wrong. But then they were not a proper family. They had never drawn the moral lines that every child so desperately needs. Instead, she had been beaten and abused whenever she committed a wrong doing. No one ever explained why. Often Bobby would be locked in her room as a child and visited by her grandfather when he wanted to hurt her or have sex with her – or worse.

On other occasions, Bobby's family could look straight through her, as if she didn't even exist. They never provided any warmth, comfort or security. Instead, she was told how bad she was. How the very mention of her name would make them feel sick. How she was a lazy, no good, evil little brat.

They would take out the belt and thrash her. Now, she wanted to show them, show them all just how evil she really was.

But Bobby was sure her horrible family would understand why she could not control herself on this night. They might not forgive her, but they would inspire her to commit the deed. Bobby reckoned she knew where all those relatives would have ended up – and it certainly was not heaven.

Then the girls pounced.

Ted buckled and thrashed as he fell onto his back but he couldn't shake off the assault. He no longer had the strength. He gurgled and spluttered as his mouth filled with blood and rapidly his convulsions became less violent before fading altogether.

Fifteen times Bobby plunged her two knives into Ted's shoulders. A soft ripping sound came with each stab. One after the other they rained in on him. The blood seeping out of each wound. Bobby was now pomelling the knives, rather than grinding them, into his body. It was the same action as if she were thumping her fists on a table. She could not stop. Ted lay motionless on his back, but it didn't stop Bobby. She attacked his neck and chest just to make doubly sure there was no more life left in the mutilated corpse.

In a way this part of the attack was even more frenzied. Ted could not fight back and that invited a more ferocious response.

All the time she was stabbing with the knife she thought of her family. Of how she had begged them for love. But none of them would forgive her for inflicting herself upon them.

Ted was now a tangled mound of a body, crumpled on the grassy embankment. With the ninja knife, Bobby coldly and calmly slit Ted's throat from ear to ear. Lisa watched in fascination. She was so excited by the sight of her lover's naked body. She knew all about her urges and she wanted to see those cravings satisfied.

Bobby crouched over the body and began to lick and drink the blood that poured from the victim's throat. More memories came flooding back. Bobby recalled how she had discovered her grandmother was not her real blood relative. How she was told her mother had abandoned her. None of her seven brothers and sisters were related to her. Life had been one long betrayal.

No one could be trusted.

She swirled her tongue around the inside of the gaping wound, trying to devour every last morsel. But there was more than enough there.

She pushed the severed head further back to expose the throat wound even further — giving her more access to the blood. Now she was devouring the flesh like a shark in a feeding frenzy. The skin ripped open like a PVC dustbin bag when it's been overfilled.

Bobby then turned to Lisa. She had a lip curling smile that showed she had fed sufficiently — for the moment.

Businessman Scott Evans Gamble was sitting on the opposite side of the river bank when he heard the groans. A wry smile came to his face as they grew in sound to reach an ecstatic peak of what he presumed was sexual climax.

Lisa was now breathing in short and sharp gasps. She watched admiringly as her lover washed her body in the warm river water. Calmly, Bobby splashed water over her breasts and legs as if washing in a shower or bath.

She was only allowed one shallow bath a week at home. This was fantastic. A whole river to lose oneself in. A torrent of never ending water deep enough to swim in.

Once, at home, she was banned from eating at mealtime because she urinated in the bath. Now she could do it to her heart's content and no one could stop her.

Soon the blood marks were washed away, but Bobby still had some other unfinished business to attend to. She strolled naked to the river bank where she picked up both the knives used in the killing and washed them lovingly in the river before carrying them back on to the river bank where the mutilated torso lay twisted on its back by the muddy verge.

Both lovers stood there for a moment in the darkness, enveloped by the pungent aroma of blood. The smell was particularly strong when Bobby's breath wafted towards Lisa.

She could feel the globules of blood and flesh mixed together after

17

becoming caught between her teeth. Using the tip of her tongue, Bobby tried to push them out from between the gaps.

Her first real taste of blood had come when she was swept up into a witch's coven near her home in Rock Hampton. She had been fascinated by the man and wife, whom the locals used to refer to as the witches.

They offered her a place to sleep. It was nicer than her foster parents home. They often made sacrifices of animals like goats. They extended her education … in blood.

Bobby put on the jeans and tee shirt that were her regular 'uniform' around town. She was remarkably calm. Spent and satisfied like a lover who has just climaxed.

They walked back towards the car … hand in hand.

Watching them from nearby was The Observer. She was astounded. How could anyone do such a thing? A feeling of utter contempt and disgust came over her. She kept repeating those eight words to herself. 'How could anyone do such a dreadful thing,' over and over. But she was powerless to act.

'I have just feasted. I have just feasted,' Bobby screamed again and again as they drove the 30 minute trip back to their homes.

The journey was truly bizarre. Tracey Waugh, close to tears, sat soberly in a corner of the back seat, terrified to speak. No one said much. All three women later recalled how they smelt the overwhelming aroma of the blood on Bobby's breath. It was pungent and nauseous. They said Bobby looked and behaved as if she had just enjoyed a three-course dinner.

Two boys were sitting in the back of a police squad car, shaking with fear. But this was not the fear of arrest. This was the shock of just having found the mutilated body of Ted Baldock.

Just a few yards away, behind the impressive facade of the South Brisbane Yacht Club, Detective Constable Danny Murdoch grimaced. He was a well built cop with the likeable smile of a perennial optimist; but even his cheerful outlook on life was strained to breaking point by the sight that greeted him.

'The guy looks like he got the ultimate head job,' said Detective Constable Barry Deveney. Nobody laughed. It was six a.m. on Saturday, October 21, and every detective called to the scene that day had been dragged in on a day off to join the murder inquiry.

The forensic team were already examining the area around the body for any minute clues. Murdoch leant down to examine Ted's clothes, which were still in a neat pile.

Policemen were cordoning off the area with white plastic tape. A small crowd had gathered just a few yards from the yacht club.

As the coroners' officers lifted the body into a zippered plastic corpse bag, some of the crowd grimaced. But they still continued to stare, fascinated by the macabre scene. They were detached from the emotion of losing a loved one. Just curious to take a look. To tell their friends they saw a body on the riverbank. It would be something to brag about when the conversation ran dry in the bars and pubs of Brisbane that night.

Murdoch picked up Ted's scruffy shoes and heard the unmistakable, jangling noise of a set of keys. He reached inside to take them out and found a credit card. The name on it clearly read: Tracey Wigginton. That was Bobby's real name.

Detective Sergeant Glenn Burton, forty, was looking forward to a nice family Saturday at home. He had almost finished washing the car with his three children. And, unlike most husbands, he was more than happy to accompany his wife and kids to the supermarket. Their home at Wynnum was a picturesque spot right on the bay. Beautiful views, beautiful weather. What more could a man ask for?

Glenn was putting the finishing touches to his car when he heard the phone. It was still early, so he knew it was unlikely to be family or friends. On occasions like this it was tempting not to answer or let one of the family say he was out. But Glenn Burton was not that kind of guy.

He was a straight man who knew that a policeman was never really off duty. He was just 'resting' between cases.

It was, therefore, hardly surprising when one of the kids said the call was for him. His assignment was to go and arrest the owner of that credit card.

Within minutes, Glenn was heading for Enoggera and the home of Tracey Wigginton. The police had a simple theory. Ted was murdered by a girlfriend and her other lover.

The clues were pretty well there for everyone to see. The tyre marks from the car. The footsteps of two other people besides Ted. The ferocity of the stab wounds implied a woman had stood by and watched while her lover/husband carried out the killing.

As Glenn and five colleagues walked calmly up the stairs of the apartment block where Tracey Wigginton lived, it all seemed pretty clear cut.

Bobby was watching television. She had not slept well – mainly because Lisa did not stay the night with her. Bobby's three flatmates were sitting around drinking coffee, relaxing. It was a Saturday morning and they were all taking it easy.

There was a knock at the door. It was a firm, officious knock and Bobby knew instantly who it was. She went to answer it.

'Tracey Wigginton?' asked Glenn Burton.

'Bobby' had gone back into the subconscious of Tracey. She had taken on her real life persona once more. There was no more eight-year-old Tracey to show innocence. Even The Observer was gone.

They had all returned into the mind of twenty-three-year-old sheet metal college student Tracey Wigginton. The moment the police came calling, her four-way personality had dispersed. She could no longer hide behind those weird characters.

They were a part of her alter ego. Not even the dominating force of Bobby could help. Tracey was going to have to cope with this living nightmare herself. There was no one else to turn to. Bobby never existed. Little Tracey never existed. The Observer was only her common sense telling her, warning her, what she was doing.

But this was reality. A reality that would cost Tracey Wigginton her liberty for the horrendous crime she had committed.

Bobby may have been in charge when those knives rained down on Ted Baldock's back. Bobby drank the blood and virtually severed the head to get more blood. Bobby seduced and lured Lisa Ptaschinski into joining those evil forces. But they'd all gone now, crawled back into the dark recesses of Tracey's troubled brain.

Tracey knew that as she opened that door, but she did not flinch. Her cold eyes stared confidently ahead as she faced Detective Sergeant Glenn Burton.

However, none of this was familiar territory for Glenn Burton. He still thought he was interviewing the estranged lover of Ted Baldock not a multipersonality lesbian vampire with a lust for blood and murder.

The real Tracey Wigginton was a cold calculating killer, who knew her legal rights. She may have gone along quietly to the police station but she was not about to confess her evil deeds to Glenn.

Kim Jervis and Tracey Waugh were worried. Neither of them had managed much sleep that night. Their consciences were beginning to get the better of them. And to make matters worse, they had heard about Tracey Wigginton's arrest.

Waugh was the most terrified. At her flat in Clayfield, she cried herself to sleep many hours after the killing of Ted Baldock. She really never wanted any part in the horrific murder.

Jervis – who lived in a separate apartment, also in Clayfield – was equally scared. But she had even more reason. Her knife had been used by Tracey Wigginton in the frenzied attack. She knew it was only a matter of time before the police came looking for her.

Ptaschinski was an all together different animal. She saw the killing and encouraged Wigginton by not trying to stop her murdering Ted Baldock.

To Lisa it had all been a game, a joke. Even now, with the reality of the situation fast encroaching, she still thrilled at the very thought of her love for Bobby.

In Bobby, she had a strong lover with whom she was willing to do anything. As she later told psychiatrist Dr Terry Mulholland: 'If you are going out with someone you do whatever you can to please them.'

The brutal sex. The blood letting. The murder. They were all just part of the thrill of an intense relationship for Lisa. She said later she was infatuated. Obsessive love can cloud judgement. Lisa had lost touch with reality for eight torrid days.

Now she had to try to work out if she knew the real Tracey Wigginton. Not Bobby the he-man, not eight-year-old Tracey and certainly not The Observer. Lisa needed to be able to predict Tracey's behaviour but she never somehow managed that. The fact remained that she couldn't tell if Tracey had started singing to police.

Tracey had had an inbuilt fear of looking at herself in the mirror since her earliest years. She hated to look at herself. Her confidence was shattered by the cruel jibes of her stepfamily. She convinced herself she was ugly and never even bothered to make the effort to smarten herself up.

Her family would frequently punish her for not brushing her hair before school. Tracey began to believe that mirrors were evil objects which reflected her true self – something she could not face up to. Maybe her family were right? Perhaps she was evil? But she didn't really care.

Now here were the police joining a long list of her castigators. She knew just how to act. Calm and detached.

Glenn Burton was puzzled. Having raided Wigginton's flat, it had become blatantly obvious that she was a lesbian living in what locals call 'a dyke's commune'. Even when officers later returned to her flat and found a black cape and other satanic style clothing, they were still baffled.

'After all, black is a trendy colour these days. To link it with vampires seemed somewhat excessive,' explained Glenn later.

Glenn wanted to know why poor old Ted had stripped down for sex with her by the riverbank. Wigginton was not telling. Her only response was no response. She simply refused to speak.

Glenn feared this was going to be a tough case to crack. He stood over Wigginton as she sat at one of the two desks in the white-walled dayroom at Wooloon Gabba police station.

As the warm midday sunlight dazzled through the office windows, Tracey blinked and squirmed in her seat. It was not the presence of the officers that bothered her, she just felt uncomfortable in direct sunlight. It was a bit like her fear of mirrors and it fuelled the vampire involvement that scandalised Brisbane.

Ironically, on that day, she was relatively well dressed with a pretty white blouse and jeans. Despite the severe haircut she still retained a certain femininity about her.

She'd been there for more than four hours and all they'd got so far was her name and address. But Glenn was still under the impression they needed to find a boyfriend.

The idea of a woman killing at random just did not add up. Men were the cold, calculating murderers. They were the ones who often picked out complete strangers as their victims. No woman could commit such a brutal crime as this. Surely?

Tracey Waugh couldn't take the pressure any more. She had always been the least likely member of the group. Never quite as keen as the others. Always holding back. At one stage her fears led her to believe that Wigginton planned to make her the next blood victim. Waugh was the one who most shied away from the actual murder. She was the one who was close to tears in the back of the car the previous night.

She was painfully aware that Wigginton was sizing her up, imagining the taste of her blood. Or maybe she was lusting after her for sex as well?

Waugh pleaded with Jervis to turn themselves in. As they sat agonising at Jervis's tiny apartment, the two women became increasingly agitated by their situation.

They could not quite believe all this was happening. Would Wigginton incriminate them?

But at the home of Wendy and Wayne Sugden, Lisa was starting to wonder as well. One moment she imagined that Bobby/Tracey would walk through the door and sweep her off her feet. The next moment she recalled the look of terror on the face of that victim as he was punctured to death.

The Sugdens knew that there was something bothering Lisa. They wanted the truth and they were prepared to coax it out of her. Earlier in the week, she had told them all about Tracey. They were worried.

Not only about the lesbian relationship but the fact that Lisa was so easily lead. She liked to be dominated and Tracey was definitely doing that.

They were especially concerned when Lisa told them about the blood lust and Tracey's claims to be a vampire. Now, the look on Lisa's pathetic face said it all. She seemed to be in a trance. Out of touch with everyone and everything.

But that didn't stop the Sugdens being shocked when she blurted out 'Tracey's murdered someone.' Wendy Sugden was stunned. At first, she failed to comprehend the full meaning of this statement. 'Was it an animal?'

Lisa just muttered: 'A man.'

Wendy and her husband were sickened by what they heard. But they knew instinctively it must be true. They had little difficulty in convincing Lisa to turn herself into the police that afternoon.

The same dilemma ultimately sealed all their fates. For less than an hour later, Tracey and Kim also walked into the same police station. Until their appearance, Wigginton had sat in stony silence, refusing to cooperate.

If the others had not come forward then maybe Tracey would never have been convicted.

By one a.m. the next morning, an exhausted Glenn Burton left the station for his bayside home having solved what was probably the most horrific killing ever committed by women.

In October, 1990, Tracey Wigginton pleaded guilty to the murder of Ted Baldock at Brisbane Supreme Court and was jailed for life.

In February, 1991, Lisa Ptaschinski was found guilty of murder and also sentenced to life.

At the same hearing, Kim Jervis was convicted of manslaughter and jailed for eight years.

Tracey Waugh was cleared of murder and freed.

2

TWIN OBSESSION

It was hardly a grand affair – as weddings go. But then Graham and Gillian Philpott would not have wanted it any other way really.

As they walked out of the quiet suburban registry office into the autumn sunlight, they felt a sense of relief that they had finally done it.

After all, they knew each other pretty well, having lived together for five years. Hardly a sin, but for most of that time, bank manager Graham had pretended to be married to avoid the bigoted gossip that their neighbours loved to indulge in.

It just would not do for a forty-five-year-old, recently divorced father-of-three to be setting up home with the pretty twenty-one-year-old clerk from his branch of a major high-street bank.

For Mungo Park Way, near Orpington, in Kent, was one of those sort of places. Lots of net curtains and perfectly mowed lawns. A veneer of respectability hiding a multitude of sins.

Graham Philpott's house was a classic example of early 1970s architecture. Functional, practical and entirely lacking in style. But then it did have a built in garage – and that was very important in Mungo Park Way.

Now Graham and Gillian had got married at last. With two failed marriages behind him, Graham wanted to start afresh. Gillian made him feel so much younger.

For her part, she'd put her spotless past on the line to marry a man more than twice her age. Not surprisingly, her parents did not entirely approve of the match.

Her father, retired special branch police detective Leslie Smoothy, was philosophical. 'They seem happy,' he observed dryly. Gillian was old enough to make up her own mind whom she should marry.

In her stunning off-the-shoulder wedding dress complete with lace veil, she really looked the part as they left the ceremony to a cheery send off from a handful of friends and relatives.

She was an attractive woman in a chiselled sort of way, possessing one of those faces with sharp features that people either love or hate. There was no middle-of-the-road reaction about Gillian.

At work, she was always immaculately dressed and bubbled enthusiasm wherever she went. Her gregarious behaviour certainly caught the eye of her colleague Graham. Balding and nearly always wearing the same style of grey flannel suit in the office, he looked the archetypal bank manager.

Within a few months of Gillian joining the bank, they had become a definite couple. Soon, they were openly holding hands and kissing and cuddling as they travelled to and from the City by commuter train each day. No one objected so long as it did not interfere with their work – and Graham made sure of that.

Now – five years later – she had actually persuaded him to marry her. They had learned to live together. To accept each other's habits. To enjoy each other's company. They were probably much better prepared than most other couples. The marriage meant something really special to them despite having been live-in lovers for so long. They wanted the ceremony to be an occasion to remember. A time of great happiness.

So when Gillian's sister Janet turned up at their house just a few days before the wedding in tears, it pained them both to see her in such distress. It was only natural that they should offer her a shoulder to cry on.

Janet had just finished a particularly turbulent love affair and her life seemed in tatters. She did the only natural thing – and turned to her twin sister for comfort.

They were not absolutely identical. But the facial resemblances were startling similar. The nose, the eyes, the mouth, the shape of the face. If you met the sister you did not know in the street, you would be sure you had seen her before.

They did not dress identically because they abhorred the habitual obligation that so many twins seem under. They were individuals and they wanted to be treated as such.

If anything, being twin sisters had made Gillian and Janet more determined to succeed on their own. Throughout their childhood, they had suffered the pressure of always being expected to perform like circus clowns. People tried to make one person out of two. It was so infuriating they promised each other they would never treat their own children that way.

It was no surprise, then, that they went their own separate ways. Even so, despite the distance they kept from each other, Janet still managed to have exactly the same job as her sister, for the same bank – but at a different branch.

Perhaps that was why the guests at the wedding that day were not the least bit shocked to see Janet sitting with her sister and brand new husband in the back of their chauffeur driven limousine as it drove off to London Airport.

Earlier, Gillian had been relieved when her husband had put up no resistance to her suggestion that Janet should accompany them on their honeymoon to beautiful Bali. It wouldn't mar the holiday. In fact, she thought, it would be quite nice to have some female company. Graham could be awfully staid at times. And Bali sounded like such a wonderful place. Situated just south of Indonesia and west of Java, it really promised to be the trip of a lifetime.

Graham Philpott had been bemused by his wife's suggestion at first. Slightly irritated that the romantic holiday was going to be with someone else. But, when she had explained the anguish her sister was going through, he thought it would be heartless to object. In any case, Janet was going to return to London after two weeks – to leave them with a full week to themselves. As they sat together chatting on the flight to paradise, Graham studied Janet more closely. They really were identical twins in more ways than he had at first realised. Talking to Janet was just like talking to a more sophisticated version of Gillian. She seemed less hard-faced. More demure. More ladylike in the way she dressed and behaved. He examined all the features of her body. It was her eyes that struck him most. They were so inviting. She would look at him in such a way that he felt as if she were reading his mind.

Janet possessed something her sister lacked. He wasn't entirely sure what it was. But he thought he might like to find out.

Graham and Gillian had the honeymoon suite. It was a sumptuous place. Servants at your beck and call. Food, drink, sunshine, even massages on tap.

At night the two newly weds walked barefoot along the endless palm-fringed beaches, golden sand scrunching beneath their feet.

Bali has been called 'The Morning of the World.' An enchanting island, it is without doubt, one of the most magical places on earth. Scattered between the trees are tiny villages where craftsmen build countless temples in honour of their gods. Every night, after the sun goes down, traditional Balinese dancing takes place. The perfect place to relax. The perfect place for a honeymoon.

There was so much for the newly-weds to do. Then there was Janet. She was always around. Laughing. Joking. Playing a hostess-type role to the two lovers. Whenever she felt in the way, she would disappear, sensing it was time to leave Graham and Gillian alone.

As the honeymoon went on, however, they both felt they couldn't just cut Janet out of the picture. More and more, they insisted she joined in with them. They wanted to make sure she didn't feel awkward with them. This was her holiday as well.

So she became an essential part of the proceedings. No mealtime was complete without her. The three of them would laugh and joke at all the same things. They had built up a remarkable rapport.

Graham was becoming convinced they were all having an even better time — thanks to bringing Janet along. If anything, he began to think, she was an improvement on Gillian. No, he didn't really mean that. Not *really*. It was just that she kept flitting into his thoughts — he couldn't help it. Every time he looked at Gillian, he saw Janet shining through. Maybe it was because they were so similar.

At first, he dismissed it as a natural fondness for his wife's sister. They were twins and it was obvious that he would find them both attractive. He would watch as Janet plunged into the pool for a swim. Looking at her body. Examining every minute detail — comparing it all the time to Gillian.

Janet seemed to hold herself much better. Her breasts seemed firmer. Her body seemed more shapely. But then again …

Both Graham and Gillian became quite depressed as the day of Janet's departure back to London approached. They both enjoyed her company immensely but for entirely different reasons. They didn't want to see her go. But the plane ticket was booked. It would cost a fortune to change it.

They all decided to go out for an extra special dinner the night before she was due to leave. It was like a leaving party in a way. Gillian was sad. She was going to miss her sister's company during those long, hot, sunny days on the beach.

As they sat in the corner of the restaurant, Graham proposed a toast to his sister-in-law. It was a nice gesture and Janet smiled warmly at him. He stared intently at her. Delighted that she had responded to him so openly. Gillian paused for moment. She frowned at Graham, then dismissed her suspicions as ridiculous. The dinner party continued.

Graham told a joke and the two sisters listened carefully to his every word.

After the punch line delivery, they both laughed in unison. Janet grabbed Graham's arm purely as a reaction to the wisecrack. She felt good about her brother-in-law. He seemed a fine person. Someone who would bring nothing but happiness to her family. She was pleased.

Her hand squeezed his arm gently. It was an act of fondness for a new relative she was only just beginning to get to know, but to Graham it was a significant sign. Evidence that Janet was starting to return the feelings he had for her.

If anyone else in the world had squeezed his arm in such a way, he would have thought nothing of it, but when she did it … it had to mean something. A deliberate flirtation. He couldn't accept it as anything else.

If only Janet had realised what thoughts were rushing through his mind at that moment, then maybe she would not have inadvertently brushed his leg with the toes of her shoe just a few minutes later. To her, it was an innocent movement. Not intended in any way to be interpreted as a show of affection. She didn't give it any thought at the time. She just pulled her foot away gradually so as not to appear rude.

When Graham felt the movement of her shoe on his leg, it left a completely different impression. He saw it as even more evidence of her attempt to tell him that she fancied him. That she could not wait for him to get back to England so they might make wild, passionate love.

He looked up and glanced at her as her toe rested, momentarily, on his leg. He smiled discreetly, so Gillian would not see. Janet saw the look on his face and pulled her foot away immediately – but it was already too late. The damage had been done.

Graham's obsession had begun.

The next day was a sad occasion for everyone. Graham and Gillian were both at the airport saying fond farewells to Janet. It was more like saying goodbye to a relative who was emigrating to the other side of the world, than a sister whom they would both see just seven days later.

Gillian had thought it ludicrous to take Janet to the airport. She was a grown up person, perfectly capable of looking after herself, but Graham had insisted. He told his new wife that he would expect her to do the same thing if the situations were reversed. That was just a smoke screen for the searing passion he felt for Janet. Any excuse just to spend that extra hour in her company. Just to be sitting next to her in the taxi. To feel her leg brush against his own as they got out at the other end. To smell her perfume. To see her smile. To feel her lips.

When Gillian kissed her sister fondly on the cheek before she went through passport control, Graham could feel the excitement in his stomach, anticipating the hug and kiss he knew he was about to receive. It was a rare opportunity for him to feel her in his arms. Gillian looked on, completely unaware of his innermost feelings.

When the time finally came for his turn to say goodbye, he was like a schoolboy about to experience his first kiss. He felt awkward. Almost embarrassed by the situation. After all those days and nights of fantasy, the reality was now staring him in the face.

He bent to kiss her gently on the side of her face. He wanted desperately to move his mouth over to her lips. He watched them. They were covered in just the right amount of red lipstick. He was certain that for a moment he saw them quiver with expectation but he couldn't bring himself to do more than brush the side of her cheek with his lips. He waited for a split second, breathing in her scent. Then he pulled away, once more aware of the presence of his young bride. She did not notice his reaction.

They both watched as she waved back at them while walking through customs, all the time completely unaware of the effect she had already had on their lives and the tragedy she had inadvertently set in motion.

Graham had always been an incurable romantic. But now his thoughts were working overtime. Janet consumed his waking hours. When Gillian turned to ask him a question, he ignored her – stuck in a fantasy trance. But this was no fairy tale. He was on his honeymoon, transfixed by another woman.

'Let's have a drink at the airport bar.'

Graham snapped out of his daze. Gillian sensed something was wrong.

However, that request to stop for a drink had an ulterior motive. For Graham wanted to see Janet's plane as it took off for London. Like a child watching a huge airliner lift into the sky, waiting for a wave from one of those tiny round windows, Graham actually believed she might look out and see him down there.

He was already beginning to lose all sense of reality. He did not even know which side of the plane she would be sitting on. How on earth would she see him?

None of that mattered to Graham. He just wanted to feel that there might be a chance. That was enough to keep him there. Waiting for the opportunity of a glimpse.

They sat in sad silence at a table in the bar. Graham's eyes kept darting towards the runway every time an aircraft taxied for take off. Gillian did not realise how attentive he was being because he wore sunglasses. Finally her plane appeared on the tarmac.

He watched as the jet engines thrusted it forward, faster and faster towards the end of the runway. For a split second, it seemed to falter and Graham caught his breath with fear. Surely it wouldn't crash. Please. God. No. The momentary jerk was a perfectly normal motion for the plane but Graham had feared catastrophe.

He stared through his sunglasses as it passed overhead. He felt as if someone had torn out his stomach. He would not see her again until they returned to Orpington! He wasn't sure he could cope. The pain was so great he doubled up as if suffering from some awful bout of indigestion.

Gillian looked over, concerned that he was in agony. If she'd been able to see behind those dark glasses, she would have noticed the tears welling up in his eyes.

He managed to wipe them away before they reached his cheeks. Gillian Philpott presumed her groom was in the middle of a hay fever attack.

That night, Graham Philpott lay in bed next to his wife wide awake. She had long since fallen asleep. But he could not relax. He could not switch his mind off.

Janet. Every minute. Every second. There she was. In her bikini. Smiling in the bar. Winking at him. Embracing him, running her fingers down his chest …

His appetite had gone. He told Gillian he had a stomach bug. But he knew he'd feel hungry when he saw Janet again.

He was tense. So anxious to see his wife's twin sister. To feel her in his arms. To love her.

After hours of lying awake in the hot Bali night, Graham quietly slipped out from between the covers and crept across the room. The only noise was the constant blur of the air conditioning system and the crickets out on the balcony.

He sat down at the desk and took out some of the hotel notepaper. He stared out of the window as he tried to put his thoughts in writing. After a few minutes the words started to flow.

'When I looked into your face you had such a lovely look when I was stroking your cheek.'

He stopped writing for a moment. Pausing to make sure that what he had just written made sense. Then he went on.

'It was such a soft expression and I think that must have been the first time certainly that I saw that and knew certainly that I must have completely fallen in love with you.'

It was a clumsy sentence but she would know what he meant.

Graham Philpott wrote for hours. He became so immersed in it, that he just gave up worrying what he would say to Gillian if she stirred from her slumber in the bed, just a few feet away.

Luckily, she slept soundly, unaware of the passionate love letter her husband was writing to her twin sister.

Janet wasn't there to meet them at the airport. That was the first disappointment. He was desperate to see her. He needed her so badly. But at least he had the letters to give to her.

Then she did not respond when he tried to call her. Perhaps she did not want him after all. Was it possible that her loyalty to her sister over-rode her feelings for him?

Graham was worried. He did not want to give either of them up. But, if he had to, he had already decided he would choose Janet first. She was the one who would become his lover. It was only a matter of time.

Then an incident occurred that seemed to confirm all his wildest fantasies. Janet asked if she could stay on at their house. The break up of her long term relationship had had a traumatic effect on her, she explained. To Gillian, it seemed a perfectly sisterly thing to say: 'Yes.'

Graham could hardly contain his excitement. When she arrived at the front door, he took all her bags upstairs to the spare bedroom and laid them all out lovingly on the duvet.

Janet was surprised. Men normally didn't bother. But she gave it little thought.

Those slightly wary feelings she had about Graham in Bali were long since gone. She was just grateful to have a place to stay. She did not really think he had a serious crush on her. Gillian, on the other hand, noticed that things seemed well ... different.

A few weeks later they accepted an invitation to a neighbours' party. It was a rare treat for the twins. Graham was not a great spender and the chance to dress up came but once or twice a month. As Janet came down the stairs wearing a pretty red dress, Graham looked up from the hallway.

'Janet. You look marvellous. What a beautiful dress. You really know how to look good don't you?'

His smile seemed never ending. He could not stop looking at her body. Admiring every aspect of it as she gave them both the customary twirl.

As Graham poured compliment after compliment out, Gillian stood beside him in the room. He had not said one word about her outfit. She felt upset by his neglect. But she put it down to thoughtlessness.

Parties in Orpington tended to be pretty staid affairs. When Gillian,

Graham and Janet turned up at their neighbour's semi-detached home, they were a breath of fresh air compared to the grey-looking people at the gathering.

Smartly, but sexily dressed, the two sisters prompted a number of glances from the mainly middle-aged men assembled. Graham was lapping up the attention. In his mind, he had not one, but two of the prettiest girls in the street on his arm.

More people began to arrive and the party picked up. Then the hosts turned up the music. The sixties sounds brought a lot of memories back for Graham. He watched as some of the couples danced in the front room. The effect of the alcohol had loosencd their suburban outlook and some people were actually enjoying themselves. Gillian wandered off to talk to a friend. It left Graham on his own with Janet. For a moment, there was a difficult silence between them. He was lost for words. His love for her was so overwhelming that he didn't know what to say. Anything would have sounded ridiculous. He could hardly blurt out 'I love you' in front of a crowded party.

Janet construed his silence as shyness. She decided to break the ice.

'Why don't we dance?'

It was an innocent enough request, but to a man as besotted as he was, it sounded like a gift from god. A confirmation of his delusion.

It was not as if they were even about to dance closely together. Janet would never have even considered that option. She simply intended to bop around to the music for a few minutes. Nothing more. She now knew he had a crush on her. It was obvious. She just hoped it would go away.

As they danced, Graham watched and soaked up the way she moved. From the twisting of her hips to the movement of her thighs, he could not take his eyes off her. Like a lot of men when they dance, he was barely moving. She had no idea he was examining her every move. Lusting after her. Imagining she was making love to him. But when she saw his eyes, they were a dead give away. They were boring deep into hers. She thought it was probably the effect of the drink. But it made her feel uncomfortable. She did not like being stared at so intently by any man – certainly not her brother-in-law.

To Graham there was no going back.

When a person is obsessed they lose sight of reality. They believe that every sign is significant. Every movement becomes yet more proof of affection.

Later, he tape recorded a message to her – referring to that fateful first dance.

'It was the first time I really had an opportunity of dancing with you the way I really wanted to. God, I can feel it now. I think it is probably the best way I have ever danced. I was moving to the way your body was moving and I was certainly responding the way you were. If anyone was watching my eyes they must have known I was so in love with you.'

To Gillian Philpott, the signs were also becoming all too apparent. She had played the good Samaritan and allowed her sister to stay at their home. Now she was abusing that hospitality by having what appeared to be a love affair with her husband. Gillian just could not believe the relationship was only one-way. It took two, that was her attitude. And now she was building up a hatred for them both.

It was December, 1989, and after just one year of married life, Gillian wished she had never agreed to the wedding. Everything was going wrong for them.

The marriage had just been a piece of paper, a confirmation of what they already knew. But now it seemed to have sealed their fate. She felt the relationship crumbling the moment they had returned from the honeymoon. He no longer listened to anything she said. Instead, he heaped praise on Janet constantly while barely acknowledging her existence.

Gillian would walk into rooms where they both were and become immediately struck by the overwhelming silence – as if they had been talking secretly until the moment she entered. At meal times, Graham would respond so lovingly to Janet's conversation. Always looking deep into her eyes whenever they spoke. Gillian would just sit there. Neglected. Unwanted.

In bed at night it was just the same story. He wasn't interested any more. Gillian came to the same conclusion millions of wives the world over do every day. She decided he must be seeing another woman – and it could only be Janet.

But, so far, she had no firm evidence. She had never caught them actually kissing. Not even touching and certainly nothing sexual. The torture of not knowing for sure was, in some ways, even worse than knowing for certain. At least then she could get on with her life and find another man. Start afresh. She was only twenty-seven. Easily young enough to meet and marry someone new. Someone who would make her happy. But, without any evidence, it was difficult to confront them.

Once, she cornered Janet on her own, while Graham was outside washing the car.

'Are you having an affair with him? Just tell me the truth.'

Janet was astounded. She had no idea what her sister was thinking. As far as she was concerned, Graham had a silly crush. She would not have even entertained the thought of having an affair with him. As far as Janet was concerned, she had never once encouraged Graham. It was all in his head.

She assured her sister there was 'no truth in it whatsoever'. But she knew that the atmosphere in that house could only get worse.

Gillian kept watching, waiting for the signs.

She became convinced her sister was lying. How could he get that infatuated with her unless she was returning his affections?

Gillian could not get the relationship out of her mind.

Janet and Graham had just gone out Christmas shopping together. That would give them all sorts of opportunities for a liaison. A chance to express their love for one another. He could even be assuring her that he would leave his wife.

All these thoughts were rushing through Gillian's mind as she sat alone at the house one afternoon. She had to know one way or another. The anguish could not go on much longer. There had to be a way to find out for certain.

She went upstairs to Janet's bedroom, determined to discover the truth. She felt no guilt as she systematically rifled through her twin sister's bags. There had to be some evidence. Some shred of proof that they were having an affair. Underneath a pile of clothing in one case, she found an envelope. Inside it was a card. Something within her cried This is it.

On the cover, it looked like a perfectly normal Christmas card. But inside, the message was loud and clear 'To my darling, I wish you every happiness at Christmas. I am so fortunate to spend my life with you always.'

Gillian began to cry. Now she had found out the truth, it really hurt. Maybe she should never have gone snooping for it in the first place.

Then she could have carried on in the hope they could mend their marriage. Now she was faced with the facts. But she had wanted to know. She had to find out.

The tears streamed down her face. The feeling of betrayal. The disappointment. But she had to get a hold of herself. She had to confront them. This was it. This was all the evidence Gillian required.

She went back downstairs and waited. She knew they had to come back from that shopping trip eventually. Then she would destroy them. She would tell them what she thought of them.

She first heard them approach as they walked up the short driveway to the house. Janet was laughing. Graham was telling her a joke and she was responding warmly. Gillian watched through the net curtains that hid so many secrets in the suburban world she lived in. It incensed her to see them so happy together.

As she heard the key being turned in the front door lock, she braced herself for her onslaught. This time they could not deny it. There was no way they could claim this Christmas card was anything other than a token of their love for one another.

Janet and Graham looked up and smiled as Gillian approached them in the hallway. But, within moments, they could tell that something was wrong. Gillian looked flushed with fury. The tears had long gone. Their place had been taken by seething anger. The time had come.

'She's got to go.'

Janet was stunned to hear what her twin sister – her own flesh and blood – was saying.

Graham was not so surprised. He knew it would come to this one day. He wanted it to reach a head, so that Gillian could no longer control it. 'Then you will have to go as well.'

Graham's voice was cool, collected. The words spoken almost silkily, but with menace underneath. The tables had turned. Gillian – the one who had just discovered her sister was having what she thought was an affair with her husband – was now being made to feel like the villain.

For a few moments these three relatives looked at one another.

But the anger that had been building up inside Gillian had turned to fear. Fear that she was about to lose her home and her husband. Underneath it all, she hoped that by confronting them both she could drive Janet out of the house and then they could start afresh.

But now her world had been turned upside down. She was confused. She knew that deep inside, she still loved Graham – no matter what he had or had not done with her twin sister.

'Please love me.' She begged. 'Not her.'

Gillian was feeling desperate now. Her sister had run upstairs to pack her things leaving the couple alone to face each other.

'Have all the affairs you want, if I don't satisfy you. But you'll never find another woman who would do all the things I did for you.'

Gillian was getting hysterical. She was straining her face to avoid crying.

'I'll do anything you want to make our marriage work. You must believe me. I love you so much.'

Graham Philpott did not react to her pleas. Instead, he said coldly, 'I want a divorce from you.'

Gillian was allowed to continue sleeping in the house – but only in the spare bedroom where her sister Janet had once slept. To all the neighbours in Mungo Park Way, who wished them 'Happy Christmas' when they passed in the street, Graham and Gillian Philpott seemed as close as ever that December. They went to a stream of parties in the area as man and wife –

never once revealing the anguish of their break up. Janet had left the house on the day of their big confrontation, never to return. She was as bemused as she was hurt by the whole episode. Graham flooded her life with cards and messages. His obsessive love had not in any way been dampened by those scenes at the house. Instead, he thought about how they would be together one day. He sent her a loving note saying, 'Thank you for giving me a lovely year. It is so lovely living with you.'

It was signed: 'From your loving Graham.'

Now, Gillian and Graham were keeping up a huge pretence to the outside world. Deceiving everyone into believing they were as happy as ever.

Christmas Day was a disaster. They barely spoke to one another. It was supposed to be a time of year for rejoicing. For Gillian and Graham it was a time for silence.

The only respite for both of them were the parties they attended in the neighbourhood. These seemed to provide them with an escape from the appalling situation at home. As soon as they arrived at any party, they would split up and head off for conversations with people on opposite sides of the room. It was a bizarre existence. No communication at home but a smiling veneer at every public function.

By the time New Year 1990 was almost upon them, the strain was really starting to tell.

On December 30, Gillian and Graham managed just enough conversation between themselves to agree to go to a neighbour for a drinks party. As usual, within seconds of arriving, they split up and headed in different directions.

But, as other guests were later to remark, they still made a point of making it absolutely clear just how much in love they still were. In one extraordinary conversation, Graham told a friend, 'We are thinking of going to Bali for a second honeymoon.' Perhaps he was thinking of Janet at the time? It was an astonishing remark to make when one considered the circumstances. Gillian may have hated him for his obsession, but she still longed to live the rest of her life with him. She still wanted him to love her. To adore her. To want her. Even though they had not even slept in the same bed for weeks she lived in hope.

But the pressure of the situation was leading them both to drink excessively. And at that neighbour's party, they both went over the top …

It was 2.30 a.m. by the time they stumbled into their house.

Graham was looking for an argument.

'I just don't care for you any more,' he said. 'We must get a divorce.'

They were standing in the hall. He was not giving her a single ounce of compassion.

Gillian longed for him. She really wanted to sleep with him that night. Feel his body next to hers. Feel the warmth and security they had enjoyed together for so many years.

'Can I come to bed with you. Please.'

He did not reply.

'Please let me sleep there tonight. I won't go near you. I won't touch you if that's what you want.' But Graham's thoughts were only for Janet – even then.

'I don't want you. Can't you understand that?'

He was shouting fiercely now.

'I don't want you.' He kept repeating it over and over.

Even then Gillian felt a compulsion to try to please him in any way she thought might bring him back to her.

'I'll bring Janet back into the house. Anything.'

'You're a bitch. You should never have thrown Janet out.'

Gillian still kept pleading.

'But surely this isn't worth giving up eight years of happiness for?'

She was trying to appeal to his good sense now. The sensible side of him that made him such a right and proper person for his job. But he only wanted one thing now – the divorce settlement.

'I've lost a house and money before. But this time, you're entitled to nothing.'

That was the final straw for Gillian. He had switched this screaming match from the subject of love to money. In her mind, it showed just what he really thought of her. It proved that he was a cold, calculating man. Not the loving person she once knew so well.

He was shouting more at her now. He kept on and on about the money. She took the pink dressing gown cord from around her waist and gripped it tightly in her fist – just in case.

He was losing control. Everything he said was becoming increasingly hurtful. Then, as he swayed around in the room, he grabbed Gillian by the neck. She did not know if it was because he was falling or trying to throttle her. But she grasped the dressing gown cord in both hands and twisted it around his neck. He felt his throat tightening as the cord dug into his windpipe. Nothing would stop her now. There was no marriage to look forward to – he had seen to that. Gillian Philpott felt the urge to pull that cord tighter and tighter. She could see his eyes bulging outwards as he tried to free himself. But the surprise element had given Gillian just a few moments in which to seal his fate. He had already begun to die. He simply did not have the energy left to fight back.

She gave the cord one more sharp pull and her husband was dead.

It had all been so quick and, in a strange way, so painless.

For a few seconds she sat there stunned by her own actions. What had she done? It was awful as the feeling began to dawn on her. She had just killed Graham – the man she once loved so dearly. The man who had given her the happiest days of her life.

But he had taken his own life. He had demanded death and been given it in the end.

Gillian looked at his twisted body on the floor and knew she had to do something to make him look as if he'd committed suicide. She wanted to die with him.

Using all her strength, she picked up his lifeless body by putting her arms under his and pulling hard. She stopped by the bannisters at the landing and tied a fresh, longer piece of cord around his neck.

Then she knotted the other end firmly to a bannister. It was no easy task to lift his 12 stone body over the edge of the rail. For minutes she struggled until, through sheer will power she managed to tip it over the edge.

Exhausted, she sat down on the bed for a few minutes, trying to compose herself so she could plan the next stage. She thought about Graham. What he meant to her. What, ultimately, she had ended up meaning to him. That gave her the strength to carry on. She got out a sheet of their headed notepaper and paused for a few seconds to decide what to write. It was not that difficult.

'We couldn't live separately. We wanted to die together. Please keep us together – I beg of you. We love one another so much.'

And she meant every word.

Gillian Philpott grabbed at the bottle of aspirins in the medicine cupboard. She was going to do it. She was going to kill herself. End it all. There was nothing left to live for.

She had lived through the worst nightmare of all and now it was time to say goodbye. To leave this world and all her problems behind. The note was written. Now she had to go through with it.

She struggled with the childproof cap of the aspirin bottle for what seemed like minutes, in a desperate effort to get at the tablets. Finally she managed to pull off the lid and put the bottle to her lips. The bitter tasting pills cascaded smoothly into her mouth. She stopped and took a huge swig from the bottle of whisky that stood on the table besides her. Soon she had finished off the bottle of about thirty pills and sat down to die.

She presumed that the tightness in her stomach was a sign that the tablets were getting into her bloodstream. Poisoning her permanently. She hoped it would be quick. Suddenly, a terrible nauseous feeling overwhelmed her. Her stomach began to spasm. Uncontrollable jerking movements. She could feel the bitter taste of the pills against the roof of her mouth. She vomited everywhere. A steady stream gushed out of her like an oil well.

She would have to try something else. The determination to end it all was still there.

It was early morning on December 31, 1990. Gillian Philpott was trying to concentrate on the road as she drove the couple's Ford Orion on the busy 'A' road full of New Year's Eve traffic.

Just a few hours earlier, she had killed the husband she had always loved so much and then tried to kill herself. Unsuccessfully. Now she intended to finish off the job in such a way there would be no room for failure.

As she approached the cliffs of Beachy Head – a picturesque beauty spot on the Sussex coast renowned for suicide bids – she kept rehearsing her death plunge plans.

She wanted to make sure there was no mistake this time. She wanted to join Graham in heaven. At least Janet was not there.

There were quite a number of sightseers at Beachy Head that day watching hang gliders sweep majestically up into the skies from the cliff edge, hundreds of feet above sea level.

Gillian clutched onto the steering wheel as the car mounted the grass verge that led to the cliff edge. Her foot flat down on the accelerator, she willed the car forward as fast as it would go. This was the worst part. The waiting. The waiting to die.

She felt the car rear forward as the engine over-revved. Getting closer and closer to that leap into the unknown.

No one was watching the Ford. All eyes were on the hang gliders soaring on the thermals.

Gillian felt a weird sensation as the car got near the edge. It was a mixture of elation and fear. She was relieved it would soon all be over. But she was terrified of the pain she might have to endure before the moment of death.

Then it happened. The car lifted over the edge of the precipice. She was flying through the air. Totally out of control now. Completely unable to stop fate from taking a hand.

She felt her head hit the steering wheel as the car smacked the ground. Then everything went dark.

'There's a car in the bushes.'

The voice of the hang glider pilot was most emphatic. Amateur photographer David Payne reacted immediately by rushing over to the place where the pilot had pointed.

Two policemen followed just seconds later and scrambled down to the Ford Orion. Gillian had been sick and was naturally distressed. But there was no lasting damage. Incredibly, she only sustained minor injuries after smashing her head on the steering wheel. The car had dropped only 20 feet onto a ledge that jutted out of the cliff.

It did not take long for forensic scientists to conclude that Graham Philpot had been murdered.

At the Old Bailey, in January, 1991, Gillian Philpott was found guilty of the manslaughter of her husband and sentenced to just two years imprisonment. Her sister Janet always emphatically denied having any sexual relations with Graham Philpott.

3

THE BLACK WIDOW

Winnacunnet High School was the sort of place educationalists dream about.

Nestling on the edge of the quiet New England town of Hampton, it enjoyed a reputation as one of the finest schools in the North Eastern United States. None of those classic inner city problems of violence and truancy existed here. This was middle America. Simple. No frills. A pleasant environment where people were at peace with themselves.

The white-wood detached houses with their neatly trimmed front lawns that dominated the area, were classic evidence of that harmony. The immaculately clean streets throughout the picture postcard town centre summed up the pride which residents of Hampton had in their town. It was a relatively small, tightly knit community where everyone knew each other. There was a familiarity about the place that made you feel instantly at home.

All in all it represented a fairly large chunk of the American dream. Virtually no crime and even fewer scandals.

And the sons and daughters of Hampton residents were brought up to honour and obey those rules. While many of them were allowed their own car by the age of sixteen, there was a strictly enforced alcohol rule that prevented any person under the age of thirty from buying booze unless they provided an ID card.

Parents were determined to bring their children up in a responsible way.

Constantly lecturing them about the evils of drink and drugs. Always preventing them from doing anything wild.

It was the same in the classrooms of Winnacunnet High. That strict moral code was abided by to the letter. And anyone who stepped out of line was severely punished. But, out of all this discipline, there were, inevitably, the rebels. The youngsters who only wanted to do the opposite of what their family hoped for. The teenagers who saw that all these rules and regulations were made to be broken.

Bill Flynn, Patrick Randall and Vance Lattime were weary of being repressed by their parents. They were sick and tired of conforming. They wanted to be different.

As the three fifteen-year-olds hung around in the school playground one cold November day, discussing how awful their families were, there seemed to be little in life for them to look forward to. College exams were fast approaching and they were under constant pressure to perform well. To them, learning was not an interesting pastime. It was that common bond of apathy that sealed their friendship. They had all recognised in each other a total disdain for schoolwork. It drew them together.

Each time one of them was in trouble in class, it became a very special mark of distinction. The other two would look on proudly when their friend was punished. They saw it as yet more evidence of why they had to get out of school as quickly as possible – which was quite a problem for the three friends.

The staff at Winnacunnet pushed relentlessly for their pupils to go on to college – no matter what. Academically and sportingly, they were all expected to excel. But Bill, Patrick and Vance had other ideas. In an attempt to separate themselves from the majority of hard working classmates, they even decided to call themselves 'The Three Musketeers'.

'That way people will know we are different,' said Bill. He had become the self-appointed ringleader despite looking even younger than his years.

Basically, Bill, Patrick and Vance were more intrigued by the girls in their grade than the history of art. Their idea of fun was discussing the prowess of their favourite girls – even though they might never have even touched them.

'Hey. Wouldn't you just love to …' Bill was trying to get a response out of his quieter friend Vance. They were discussing what they would like to do to one particularly sexy looking blonde classmate. She was glancing over in their direction from the other side of the playground. She seemed to be encouraging them. Maybe she could hear what they were saying?

The boys were smirking. Excited at the prospect. They had interpreted the girl's acknowledgement as a certain invitation for sex – even though none of them had uttered more than a few words to her. In truth, she was just flirting in that inimitable way only teenage girls can. Just glancing every so often. Encouraging the boys' adolescent minds at every moment.

The Three Musketeers had another good reason to get out of school at the earliest opportunity. They were all virgins. But they didn't like admitting it to themselves – let alone their pals. They tended to swap imaginary tales of their sexual conquests in the hope it would convince their pals what experienced men they really were.

'Maybe she's just after your body Vance,' said Bill when he spotted Vance staring wistfully in the direction of that pretty classmate.

From the opposite corner of the playground, another older woman was watching the three boys. But they did not notice.

Class was about to restart – and that meant more mindless learning.

They quickly shared a cigarette butt in the corner of the vast grey concrete covered playground and all agreed there must be more to life than just school. They were all about to find out. A lot sooner than they realised.

The older woman was still watching the threesome. Holding back. She was waiting for the perfect moment to make her approach. When the bell rang, The Three Musketeers hastily stubbed out their sneaky cigarette and sloped off towards the double doors that led to the main school corridor.

'Hello Billy,' teacher Pamela Smart had just caught up with the boy.

Bill was slightly embarrassed in front of his pals. It was all very well talking about women, but it wasn't so easy when they confronted you head on.

He had met Pamela Smart for the first time the previous evening when she ran a self-esteem class for teenagers from the school. She seemed so mature and adult to Bill – even though there was only five years between them. He had found himself glancing incessantly at her legs as she leaned against the teacher's desk in that classroom the night before. She had good legs for a teacher. Even a pretty face with a fashionable streaked blonde hairstyle.

He had tried to make out her breasts beneath her loose fitting knitted jumper, and when he lay in bed that night, Billy thought about those brief glimpses of her upper thighs. It might not have been reality but then he knew, from her wedding ring, that she would never become anything more than a figure to put in that memory bank, which can provide the perfect fantasy on demand.

Now, here she was approaching him in the playground.

'Will you please come to my office after school Billy. It's important,' she said almost coldly. Pamela Smart then walked off in the opposite direction.

The other two Musketeers were sniggering.

'Hey. Billy baby. Maybe it'll be your lucky night!' They were amused by the use of the name 'Billy', as opposed to the macho 'Bill'. But that adolescent theory on why she wanted to see Bill seemed a far-fetched notion at the time. His thoughts were completely opposite to those of his friends. He was furious that he was going to have to stay on at school. He never liked to spend a moment longer than was absolutely necessary inside those four grey walls.

But he was puzzled all the same. She had offered no explanation. Just a direct order. It was as if she didn't want to hear any reply. He just had to obey. It was as simple as that.

Pamela's office at Winnacunnet High School was hardly a grand affair. Surrounded with shelves crammed with schoolbooks, it consisted of a table and two chairs – just enough space for her to type undisturbed.

As media studies teacher at the school, she was afforded the luxury of her own office, because she had other duties besides teaching. They included the onerous task of writing and then distributing press releases to the local newspaper and television stations about certain school events.

It was a relentless battle. And there were times when Pamela really wondered why she bothered. So little of her material was ever acted upon. She had landed the teaching job thanks to her own virtually obsessive knowledge of the media. And this was one of the drawbacks.

It was her work as a DJ on a local heavy rock station, that had sparked off her interest. She regularly indulged herself by playing her own special brand of really loud, raucous music to an audience of listeners who really appreciated her efforts. It was a part-time, unpaid job. But just to get the chance to play her favourite band Van Halen over and over again was reward in itself. It was her way of turning the clock back to her teenage years. Something she seemed to be doing more and more.

The staff at the radio station particularly enjoyed Pam's visits, because she always went to great effort to wear really sexy clothes – like skintight jeans and lots of leather.

Pam loved the heavy thudding bass lines and the screaming vocals. Heavy metal music made her feel really good if she was down. She idolised Van Halen in every way possible. She would have done anything to meet them in person.

Pam also had a softer, more charitable side to her nature in sharp contrast to her passion for those brutal heavy metal sounds. She used to be happy to help out at the school by teaching to the school's self-esteem programme for teenagers. After all, she herself had only just come out of her teens and she knew just what it was like. She got a real buzz out of helping the kids to discover themselves. It was a vital part of the growing up process as far as she was concerned.

The past few months had been a time of great upheaval for Pam. The previous May she had married her college sweetheart, Greg. They had moved into a comfortable apartment in nearby Derry, New Hampshire. But, as a salesman, he was often away and she found it difficult being on her own at home so often, with only the dog for company. That was another reason why she had volunteered to teach the programme.

In the class that previous evening, she had clearly noticed Bill Flynn studying her body. She did not think Bill noticed the wry smile that came to her lips at that moment. Maybe it was just as well.

It was hardly a new experience for Pam. As a young female teacher, a lot of the boy pupils would lust after her. Imagining what they would like to do to her. Stripping her with their eyes. Fantasising about bedroom encounters.

It amused her. When she was a pupil at school herself, she had always been the girl who would flirt in the playground. She used to love teasing them by leaving a button undone or pursing her lips. It was fun. So good for one's confidence. She missed the attention she used to get from all those boys. It just wasn't the same once you had grown up. People expected you to behave more responsibly. You could no longer act wild.

Pam would often flashback to those days when she found herself jealously watching the kids in the playground at Winnacunnet doing exactly the same thing. She wished she could do it all over again.

When Pam spotted Billy in the playground that morning, she felt compelled to do something. He was such a nice looking boy with that mane of dark wavy hair and those sea blue eyes. She had watched as he and his friends flirted with that blonde schoolgirl on the other side of the playground. She wanted Bill to notice her and flirt with her – but he didn't.

Now she had him all to herself here in her office. 'Sit down Billy,' said Pamela, as the teenager stepped nervously into the room.

Bill was still puzzled. He could not quite work out why Pamela had made him stay late. Maybe she had noticed him leering at her the previous evening and wanted to reprimand him? If that was the case, he felt highly embarrassed. It was all very well thinking those dirty thoughts but he didn't want to be confronted with them by the object of his fantasies.

Few words passed between them before she produced an envelope and gave it to him. He did not question why. But just opened it.

'I hope you like them,' was all she said.

It was clear from the package they were family snap shots. Perhaps she was trying to relax him by showing him pictures of her family before she punished him. Bill was very confused. What on earth was she handing them to me for? he wondered.

'Go on. Go ahead and look,' insisted Pamela. Before opening the package, Bill hesitated for a moment. None of this made any sense. It was ridiculous. He was about to ask why when Pam repeated 'Go on. Open it.' He felt compelled to do as he was told. As he took the snapshots out of the packet, he froze. His eyes were feasting upon the photograph on top of the pile. Bill was speechless. Stunned by the contents. He could not believe what was happening. Picture after picture showed Pamela in just the way he had dreamt about her the previous evening. But she had an even better figure. He did not realise teachers could have such fantastic bodies.

She was wearing the briefest of bikinis in every shot. But it was the look on her face that said it all, loud and clear. She had a sensual gleam in her eyes. They said: 'Come here. I want you.' For a moment, he wondered if these were taken just before she had sex. All the evidence seemed to point to that conclusion.

Her body was far more sensational than it could ever seem in the classroom. His pals would not believe him if he told them.

Bill was having trouble keeping his hands from shaking. He was still bewildered. Here he was sitting in a teacher's office at school while she showed him the sexiest set of pictures he had ever seen in his life. They might not have been as graphic as the soft porn mag he had flicked through at a friend's house only a few days previously, but this was a real person – not some dolly girl whose name in the captions probably did not even exist. The model in this case was sitting opposite him in that very room.

Pam was watching his reaction with interest. She could see him fidgeting uncomfortably in his seat. She wanted him to relax. She knew she was going to have to lead the way. She wondered if he really was a virgin after all. Somehow, she thought, he was.

She stood up and walked around to the side of the desk where Bill was sitting. He looked at her in a daze, unable to cope with what was happening. The photos still clutched in his clammy hands.

She knew he was bewildered. It was exactly how she wanted him. She wanted to be the dominating force. Leading the way with every move. Only deciding what *she* wanted to do. He just had to obey her.

Then she leant against the desk in exactly the same way she had done on the previous night. It was a deliberately provocative act. She wanted an excuse. She needed to have that control over him.

She kept repeating the lines to her favourite Van Halen song 'Hot For Teacher'. It was all about the seduction of a pupil by his teacher.

Pam wriggled her hips ever so slightly to losen up the tight fitting skirt she was wearing. Bill was at last beginning to realise that his teacher had seen every one of his reactions the previous evening. She had obviously enjoyed every glance. Now he had an extraordinary opportunity to translate those fantasies into reality.

Pam stroked his hair gently. Touching and probing with one hand. The other traced circles around the inside of his ear lobe. Then she picked up the photos and handed them to Bill. 'Find the one you like best.'

To Bill, every picture was too hot to handle. They were all as suggestive as each other. He wasn't interested in the pictures. He wanted the real thing.

'You've got to pick out the best one Bill,' she repeated her request. But, by now, it had become an order. Bill showed her a shot of her on all fours taken from behind. It was an incredibly provocative photograph.

On the day she posed, Pam had been determined to act as sexily as possible – twisting her body in a way that would maximise her ultimate message to whoever she showed them to. As her best friend Tracey Collins took the photos, she kept repeating: 'Do you think they are sexy enough. Tell me they are. Tell me they are.'

She hoped it would turn on her husband Greg. But, instead, he was appalled and demanded that she destroy the pictures. He craved respectability not all this sordidness.

'Well if he doesn't like the pictures I'll find someone else who will,' she thought to herself.

Now she was about to put those pictures to the test by using them to seduce a fifteen-year-old boy.

Bill sat there in her office, still drifting in and out of reality. At one point he decided it must all be a dream. His mind began to wander. Then he felt Pamela's hand stroking and caressing. It was all becoming very real once more.

Suddenly, Pamela pulled her hand away from Bill's lap. She had heard voices outside the door to her office. Bill came to. Snapped out of his sexual trance. Perhaps taking a split second longer to register the disturbance nearby.

'Don't worry Billy. You'll have me next time,' she whispered.

Next day found Billy wandering around the playground in a trance of disbelief. Had she really shown him those photos? His fellow musketeers were worried. 'What's wrong Bill? You ill or something?' Vance said.

Bill's mind was elsewhere.

He could not stop thinking about her. The chance to break his virginity had been so close and yet so far last night. But at least he now had a chance to actually lose it with a real woman – not some giggling classmate with as little experience as him.

The strange aspect was that Bill also felt a great deal of affection for Pamela. He didn't see her as a grand seducer only interested in satisfying her own sexual desires. Rather, he portrayed her as a beautiful woman who actually wanted him for more than just his young, lithe body.

It was for that reason Bill decided to break his code of friendship within The Three Musketeers and not tell them about his encounter with her – for the time being at least. If she ever found out that he'd been blabbing he'd lose his chance for good.

Across the other side of the playground, Pamela was watching and waiting once more. This time Bill noticed her instantly. That delighted her. She wanted that attention – and now she was getting it.

Minutes later, in the corridor, she touched his arm gently and said: 'Come to my home tonight.' She passed him a scrap of paper with her address. The appointment was set. It was now only a matter of time. Bill was ecstatic.

Pamela had been planning this moment in her mind for a long time. She was fed up with those lonely nights in front of the TV screen with only her mongrel dog for company. She had kept asking Greg to change jobs so he could be around more. But, as he continually explained to her, it was not that easy. She was resigned to spending at least half the nights of the year alone. Once a week, she would host the heavy rock radio show. That was real fun. She adored the music and people at the station. They all seemed to have a much better life than her.

But the rest of her life seemed painfully empty. When she had first met Greg at that teenage party, all those years ago, he had seemed just like her. With his shoulder length hair and love of heavy metal music they seemed to have so much in common. Both loved nights out with their mutual friends.

Greg looked like Jon Bon Jovi, and behaved like him sometimes. She liked that badness in him then. It was such a happy time for Pamela. She used to love dressing up in her heavy metal studded leather jackets and skirts, often adding fishnet stockings – oozing sex to all around her but still retaining a one-woman one-man passion for Greg. At rock concerts around the entire country, they and their friends would head bang to the hypnotic sounds, like millions of other teenagers.

Then Greg took a job as an insurance salesman and cut off all his long locks. He wanted to turn the clock forward and grow up. Pamela wanted to stay young and carefree.

Calling herself the Maiden of Metal, she took on the part-time job at the radio station and kept playing her Van Halen tracks. She began to think more and more about their message. They would always be her inspiration.

While Greg was settling down, with a safe career and a nice home, she was still firmly anchored in a teenage world of heavy metal, wild friends and all night parties.

Only a few weeks earlier, they had had an awful row when Greg announced he was going sking with some friends. Pam was furious. How could he leave her alone after all those nights he had been away for work? They really screamed at each other that night. She even told Greg she wished they'd never got married.

'You've just become some boring yuppie. You're not the man I married.'

To Greg, it was a painful insult. He retaliated in a crushing outburst and poured out the details of a sordid one-night stand he had had some weeks earlier.

Pam was horrified. She felt betrayed. But that feeling turned to anger when he explained: 'I was really drunk at the time. I didn't know what I was doing.'

In her eyes, that was no excuse. From that day on her hatred for him grew like a cancer, gnawing away at her insides.

Now she waited for her fifteen-year-old virgin pupil to arrive so she could give him her lessons in love. Just the mere thought of what she would do to Bill excited her as she waited there in the modest two-bedroomed apartment.

She had planned it all with great precision. Greg had hurt her. Now she was intending to get her revenge. Earlier that evening, she went to the video store to rent Nine and a Half Weeks. Pamela had seen it once before with husband Greg. They had both found it a real turn on. Now she was hoping it would have the same effect on Bill. Even the fridge was filled with beers to guarantee that the teenager would feel completely in the mood.

The stage was set. It just needed the other player.

The other player was feeling very nervous. The air of expectancy that he had felt earlier had now dissolved into a very real masculine fear that he might not be able to perform. After all, he had never had sex before in his young life. What happened if he climaxed too soon? How would he know what parts of her body were the most sensitive? He knew she would have to lead him and educate him.

As he rang the doorbell something inside him half wished she wouldn't be there. Then he could just turn round and walk home. Escape the embarrassment of not being experienced. He genuinely feared that she thought he had slept with at least three or four women already.

But Pam was only too well aware of his limitations. It pleased her to think that she was going to teach him so much. It made her feel wonderful that she could influence every aspect of their relationship. She had complete power over him. Perhaps even enough power to persuade him to carry out the ultimate sacrifice?

As she opened her front door she felt a surge of excitement rushing through her body. She knew he was hungry to learn — and she wanted so badly to be his teacher. Bill also felt an instant rush of adrenaline. But it was for a different reason from her. In those few moments it took her to open the door, his attitude had undergone a complete about-turn. His guilt had evaporated. He was now desperate to have her. This was going to be it. All those fears about sex had been stupid. Now he just wanted it. Wanted it really badly.

Pam's medium length hair was no longer tied back. Instead she had it falling neatly around her face. The make-up was more elaborate than at school. Her lips were glossed. They had seemed thin before. Now they were much fuller. Enveloping. Coaxing. She licked her top lip. Her tight fitting skirt was much further above the knee than any skirt she had worn to school. She was wearing flesh coloured tights, or were they stockings? He was desperate to find out. He could see just a hint of her bust and a bra through the opened top three buttons of her blouse.

Pam and Bill were not even inside the apartment yet. But the atmosphere was clearly sexually charged. That much was patently obvious to Pamela's friend Cecilia Pierce. She was sitting on the settee in the lounge when the couple walked in from the hallway.

Bill was taken aback. He had not expected to see Cecilia here. Perhaps he'd got it all wrong? Maybe Pam's behaviour the previous night was just a tease? How could she invite a friend along when she was planning the great seduction? It just did not make sense.

A look of obvious disappointment came over Bill's face. Both women could see it clearly.

'Hey. Billy,' said Pam. 'I got a really hot movie for us all to watch.'

But Billy wasn't listening. His mind was racing ahead. Either he had imagined the incident in the office or perhaps he was going to end up with both these women tonight? What an experience that would be, he thought.

Soon, all three were sitting back, transfixed by the video of *Nine and a Half Weeks*.

Basinger's character Elizabeth begins the film by rejecting sex-mad Rourke, saying: 'You're taking a hell of a lot for granted.'

In Pam's sitting room that evening, Bill was just praying he could.

But, back on celluloid, it wasn't long before Rourke got his woman in a sex scene that is said to have been one of the steamiest in Hollywood history.

Bill watched open mouthed as Rourke's character 'John' blindfolded 'Elizabeth'. Perhaps that's what Pam wanted to do to him?

The atmosphere in the sitting room was expectant, to say the least. All three were transfixed as 'John' took an ice cube out of a glass of whisky and began dripping drops of ice cold water onto Elizabeth's body. Then he rubbed the cube over her lips before sensuously stroking the beautiful actress's nipples. Finally, he traced the edge of her panties with an ice cube between his teeth.

It was an outrageous scene, deliberately scripted to give maximum titillation to the audience. It was certainly having the desired effect on the three watching.

Pam was already planning precisely how she would make Bill re-enact the film in her bedroom. As Kim Basinger performed a really hot striptease as part of yet another seduction scene with Mickey Rourke, Bill hoped Pam would do the same for him later on. At one stage, Kim became Pam as his imagination began to work overtime.

They watched spellbound as Mickey Rourke ravaged Kim Basinger up against a wall in a street. Torrents of water cascaded over the two stars as they tried at least six different positions.

'Wow. He's got a great body,' both the girls were giggling in schoolgirl fashion as the camera followed the contours of Rourke's body.

Bill looked away embarrassed for a moment by the naked male form. But soon his eyes were once more glued to the TV set, as Basinger's figure was exploited to the full.

It was clearly one of Pam's favourite movies. She fidgeted and crossed, then uncrossed, her legs throughout. Her tight skirt rode higher and higher up her thighs. She knew it was happening but she did not care. She could feel the rush of cool air going between her legs.

Bill knew that if he had to stand up it would be embarrassing because of his huge erection. He looked over toward Pam. He could clearly see her stocking tops and the contrasting bare flesh above. At that moment, they watched Basinger – dressed in black stockings and figure hugging pencil skirt – masturbating while she fantasised over Rourke.

Earlier that day, Pamela had informed Cecilia she was inviting the youngster round, telling her in no uncertain terms that she wanted to have the boy. But she wanted Cecilia to pretend to be his girlfriend if anyone called round unexpectedly. The irony was that Cecilia was nearer to his age — she was just sixteen. But she realised that Pam needed to have her around as cover in case Greg got back from a ski-ing trip early. It certainly would not do if he walked in on Pam and Bill alone. Greg was a jealous man.

'It must be giving you a few ideas Bill.' The movie was almost over but the real action was only just beginning as far as Pam was concerned.

On the screen, Basinger was walking away from Rourke, having rejected one of his perverse requests for the last time. She had decided they had to finish before it was too late.

As the end credits rolled, Pamela got up and went into the kitchen. Cecilia smiled knowingly. She knew she was playing the extra on this occasion. But it did not bother her.

Bill was lost for words. He just hoped this was all going to lead to what he had earlier envisaged. The sexy message of the movie was loud and clear. But where did Cecilia fit in?

Pamela swiftly answered that when she returned from the kitchen with a tray of ice cubes and took his hand. 'Let me show you the rest of the apartment ...'

Bill just couldn't believe it was finally actually happening. All this expectation and now they were really doing it.

Pamela was firmly in control. Bill knew his place the instant she peeled off her skirt and blouse to reveal a turquoise set of silk lingerie.

As she undid the belt of his trousers, he felt like her pupil once more. It was a nice, secure response. He was unsure. He wanted to be led. She seemed so powerful. So strong. He just did as he was told.

In the first few moments, Bill was embarrassed by his own nudity. But he soon shed his inhibitions as Pamela explored every part of his body in the dimly lit bedroom.

The partly empty ice cube tray was on the bedside table. Bill had smothered the freezing cold pieces all over her body. He was fascinated by the erectness of her nipples when he touched them with the cubes.

He was pushing them gently over every curve, then licking the watery remains with his tongue in a really teasing fashion. It was driving Pamela into spasms of excitement. It was the only time Bill ever got anywhere near being in complete control.

He stopped to put the ice cubes back in the tray, desperate to actually make love. He understood the importance of foreplay but he really wanted the real thing. Each time he tried to stop though, she would insist he carry on with the ice cubes. She wanted him to put them in her mouth and drip tiny droplets onto her body – just like in the movie.

It was time for Cecilia to go. She could well imagine what was going on in the bedroom next door. She had to pass the bedroom door to get out of the apartment, so she braced herself. It wasn't that she was shocked by Pamela's seduction technique. More jealous really.

For Cecilia had been equally turned on by the movie, but she had no one to turn to. As she crept past the door, that was ever so slightly ajar, she could clearly see the two naked bodies entwined and heaving on the double bed. It was an image she would never forget.

At last Bill was discovering the real thing. They were making love on the bed wildly and rampantly, totally consumed by each other's bodies.

It was a brilliant experience. Sex with an older, more experienced woman!

Pamela's appetite for lust knew few boundaries. She was training her 'love slave' to do anything she demanded.

In the background, Van Halen's 'Hot For Teacher' was blaring out of the stereo system. Reminding Pam of her conquest. How could she ever forget?

Now she wanted sex on the floor. He had to obey as she pulled him on top of her, guiding him into her because he was still clumsy and inexperienced.

As their bodies moved in rhythm on the shag pile carpet, she fantasised about Mickey Rourke. She knew she would reach a climax, just so long as Bill was half as good as Mickey was.

Bill was feeling guilt-ridden. It was a classic schoolboy guilt. He wasn't sure if he could face Pam again after their night of passion. Now he had actually experienced sex, he was not quite sure how to handle it. Should he ignore Pam and hope her husband does not find out? Or would it be better to take the affair a stage further and become her regular lover?

He could not believe that a woman would give herself to him in the way Pam had, without feeling very emotionally involved. He had read about prostitutes and sex on demand. But Pam was not like that. There was only one conclusion to draw: something special must exist between them.

As he stood in his regular place in the corner of the school playground on the morning after he lost his virginity, he felt a strange combination of elation and depression. The joy of that sexual experience was being mellowed by the ongoing feeling of guilt.

But then he snapped out of it when he sensed Pam's eyes upon him from the other side of playground. This time she was coming towards him, rather than holding back by the double doors like before. As she approached, the other two Musketeers moved away, instinctively aware of the relationship between their best friend and his teacher. Pam had been rehearsing this moment all morning. Now the time had come.

Bill did not know where to look at first. Pamela had obviously been crying. The mascara around her eyes had smudged and she looked a different person from the passionate vamp of just a few hours earlier.

They talked in low, almost whispered tones, to avoid the prying ears of the other children standing nearby.

'I want you so badly Billy,' uttered Pamela.

Bill did not know what to say. She was proclaiming her love for him.

'I've got to have you the whole time. I don't want anyone else. I want you.'

Pamela was weeping slightly throughout, but she still had that air of authority about her. The teacher in charge. There was no way he could refuse her anything. If she wanted just him and no one else than that was fine by him.

There was something wrong though. She seemed to be building up to it. As if she had some other motive for her tears ... but he couldn't be sure of it. It did not take long for him to find out.

'We've got to get rid of Greg. It's the only way.'

Bill reeled back with shock. Maybe he wasn't hearing her correctly? But Pamela was being deadly serious. She wanted Greg out of the way and she ordered Bill to do it.

The car was parked in a narrow lane off the main highway. It was eight o'clock in the evening. The windows were heavily steamed up and the car was gently rocking – only slightly – from side to side. It was just enough so you would notice if you were standing right by it.

Inside, Pamela and Bill were making love. It wasn't as comfortable as the first time. But it was just as passionate.

'Bill. If you really loved me ...'

Pamela wanted her young lover to prove his commitment to her. Bill was in a daze. He had just turned sixteen years of age, and now his married girlfriend was briefing him on how to kill her husband. In between gasps she said:

'Make it look like a burglary. Steal a few thing from the bedroom ... There's some jewellery in there ... The cops will think Greg walked in on the burglars ... It's going to be so simple ... I don't want you to do a messy job. It's got to be clean and quick ... Use a gun then you won't mess up the carpet.'

Above: Lawrencia 'Bambi' Bembeck – sentenced to life for the murder of her husband's ex-wife.

Above: She-Devil of Nancy: Simone Weber.

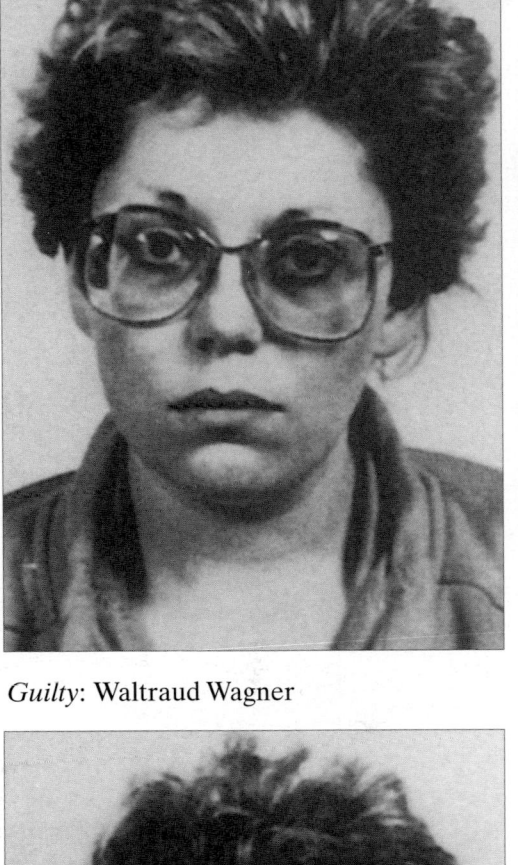

Guilty: Waltraud Wagner

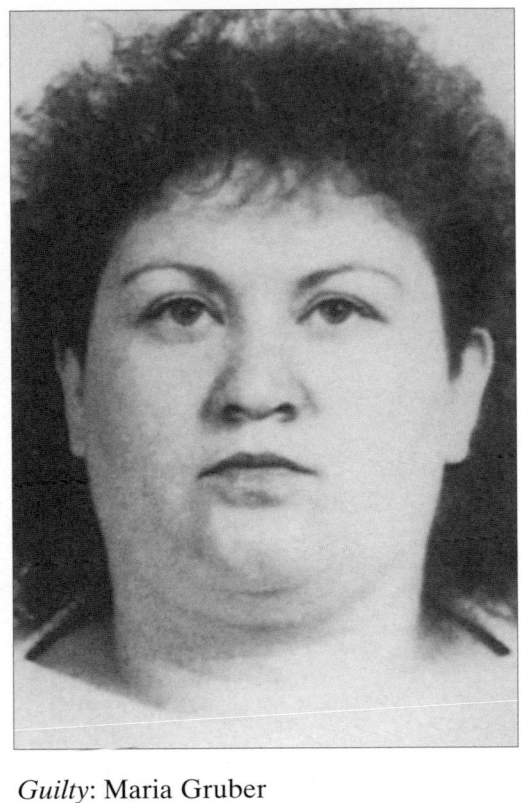

Guilty: Maria Gruber

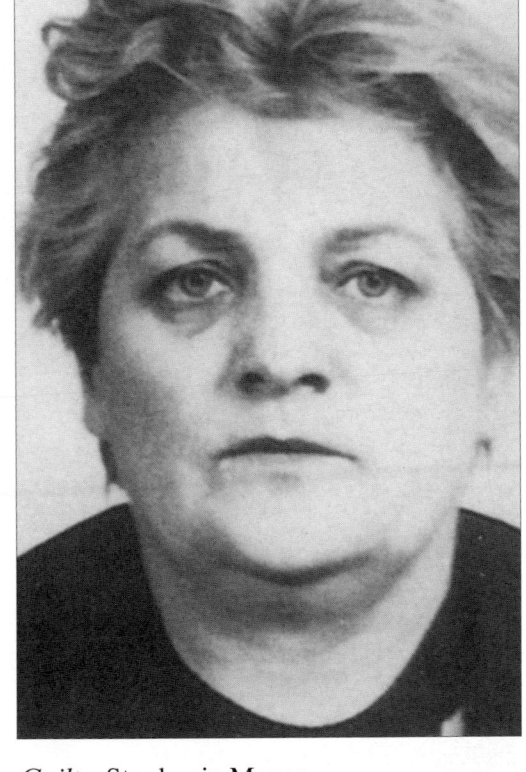

Guilty: Irene Leidolf

Guilty: Stephanie Mayen

Above: The four nurses of death.

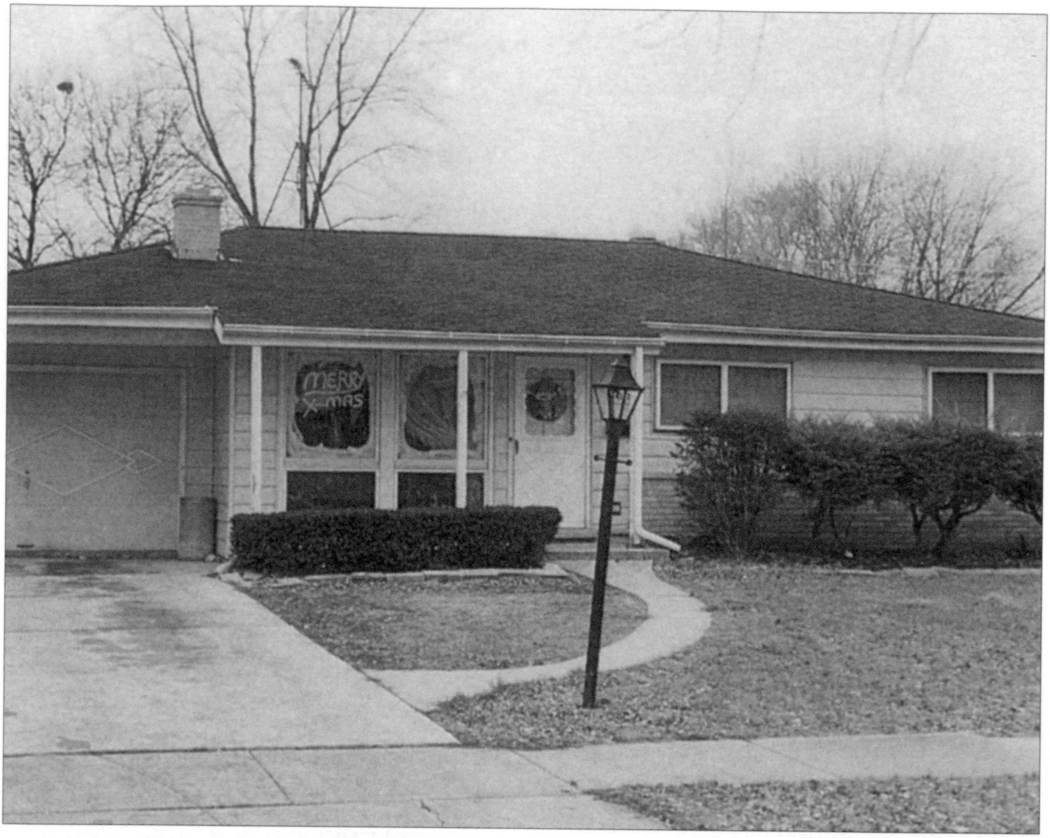
MERRY
X-MAS

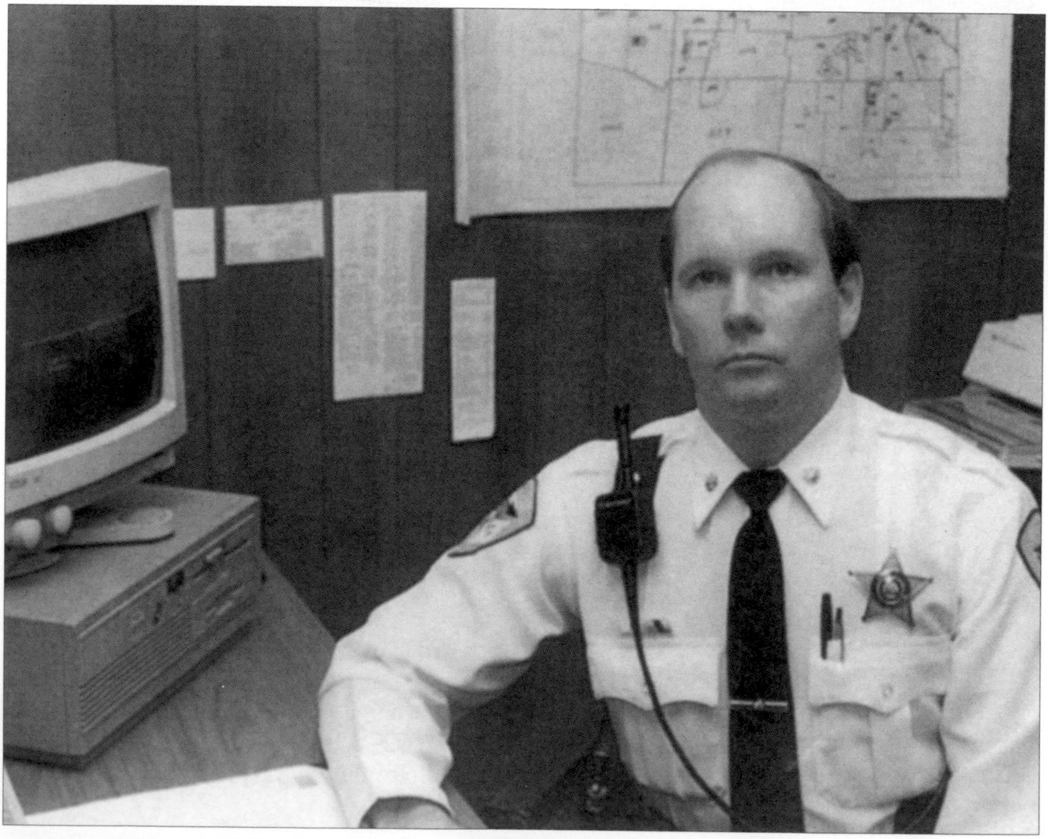

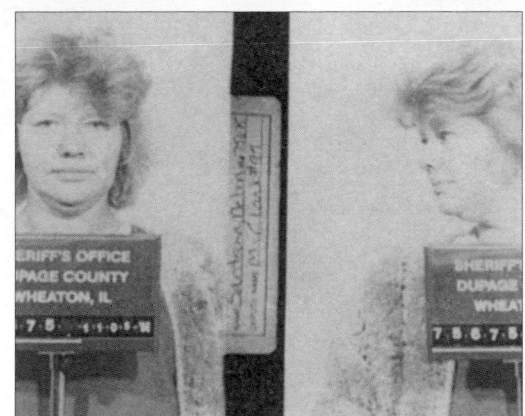

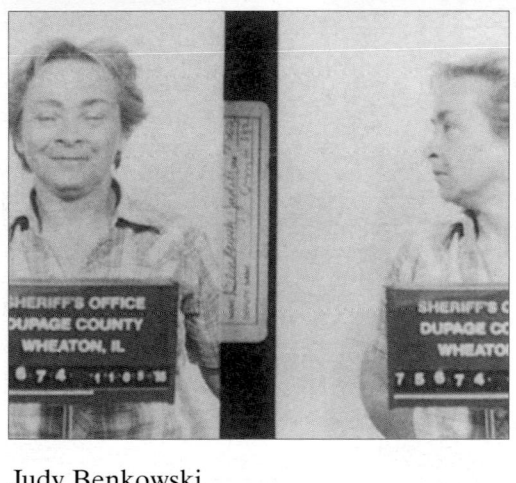

Judy Benkowski

Debra Santana

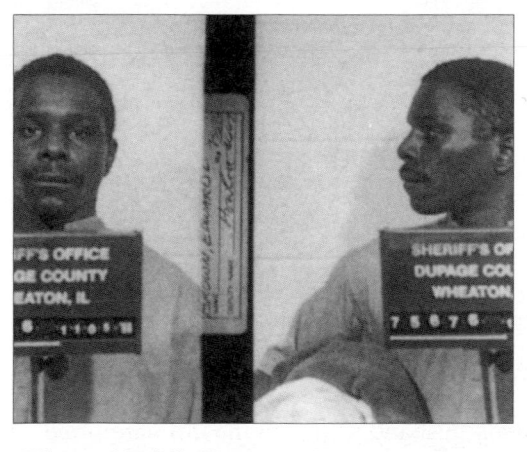

'Hitman' Eddie Brown

Top: Judy Benkowski marries lover Clarence Jeske inside Dwight Correction Institute, Illinois – August 1991

Far Left (*top*): The house in Addison, Illinois, where Clarence Benkowski was shot dead.

Far Left (*below*): Det. Sgt. Tom Gorniak of Addison Police, who immediately suspected Judy Benkowski.

Above: Paul Sainsbury – the jealous and bullying husband who paid the ultimate price for abusing his wife Pamela for so many years.

Above: Pamela Sainsbury who was placed on two years probation after admitting the manslaughter of her husband.

Above: Sara Thornton – sentenced to life for the murder of her husband, Malcolm.

She was ordering the assassination of her husband but her chief concern was her new lounge carpet.

'And don't do it in front of the dog. I don't want him scared.'

Pam always said she preferred animals to humans – now she was proving that point beyond any doubt.

Despite reservations Bill was getting what he always wanted – real sex from a woman who really knew how to perform. If he had to carry out certain, well, unsavoury tasks than so be it.

He wanted his lessons to last forever.

Vance Lattime was tip-toeing silently down the stairs of his home, desperate not to wake the rest of the family. As he made his way across the lobby to his father's study, he wondered if what he was about to do was really going to be worth it.

Only a few hours earlier, his best friend and fellow Musketeer Bill Flynn had persuaded him and Patrick Randall to carry out the cold-blooded murder of Pamela's husband Greg.

She had been with all three of them when the plan had been discussed. She made them believe it would all be so simple. Vance was not so sure. But Bill and Pam were most persuasive. They knew that Vance's father had a vast collection of firearms at his home.

As the teenager gently opened the glass case and eased the .22 pistol out, he hesitated for a moment. For the price on Greg Smart's head was a mere £2,400 each. That was the amount Pamela had promised Bill that he and his friends would receive from Greg's life insurance. The only condition was that they made sure he was dead.

As he stood inspecting the daunting array of weaponry on display, Vance knew he had made The Musketeers' pledge of honour – and that meant he was committed.

Bill, Vance, Patrick and their driver Ray Fowler were motoring up the freeway towards Derry. They were visibly nervous. They were having to face the reality of the situation – and it was terrifying them. As Ray drove, Bill briefed the other three on the roles they had to play.

No one was listening properly. Their powers of concentration were all but gone. These were not cold, professional killers. These were four school kids who had come under the spell of one determined seductress.

'Shit. Let's turn around,' Bill was back in control. Thinking clearly for a moment, he realised the enormity of their task. He could see the ludicrous side of the situation and it was time to take stock of it all. Time to reassess his true feelings for Pamela. Perhaps she was using him to kill her husband? Maybe she would just drop him like a stone the moment the murder was committed?

For the first time, Bill had his doubts about the relationship which had picked him up and swept him off his feet.

'I'm sorry. We just got kinda lost, I couldn't remember which street you lived in.'

It was a feeble excuse from Bill and he knew it. But it was all he could do in the circumstances. Vance and Patrick were cowering with him outside the front door to Pam's apartment. They were almost more scared of her reaction than the prospect of murdering someone.

Pamela was indeed furious.

'You don't love me. You got lost on purpose,' she was screaming at Bill, totally ignoring the presence of the other two boys.

He was frightened she was going to ditch him. That would mean the end of all that passion. But at least it might leave him with a clear conscience.

Bill was half hoping that perhaps this would be the end. He was worried about a lot of things to do with this illicit relationship. It all seemed so dangerous. So risky. But the over-riding guilt always dispersed the moment he set eyes on Pam. Remembering the love making they had enjoyed seemed to lull him into a false sense of security. It was all so easy.

She started to stroke Bill's neck. She was going to get her way. No matter what it took. The two other boys looked on embarrassingly as their media studies teacher kissed and caressed her pupil in front of their very eyes. Pam was well aware of the presence of those other two. She led Bill into the kitchen and told them to let themselves out ...

Soon they were making love all over the house. On the sitting room floor. On the staircase. And finally in the bedroom.

Pamela's initial anger at Bill had now transformed into lust. Her fury about the failed attempt on her husband's life was making her more frantic.

Bill could barely handle it. She was oozing with sex. She did not remove her clothes for the first bout of love making – not even her black patent leather stilettos.

She was tearing at him wildly. Wanting more. And more. And more.

By the time they had both climaxed, Pam was like a different person. All the anger had subsided. She had let it all flow out of her system during the love making. She felt immensely satisfied ... for the time being.

Gently, she stroked his chest and looked at him lovingly, as they relaxed together in her double bed. But that nagging feeling she wanted something was coming back to Bill. It was the same feeling that he had when they lay on the back seat of the car a few days earlier.

He knew exactly what was on her mind.

'You've got to try again. This time make it work. If you don't, we shall have to stop seeing each other.'

The chilling reminder made Bill's stomach turn. He wanted her so badly. Before, he had hoped the whole crazy scheme would just go away.

He should have known better.

In their Derry apartment, Greg Smart was tidying up before Pamela's return from a late evening school meeting.

He wanted so desperately to make up for the confession which had so upset Pam. He knew it was wrong to have slept with someone else. It was just one of those things. He still loved Pam and he wanted to show her how much. Now, he was looking forward to a great celebration that would wipe those bitter memories out forever.

Greg was so engrossed in his thoughts he did not even notice the smash of a rear window at first.

As the three hooded figures crept through the bedroom towards the lounge, Greg was just thinking who to call next on his round up of friends for the party.

When The Three Musketeers burst in they took Greg completely by surprise.

'Take anything you want.' He wasn't going to argue with three men and a pistol.

Bill was feeling elated. The gun. The power. The power to order someone about. Just like Pam did with him. He felt in control of his own destiny for the first time in his entire life. He knew he could get Greg to do anything he wanted. Well, almost anything.

'Give us that ring scumbag.'

He wanted that ring more than anything else. He wanted it to be his forever some day.

For a few seconds, the whole scenario was reduced to a farce by Greg's response.

'If I gave it to you, my wife would kill me.' One of the other boys sniggered.

Bill and his fellow Musketeers were flabbergasted. His wife wanted him dead – and he really did not have a clue.

'Just give us it.'

Bill tried to sound menacing. But to no avail. Greg was adamant.

He had just signed his own death warrant. Bill cocked the hammer on the gun.

'Get down on your knees. Now!' yelled Bill Flynn to his lover's terrified husband.

He pointed the gun at the back of Greg's head and uttered three simple words:

'God forgive me.'

Greg Smart fell to the floor silently.

Bill and his two fellow Musketeers beat a hasty retreat ...

She looked stunning dressed all in black. The seamed stockings added just that hint of sexuality, at a sombre occasion. She was even wearing the same black patent stilettos that she had kept on during her last bout of passion with Bill.

This was the funeral of Greg Smart, and his grieving widow was putting on an Oscar winning performance. Head down, she looked heartbroken as the wooden coffin was mechanically lowered into its final resting place in the ground. The so-called Maiden of Metal was melting the hearts of her family and friends, gathered around the graveside.

As they heard the priest refer to Greg's tragic death at the hands of unknown assailants, she shed a tear and dropped a bouquet of red roses onto the casket before it was covered up with earth.

'God rest his soul ...'

Back in the playground, The Three Musketeers were in a daze. They still couldn't quite believe what they had actually done.

The newspaper headlines had come and gone. Pamela Smart was still grieving at home – crying those crocodile tears. The whole operation seemed to have gone like clockwork. Now the teenagers wanted to collect their money. It seemed like a job well done.

But they were all starting to drop their guards.

The bragging at school began. Word started to get out that maybe Greg Smart wasn't killed by burglars after all.

'He was worth more dead, than alive,' boasted Patrick Randall to one classmate.

It was the talk of the playground. The place where, all those months ago, the whole train of events had been set in motion.

It was now only a matter of time.

Vance Lattime was feeling really distraught. He had just woken up after having a horrific nightmare, in which he kept seeing the face of Greg Smart over and over again. It was a vivid image. Lifelike to the extreme, and it really scared the teenager.

He, more than the other two Musketeers, was constantly filled with a sense of guilt that wouldn't let go. While the other boys waited for Pamela to get in contact and hand over their 'fees', he was starting to question the whole horrific episode.

At home, his parents thought it was adolescent girl trouble that was causing Vance's depression. The problem was certainly with the opposite sex. But this was no girl. She was a murderous, manipulative woman.

His parents tried in vain to help him over his anxiety. But no amount of appeals would work.

He couldn't keep this evil secret locked up inside his mind for much longer. He knew that other kids were talking about it at school. He was sure the police would come knocking some day.

Then, one breakfast time, he snapped. Breaking down in floods of tears he poured out the entire incident to his stunned parents.

Vance's father went straight to the police.

Pamela took the news of the arrest of The Three Musketeers and their driver very calmly. She certainly was not going to be panicked into a confession.

As she sat in the once happy matrimonial home in Derry, with her best friend Cecilia, she seemed in a remarkably cool state of mind.

'Who are they going to believe? A sixteen-year-old, or me with my professional reputation,' she said confidently. 'I'll get off, don't worry. I'm never going to admit to the affair.'

Unluckily for Pamela, she did not notice the electronic tape recorder that was strapped to Cecilia's back ...

On March 22, 1991, at a court in Exeter, New Hampshire, Pamela Smart was found guilty of masterminding her husband's murder. She was sentenced to life imprisonment.

Bill Flynn, Patrick Randall and Vance Lattime all admitted killing Greg Smart. Their life sentences were reduced to 28 years in exchange for their cooperation in helping the prosecution of Pamela Smart.

4

PMT

Christine English hated the mornings.

There was always so much to do. Get the kids ready for school. Make sure they ate some breakfast. Do the beds. Tidy the house. A never-ending stream of chores.

And then there was Barry.

Once both her sons had departed for school, she had to nursemaid him through the morning. In some ways, he was more like another child than her lover.

They had been together for four years. But sometimes it felt like four hundred. Their love for each other veered from hatred to total infatuation – and there was no knowing which way it would end.

All her friends kept telling her she was mad to set up home with a man six years her junior, but Barry kept Christine feeling young. When he wanted to be, he could be the most loving, caring person in the world.

She didn't want to listen to what everyone was saying. So long as the good times were more frequent than the bad, she was happy.

Lately, however, she had begun to wonder whether it really was all worth it. Barry had turned to drink in a big way. It started with beers every night in the pub but, in the past year or so, he had found a taste for vodka.

Nearly every night he would end up drunk or close to it. Sometimes he was amusing company when he was tipsy, other times he turned into an out-of-control monster who would strike real fear into Christine.

63

Barry's problems lay with his work. Like so many self-employed people he was under enormous financial strain. He owned a franchise to a bakery. Although the business was doing OK, it wasn't bringing in the return Barry had once hoped for.

Life had turned into a constant battle for him. His only way out was the bottle. When he was drinking none of the stresses and strains, however large, would enter his mind.

In the pub of an evening, he would sit at the bar, talking to his drinking partners about everything except his business. It was a great way to avoid the tensions. Drink was the great escape.

When Barry got home to Christine each night, he would start to sober up and realise that what he was doing was merely a smokescreen for his problems. Underneath it all, he was well aware that he couldn't just carry on pickling his brain in alcohol.

He had to do something to sort himself out. But how? Christine knew the answer, but she didn't know how she was going to convince Barry. Many years before, after the birth of her two sons, she had noticed her moods swinging enormously in the space of just a few hours. At first she just dismissed it as temporary post-natal depression. The man she was married to then had not helped. He wasn't interested in her 'women's problems'.

'What are you on about woman,' he'd grumble, an uncomprehending scowl on his face. Their marriage was already crumbling, so compassion did not come high on his list of emotional priorities.

Christine was desperate to break out of the constant moods that were starting to make her life miserable. Sometimes she would get so het up she would start smashing up cutlery. Throwing it around the kitchen in an inexplicable frenzy.

Afterwards, she would try to explain to her husband why it had happened. But he didn't want to know. 'He just did not care. A woman's place was clearly defined in his little world and the sort of problems I had were the sort he did not want to talk about,' explained Christine later.

Things got worse and worse at home for Christine. The moods became more frequent and less controllable. It was as if there was a different person inside her, trying desperately to get out and cause havoc.

After one particularly nasty fight with her husband, she threw a plate at him. He struck her. That was it. She had to do something before it was too late.

So Christine turned to Transcendental Meditation. It was the mid-seventies. Hippies had come and almost gone – yesterday's beatniks were today's married couples with 2.2 kids – but TM was a relic that had survived the fickle swings of fashion.

It was also the life saver Christine had been looking for. At first, she attended group meetings where everyone would sit and meditate. Learn to relax in a way the modern world rarely allows you to.

Christine was given her own mantra. It was a call-sign awarded to her by her teacher. A name that no one else in the entire world should ever know – or be called. Her teacher warned her of the dire consequences if she ever revealed her mantra to anyone else.

Within weeks, she began to feel better. Just meditating for 15 minutes every morning before breakfast and just before bed seemed to calm her so much. She was starting to look inside herself more. To understand the powers that were making her so tense. Appreciating the evil influences that were contributing to her unhappiness. Christine was starting to find an answer.

It had given her hope for the future and made her far more tolerant and understanding towards Barry's drink problems than she ever would have been with her husband.

When Barry's boozing became excessive she knew she would have to use her TM experiences to help him escape from his problems – just as she herself had done all those years before.

'In any case, Barry wanted it. He was desperate to sort himself out,' explained Christine.

One night he wept in her arms, after a particularly outrageous drinking bout, and begged her to help him find the same sort of contentment as her.

He refused to attend a TM session. He wanted Christine to teach him. No one else was trustworthy enough. He was like a child in that way, feeling he could not do it in front of strangers. Immature reservations aside, he was desperate to rid himself of his problems before they cost him his life.

Naturally, Christine was troubled by all this. She felt that he should attend proper classes but she knew something had to be done quickly, otherwise it might be too late. What she feared most of all was that superstition about the mantra. He wanted her mantra. Nobody else's. In fact he insisted that Christine shared that name with him as a pre-condition to learning TM.

Barry needed to be helped so badly. He wanted to sort himself out and Christine loved him. Reluctantly, she agreed to tell him. It was something that would haunt her forever.

Only the night before, they had had such a great evening together. It had been like old times really. Lots of cuddles. Lots of love. Lots of security.

Christine had felt, for the first time in many months, that maybe they could survive together. Barry was meditating regularly with her now. It actually seemed to be working.

Maybe all that superstition about the mantra was nonsense. Perhaps he really would start to live a decent life again. Barry had started to take the TM as seriously as Christine. Every morning they would meditate together. It was having a calming influence. She hoped it would start to divert him away from the drink.

She had gone to sleep that night feeling really optimistic. It certainly made a change.

But the next morning, Christine felt she was back at square one. All that happiness and contentment had disappeared to be replaced with a searing feeling of tension coming from deep inside herself.

However, Barry was not the instigator this time. The cause of her depression was far more simple, although just as tragic. Christine was about to start her menstrual cycle – and she felt awful.

Over the years, Christine had got used to suffering really badly. The TM had helped enormously but PMT was still something she dreaded. While many women manage to carry on their lives virtually unaffected, Christine really couldn't cope.

That pre-menstrual stage would build up until she felt like snapping with the tension. In the week or so before her period she would suffer from splitting headaches, swelling parts of the body, pimples on her skin and incredibly tender breasts.

Headaches are often referred to as the body's all-purpose distress signal. They alert you to the fact that something is wrong. In Christine's case, they were throbbing and excruciatingly painful. Like a hot knife going right through the temple.

Swollen breasts are often a woman's only symptom of Pre Menstrual Tension. But, in Christine's case, they were just part of the agonising scenario. Any hug or pressure was painful. It made her sound irritated, even when she was not. And it didn't help in any relationship with an ignorant man.

Then there was the weight gain and bloating that often accompanied the PMT. Sometimes she would put on as much as seven pounds – all as a result of her body's retention of water.

Her skin also became pink and blotchy. Boils and cold sores were frequent occurrences for Christine. These would affect her confidence and, in turn, could make her even snappier.

Worst of all, though, was the clumsiness. Things were always falling out of Christine's hands. She was forever walking into furniture and knocking things over. Most of the time she would blame herself for her awkwardness. That would put her under even more pressure. Her previous husband and now Barry never truly understood why.

There lay Christine's biggest problem.

The men in her life just never seemed to appreciate the pain and anguish she went through. They just dismissed her behaviour as 'bloody irritating'. Never bothering to really try to think about what was happening inside her body.

She suffered constant anxiety or panic attacks. She felt unloved, irritable, always on the defensive. She would lash out at people for no reason and find herself bursting into tears at the slightest provocation. Even when Barry bought her a present, she would scream at him for no apparent reason.

Then there was the depression. Moodiness, no interest in people or important events, lack of energy, lack of concentration, forgetfulness, insomnia. It all seemed to gang up on Christine and no amount of TM could completely cure her of it. But at least it relaxed her enough to make her believe she could cope.

When she meditated, her body seemed to float away from all the tensions surrounding her. For a precious quarter-hour, she could lose herself in a sea of mysticism. It was the ultimate escape. Sometimes, she wished she could do it permanently.

But the moment she woke up on December 16, 1980, she knew it was going to be a very difficult day – thanks to PMT. That tense feeling was in her head as she grappled for the alarm clock. It could only get worse.

At least she would have Barry for support. Surely he would be understanding about her problem this time? He had witnessed her foul tempers enough in the past. When she tried to explain to him what was going on, he started to appreciate the anguish she went through every month. But it was clear that he did not really understand.

On this particular morning, Barry wasn't in such a good mood himself. Although he had happily soothed Christine the whole of the night before, resulting in a pleasant evening together, he had something he wanted to tell her. And he didn't think she'd like it. She'd only been up a few minutes and she was already very stressed out.

As she meditated in the corner of the bedroom that morning, the TM helped ease the anxiety, but she still had the whole day ahead to cope with.

They meditated together, hoping a 15-minute trance at the end of the bed might be the answer to both their problems. But Barry had not been concentrating properly. Christine noticed he had other things on his mind.

The anticipation of the argument he was bound to provoke was already making Barry short-tempered – and he hadn't even told her yet.

He'd let her get the kids off to school before he broke it to her. Otherwise, she would really go to pieces – and that would not be fair on the children.

Barry had a sense of right and wrong. Maybe that was why he was so worried about telling Christine his little secret. In the time they had been together, she had proved to be remarkably possessive. She didn't like any other female even so much as looking at Barry.

He was her's – and no one else's. That was her attitude and she was sticking to it.

Even when he began drinking more and more and staying at the pub until almost midnight, Christine still regarded him as her property. She was always wary of the predators circling around him. She knew she had to keep a pretty close eye on him.

But Barry was not so keen. He liked the idea of being attractive to other women. It was good for his ego. Besides, it didn't have to mean he slept with them. Being admired is a far cry from infidelity.

He didn't like her possessiveness. It intruded on his freedom. Stopped him being a lad about town.

'I'm going to meet another woman tonight.'

Barry spluttered out the words as hurriedly as possible. It was as if he knew he had to tell her but was hoping she wouldn't hear him.

Christine heard him all right. She looked up from the breakfast table at her handsome lover. She was momentarily stunned. What the hell was he saying? They had just enjoyed one of their best evenings together in months and he was now telling her he was going out with another woman.

She was numbed. He wouldn't do that. He couldn't! Why did he want to hurt her? What right had he to treat her like this?

The tension increased by the second as his words began to sink in. Christine could feel the tightness in her stomach as the adrenaline pumped around her veins, making even her finger tips stiffen with anger.

She began to shout at Barry. How could he do such a thing? Didn't he love her? Bastard. Bastard. Bastard. She would not let him. It was as simple as that. She would not allow him to see the other woman. He would have to make his choice. If he chose this woman then he may as well not bother coming back that night, or any other for that matter.

But Barry was adamant. He wanted his freedom. She could not stand in his way.

He stormed out of the house.

'I am going to run him over. I am going to run him over.'

Christine English kept repeating it to herself over and over again. The elderly woman at the other end of the line was understandably perturbed – she was Barry Kitson's mother.

'I am going to kill him. I am going to run him over and kill him.'

Christine was adamant. The strain that had been building up inside her all day was fast reaching breaking point.

She had eaten nothing but half a sandwich at lunchtime. For a woman who suffered from severe PMT this was madness. All medical researches on PMT have long agreed on one thing – skipping meals can often worsen the symptoms. The irony is that cutting back on food is a classic response to tension and unhappiness. But the lack of food, when nourishment is sorely needed, can be particularly hazardous.

It was mid-afternoon and Christine was already at the end of her tether. She had to tell someone what she felt – so why not his mother?

Mrs Kitson knew that things between them were not good and that her son was partly to blame, but she listened in horror to Christine's threats.

Christine couldn't concentrate on anything. Her mind kept going back to Barry. She wasn't going to let him betray her with that woman. Not tonight. Not any night.

At home that afternoon she was close to tears as she prepared tea for her two sons on their return from school.

How could he just announce his decision like that? How could he be so uncaring? After all she'd done for him.

Christine sat with her head in her hands wondering what she should do about it. In the back of her mind she kept recalling the words she shrieked hysterically at his mother: 'I am going to run him over. I am going to run him over.'

Maybe that was the answer.

By the time Barry got home in the evening, Christine felt her life had been systematically broken into little pieces. Everything she relied on to help her through times of crisis had vanished without explanation. The foundations had been dismantled from beneath her feet.

When he walked in, she tried to stay calm but it was no good. She could not bottle up the anger and bitterness she felt toward him. And to make matters worse, he was still determined to go ahead with his date with another woman. They were heading for an inevitable collision.

'How can you do it? How can you?' She broke the silence within minutes of him settling down in an armchair in the living room.

'I've had enough of this. I'm off.'

Barry made for the door. Desperate to find an escape route away from the constant pressure being applied by Christine. He took the only course of action he knew – and went straight to the pub.

The Live and Let Live was the perfect retreat for Barry Kitson, and it had a particularly pertinent name for him that night. It was the sort of place where he could lose himself in a sea of alcohol. Somewhere to forget his troubles. A pub where he could be himself.

With it's beige, nicotine-stained walls and swirling red carpet, the Trueman's Ales pub was typical of the sort of bar found in a provincial English town. A dartboard offered the only exercise of the day to any regulars.

Barry took up his stool against the tatty pine clad bar – it gave a clear view through the window to the car park outside.

When Christine turned up that evening, she didn't even have to go into the pub for Barry to know she had arrived.

She walked in and tried to nag at him in front of his drinking mates. He was embarrassed and intensely irritated.

'Leave me alone woman.'

He did not want to know. In any case, he still had that date with the other woman to go to. Christine knew that only too well, but she was determined to try to do something to stop it. But the more he drank, the more obsessed Barry became with his inflated idea of freedom. Really, he wanted to see lots of other women the whole time. This was just an excuse to start playing around. Deep down, they both knew that.

Christine really did care about his welfare. She wanted him to come home and sleep off the drink. She hoped he'd forget about the other woman and they could start afresh in the morning.

'Well. If you won't come home, I'll drive you there,' Christine finally offered.

It was a bizarre way to respond, but she was convinced that so long as she was near him there was a chance he might give up his plans for the night.

The journey was strained. After all, Christine was driving her lover to meet another woman on a date. Her motivation was bewildering. Most wives or lovers would have kicked their partner out long ago. But Christine lived in hope that they would enjoy a normal, peaceful life together.

The anxiety was building up inside all the time. She was shaking with tension. She was making herself suffer. When they arrived, Barry got out of the car without uttering a word and walked towards the pub where his secret lover was supposed to be waiting.

As Christine sat in the car outside the pub, it really began to dawn on her what a fool she was being. Why had she allowed herself to drive him to meet another woman? How could he humiliate her so much? She sat in the car outside the pub with her eyes closed. Trying to clear her mind. Trying to get a hold of herself. See sense. This was all so ridiculous. She loved him so much, but what on earth was she doing waiting for him? He was probably inside there holding the bitch's hand while she sat in that car just a few yards away.

People kept walking past her car, wondering what she was doing. She ignored their stares, determined to wait for him however long it took.

After nearly thirty minutes Barry emerged. He was alone. She felt a surge of relief go through her body. He had been stood up for his date. Christine was ecstatic. Barry was furious.

She saw it as a victory. He looked enraged. It was a humiliating climb-down. He was the one who looked a fool now. He had been let down by one woman. Now he had to face the full wrath of another.

Even the drink was beginning to wear off. Even the headaches had been transferred to him.

In the car there was a tense silence. Christine was still outraged by his insulting behaviour. But at least she had her man back. Barry was sulking. It was inevitable they would end up rowing. He called her a bitch. He reckoned she was sneering because she was so satisfied at his failure to pull.

In truth, Christine was far from satisfied. She was angered by his remarks. He was trying to turn the tables on her. Make her feel guilty about the fact that he had a secret rendezvous with another woman.

Her head was throbbing with pain again. It felt as though a tight band of steel was squeezing her skull. Bright light slammed into her eyes, loud noises hammered at her eardrums, the lightest of touches felt they would bruise. To top it all, she felt nauseously dizzy.

It was Barry, however, who cracked first. He grabbed her hair, slapping her viciously across the faces She pulled the car up and started to fight back. Desperate to hurt him. To make him pay for all the awful things he had done to her.

She blasted the horn.

'Get out ... get out ...'

Barry carried on hitting her. But then he noticed they had just pulled up near another of his favourite pubs. He got out of the car. Slammed the door and marched off towards the entrance.

He warned her not to follow him. He said he just wanted to be left alone or 'I'll call the cops.'

Barry must have sensed the devil lurking inside Christine's mind as he walked away.

Christine was shaking with fear at her own rage. She felt incensed by his behaviour. Hurt. Fury. Hate. She had all those feelings going through her head. She had to stop him treating her like this. It could not go on. She kept remembering the warnings of her friends and family. 'He's a bad type. What are you doing with him?' they used to say.

She felt an urge to drive after him. To punish him for all those hurtful things he had done. Flatten him into a bloody pulp forever.

She started up the car and drove after him. She wanted to damage him.

As the car approached him, he turned and faced her. Defiant. Full of bravado.

She looked into his eyes and realised she could not harm the man she loved, so she pulled away and just drove around and around Colchester instead. She needed time to think. She had to get a grip on herself. But the heartbreak of the situation just would not release its grip on her. One moment she felt compassion and love for him, the next she would feel a burning desire to make him suffer, just as he had made her suffer.

Christine thought that, by driving around, she might be able to work off the aggression. She had been so close to killing him. She had to get that feeling out of her system.

But Colchester has only a small core. Soon, she found herself driving past pub after pub that she knew Barry would go to.

It was inevitable that she would come across him wandering drunkenly out of one. She drove through the town's one-way system. Then she signalled right, back onto the dual carriageway that skirts the edge of the town centre.

It was a repetitious journey. The constant driving was soon interrupted when she spotted Barry.

Christine immediately felt that uncontrollable surge of tension returning, when she laid eyes on him.

She stopped the car by him and they began arguing. This time, it was a ferocious row with no limit to the insults they were hurling at each other. All the time, Christine could feel the knots in her stomach tightening.

The enormous stress was exacerbating the symptoms of PMT. She desperately needed to find a way to ease her pain. All that meditation had helped. But, as she sat there, she realised it had not really gone to the root of her problems. The breakdown of every meaningful relationship she'd ever had.

Why did she feel so bad? Why did all this have to happen now, just at the most crucial time? Why couldn't she just close her eyes and wake up somewhere pleasant instead of sitting in that car fighting?

'Just go away!' Barry was yelling at the top of his voice now.

Christine felt a strange compulsion to chase after him. She wanted to wind the argument up even more. She wanted it to reach a crescendo from which there could be no return.

Barry was already at breaking point. He seemed about to explode as he sat in the car next to her. Without any warning he hit her on the head with his hand. It was a short, sharp movement. He did it again. This time smashing down on her arm instead. She tried desperately to fight back, but he was far too strong for her. They were virtually wrestling inside the car now.

Then Barry drew out his ultimate weapon. Something that would hurt her more than any punch. The threat to end all threats. Something he knew she dreaded.

'I never want to see you again.'

He slammed the car door shut and walked off.

She watched him for a moment. In her terrible state, everything seemed distorted with the streetlights and shadows and colours from the buildings and roads all converging on her, rushing towards her as though they would smack the windscreen.

Then she realised the car was moving. She felt herself press down on the accelerator.

I am going to run him over … I am going to run him over. Then a little voice inside her head said. I'm hungry! But it was too late for that now. The only thing she could feed on was revenge.

It was meant to be. Never tell anyone the name of your mantra. It will only bring misery to your life.

He knew her innermost secrets. Now fate would take a hand and punish him for that knowledge.

Run him down! Run him down! Flatten the bastard! The evil little voice had to have its say.

Christine watched Barry as he half walked, half stumbled along the street.

Do it. Go on. He deserves it!

Barry was about to cross the entrance to Sainsbury's. He never got there.

She felt the urge to press harder on the accelerator pedal. She tried to pull her foot up, but the twitching became even worse. She wanted to slam her foot hard down.

It's so easy. Bye bye unhappiness – just one small step ...

Barry helped make up her mind. He turned and, looking straight at her, thrust two fingers into the air. Fuck you, they said, you wouldn't dare.

Christine took a deep breath and pressed her foot down as hard as possible on the accelerator. Just a little bump to show him. That'll shut him up.

Barry didn't believe she would actually do it. She didn't have it in her.

As he stumbled across the poorly lit entrance to Sainsbury's, he turned and saw her face. She certainly looked determined. But she wouldn't actually kill him. He'd test her bottle. And laugh at her when she slammed on the brakes.

The front of the car hit Barry with a huge thud. Then he was swept on to the bonnet.

The bulk of his body lolled against the windscreen.

She felt no emotion. Just a determination to finish off the job properly. She could have stopped there and then. He was already badly injured. Instead, she kept her foot full down on the accelerator and mounted the pavement before smashing head-on into a telegraph pole.

The impact of the car jolted Christine out of her intense trance. She heard her lover groaning. The man she had slept with just ten hours earlier. The man she had just tried to kill.

He was pinned between the lamp-post and the car bonnet, his right leg was almost severed.

'Get it off me. Get it off me.' His voice was slight and agonising.

'Get it off me. Get ...'

He was fading by the second.

Christine English sat for a moment behind the wheel of the car, unable, for a second, to absorb the enormity of what she had just done. Then hysteria took over. It was all so unreal.

'Please, please tell me it's not true. Please God, it hasn't happened.'

Christine stood by the side of the car now. She kept telling herself she only meant to frighten him. She did not want to do this.

Two weeks later Barry Kitson died in hospital.

Christine English was given a conditional discharge for twelve months after pleading guilty to manslaughter with diminished responsibility when she appeared before Norwich Crown Court.

Before deciding to free her, Judge Justice Perchas said, 'There is no course of treatment which can be prescribed for you. But now you are aware that a dramatically minor affair like eating properly is of the utmost importance.'

5

POISON PIE

She wrapped him in her arms, burying his face in her dark, curly hair. For a moment they rocked back and forth, looking intently into each other's eyes. Then she trailed her tongue from his earlobe to the nape of his neck, stopping every few seconds to kiss and suck his young skin. She licked an imaginary line up a few inches before coming to rest at his ear. There, her tongue probed deeper and deeper. It felt as though she was touching his eardrum, exploring every centimetre before sucking the air from it gently and sensuously.

She was in control. She, the mother of three young children, could do anything she wanted with him. He was six years younger – a virgin until he met her.

Next, she nibbled his earlobe. Five, maybe six, times. He was far too excited to be able to count. They were both standing by the end of the bed, waiting for the right moment to fall backwards onto the soft mattress.

She kissed his chest, circling each nipple with her tongue before biting the end. He winced. The pain was sharp, but pleasant. She looked up at his face to see his reaction. His eyes looked glazed and distant. Her silky lips teased each breast, before sucking in hard.

Domination. That's how she liked it. It gave her more pleasure than anything else.

Her lips started moving further down now, exploring every contour of muscle beneath skin. She ran the tip of her tongue from side to side just above his penis. The lovely, beautiful power of the tease. So near and yet so far.

Finally, after what seemed like years, she went lower. Sucking. Biting. Sucking.

Susan Barber was in ecstasy. She was satisfying her young lover in a way that he could not resist. She could do anything she wanted to him and he would just whimper for more. He was so inexperienced – anxious to learn and receive.

They both fell on to the bed. She paused for a moment, making him lie on his back because she wanted to decide when it was time. Until then, she would tease and caress him to within a flick of a finger before orgasm. Each time his breathing reached fever pitch, she would pull away momentarily, just to make sure he did not come.

Soon she would let Richard get what he so badly wanted. But, until that moment she would continue pushing him to the limit. Watching him squirm with a delight tainted by exasperation.

The unmistakable sound of the front door slamming came from downstairs. Susan stopped dead. It was followed by a crash of cutlery in the kitchen.

'Shit! He's come back early.'

Susan jumped up and grabbed her nylon housecoat from the end of the bed. She could hear her husband coming up the stairs. He had heard something. He was going to find them.

Richard was panic stricken. He was not as fast off the mark as Susan. Also, he had peeled his clothes off in her front room when they had first started kissing.

'Shit!! He's seen the clothes on the floor.'

The bedroom door burst open. Michael Barber was steaming with rage. He had come home early from a fishing trip because of bad weather. It was nothing compared with the storm of fury about to erupt in his house.

There was no point in either of them denying it.

Richard was standing completely naked by the wardrobe, desperately trying to find something to put on. But then he could hardly take out a pair of Michael's trousers!

Susan's nipples pressed hard against the nylon of her housecoat. It was obvious she had nothing else on underneath.

'You whore.'

Michael Barber grabbed at her coat. He wanted to rip it off her, humiliate her. She evaded his grasp and made a dash for the door.

But Michael was not going to let matters rest there. 'Come here you slut. Come here!'

He yelled abuse at Susan, then he turned his attentions to Richard. Only two days before, the two men had played on the same side in an Essex interleague darts match at The Plough. Now, that same 'friend' stood before him stark naked after just having made love to his wife in his bed. This was the same man he had bought a pint of bitter for so often. The same man he had congratulated on getting a bullseye. The same man he had encouraged to be patient with the darts team scorer.

'She's not too good at adding up mate. But her heart's in the right place.'

'She' just happened to be Susan.

'You fucking bastard.'

Michael stood there and looked at Richard's pale and plucked body.

'Pathetic. Fucking pathetic.'

Richard stayed silent – afraid to inflame the situation. Not really knowing what to say.

'Now get the fuck out of my house. Bastard.'

Michael tensed his fists in anger. This was an insult to his manhood. His pride. His reputation. He had to do something about it.

'I'm going to kill you.'

He lurched towards Richard, just missing him with his right fist. Still completely naked, the slightly built lover made a move for the door. He was vulnerable and highly embarrassed, but he had to get out of that house if he valued his own life.

'Come here you fucking cunt!'

The two men came thumping down the stairs.

Richard slipped, rather than ran, down the stairway. Losing his balance every two or three steps in a desperate bid to escape Michael's clutches. In the hallway, he stopped for a moment, but it was a ridiculous idea. There was no way he was going to pick up his clothes from the front room *and* escape without a beating. They still lay scattered across the carpet where – less than an hour earlier – Susan had so amorously removed them. Richard lunged for the front door.

Michael was gaining on the younger, lighter man. Richard struggled with the front door lock. It was one of those Yale-type double locks. Almost as difficult to open as to close.

Susan pushed him out of the way and opened the lock for him in one quick motion. She blocked the way while Richard made a run for it. Michael barged his wife out of his path, sending her flying to the floor.

As he reached the front door step, he saw Richard's naked form desperately fiddling with the garden gate. He gave up and hurtled over it in one precarious leap.

Michael knew he would get away. He stopped chasing and watched as the nude figure ran four houses up Osbourne Road, then went up the pathway to the neighbouring house.

Michael looked at his wife.

'Now it's your turn bitch ...'

He shut the front door and hit his wife across the face.

Michael and Susan were barely on speaking terms the next morning. By the time he left the house to go to work at the nearby Rothman's factory, the atmosphere had got so tense that she had genuinely feared for her life.

The previous night he had beaten her black and blue. She couldn't face another thrashing. Rather than inflame the situation any further, she kept quiet. Praying he wouldn't pick a rematch with her.

Within minutes of watching her husband leave their modest three-bedroomed semi, she found herself thinking about Richard. He kept her going. She wanted to be with him the whole time.

There was not a lot of other happiness in her life at that time. Richard satisfied her craving for physical love. Sex was something that had been missing from her marriage for at least five years. Now she had got her sense of adventure back. She loved to feel that she was doing something exciting. Daring. Naughty.

She always felt so good when she was with him. He made her feel ten years younger than her twenty-nine years – and that was the best part of all. She could relive her lost youth by behaving as irresponsibly as she wanted.

Now, her husband had gone off to work and she wanted her lover once more. She stood by the telephone in the hallway, wondering if she should call him. Would he even want to see her again after what happened yesterday? Perhaps he'd want to finish their affair? After all, he must have been pretty scared. But then again he had left his clothes. That gave her an excuse to call.

She picked up the phone.

Susan and Richard lay next to each other in bed. Both were entirely satisfied. Content for the first time in days. Physically drained from an hour of energy-sapping love making.

'He's mad you know. One day he'll kill you,' said Richard.

Susan knew her lover was right. She had long harboured an intense hatred for her husband. The beatings. The verbal abuse. The lack of affection. The list of reasons why their marriage was in shreds was endless.

She had promised herself she'd leave him. But she'd never plucked up the courage to actually do it. Now, however, it was different. Her infidelities were out in the open and he would become even more violent towards her. He wouldn't be able to understand her need for sex. He'd given it up so why should she have it? That was just the way he saw life. Revolving around him.

Now his pride had taken a battering. The whole street probably knew what had happened that night. A naked man runs out of their house with the husband in hot pursuit. And he just happens to be the boy who lives with his parents a few doors up the road. The evidence was there for everyone to see.

It would be the talk of the neighbourhood, if not the whole of Westcliff-on-Sea, by now. Susan didn't care. Her need to be loved far outweighed her reputation amongst a load of petty, nosey neighbours. But he would.

As she lay there next to Richard, she began to realise that maybe there was only one solution to the problem. 'Kill him before he kills me.'

She got out of the bed and put on her clothes. Richard looked disappointedly at her. She beckoned him to come with her. They had some very important business to attend to.

The Barber back garden was not exactly an impressive example of superb horticultural skills. A few flower beds dotted about the place. A scrap of grass in the middle, badly worn by the antics of three young children. A few toys scattered haphazardly beside a climbing frame in the corner.

It was a garden all the same. And nearly all the gardens in Osbourne Road had one thing in common – a shed. They were a vital part of keeping up with the Joneses. The sort of shed you had was a definite reflection of your wealth. Neighbours would frequently glance along the rows of gardens, comparing their own outhouse with those in every garden for at least 100 yards in each direction.

Michael Barber's shed wasn't perfect. But it certainly had a lot of character to it. He had built it with his own fair hands out of slates of wood he got when he worked for a firm of landscape gardeners. About eight feet square, it had another very important role to play besides being the place where he kept all the tools and utensils. It was his very own very private retreat. A place where he could get away from everything. Where neither the children nor the wife could bother him.

He would often spend hours fiddling with bits of car engines in the shed, happy in the knowledge that no one would disturb him. It was the perfect place to escape if you happened to live in a town like Westcliff-on-Sea.

Now, Susan Barber was trying to find out if that shed held the ultimate escape route for her.

With Richard by her side, she was trying to find the Paraquat poison she knew her husband had left in the shed a few years back.

She remembered the day he got it, back in the seventies, because he brought it home from work and used to go on and on about making sure the kids got nowhere near it. They were younger then.

'It's a killer, this stuff. Just remember that.'

Susan had never forgotten her husband's warning. She took great care as she heaped tablespoonfuls of the powder into a small pill bottle.

Richard smiled as he watched her.

Susan had taken full heed of her husband's warning by using a bottle with a child-proof cap. You didn't want it getting into the wrong hands, after all.

Susan made an effort for Michael when he came home from work that evening. She wanted to make amends. Start all over. Try and make the next few weeks as bearable as possible. They might be his last.

She made his favourite dish for tea – steak pie. If there was one thing that just about brought a smile to his face, she thought, it was steak pie.

It needed to be cooked for hours beforehand, to make the meat as lean as possible. Michael would never allow her enough money to buy the good meat. She had to make do with that tough stuff that the butchers virtually gave away. But, after simmering for a long time, no one could really tell the difference. At least that's what Michael always said.

Earlier that afternoon, Richard gave her a warm embrace as they stood by the cooker. Together, they were hatching a plan that could give her the perfect way out of an awful marriage.

She picked up the plastic pill container, untwisted the lid and sprinkled the powder into the gravy she was mixing on the stove.

'How much do you think? Is that enough?'

'No. Put some more in. He won't be able to tell the difference.'

Richard hugged his lover, giving her an extra tight squeeze as she dropped most of the contents into the gravy.

He won't humiliate me ever again, she thought.

Michael was not particularly impressed with his favourite dish when he eventually got home from work. He was still seething with anger about the events of the day before. Furious and unforgiving. How could she expect him to just forget the fact that, only twenty-four hours earlier, he had come home and found her in bed with one of the neighbours? What difference could a bloody pie make?

Mind you, he was starving hungry - and that steak pie did smell delicious. Susan always cooked great pies. It must have covered three quarters of the white plate. The yellowing, crusty pastry contrasting with the dark brown, almost black, colour of the beef. The peas and boiled potatoes were like an afterthought really. Barely making an impression, compared with the vast quantity of pie.

Susan watched him pouring the gravy over the food. She found she just could not keep her eyes off it. For a moment, Michael looked up at her quizzically. 'What you looking at woman?'

Susan smiled and got back to her own dish of food. She never did like gravy anyway. She always made it especially for her husband.

Michael was a messy eater. He tended to hold his knife and fork like two drum sticks and shovel the food into his mouth. Usually, Susan would grimace with disgust while watching him stuff his face. But this time she actually found herself enjoying the sight of him eating. Munching, and then noisily swallowing, each gigantic mouthful. It was a lovely sight.

She tried to keep her head down in silence. That was the way it was normally at meal times. Every so often, though, she allowed her eyes to travel discreetly towards his plate of food, where he was feasting on that very special pie.

It didn't take a lot to get Susan excited when she was in a room with an attractive man. Her husband had long since stopped having that effect on her. However, as she sat at the kitchen table, watching Michael devouring his food, she felt a strange tingling sensation rushing through her body. She kept fidgeting in her chair in the hope it would divert his attention from her obviously excited state.

Crossing her legs one moment. Uncrossing them the next. She had to clench her teeth to stop herself from giggling. She could not believe he was actually eating it without a word of complaint.

Richard had said he wouldn't taste a thing. She hadn't believed it. She thought it would surely have had some sort of aftertaste.

But her grotesque lump of a husband was loving each and every mouthful.

'Got any more of this stuff on the go?'

That was the nearest he had come to a compliment in years. She took his plate and piled on yet more pie, a sparse sprinkling of vegetables and sloshed the whole lot with gallons of gluey gravy.

Her breathing had quickened. Would he notice? No. He was too busy filling his fat stomach 'What's for sweet then?'

Susan snapped out of her trance. It was probably just as well.

She served up his pudding, happy in the knowledge she had just sentenced her husband to a slow and agonising death.

Susan was irritated.

It had been three days now and there had been no sign of it taking effect. She lay in bed next to her husband wondering if she would have to give him even more Paraquat. Richard had warned it would take a few days.

She could not stand the waiting. Not knowing if his cast-iron stomach had already managed to flush every trace of poison out.

How much longer would it take? She had given him a massive dose. Surely he would start to suffer soon? Maybe they should have cut his brake pipes instead. That would have been much faster and simpler. None of this cooking and waiting around.

As she lay there, she became aware that her husband was stirring. She kept her eyes tightly shut in case he realised she was awake.

It was the middle of the night. He could hardly breath. His throat felt as if it had a layer of carpet clogging it up. His chest was pulsating with pain. What he did not realise was that his lungs had been rapidly turning hard and leathery – making it more and more difficult for any air to get through. Then he started to get awful stabbing pains in his kidneys.

He got up to get a glass of water. But the liquid just made the stinging sensation even more unbearable. He felt as if hundreds of tiny daggers were travelling through his body, stabbing his insides at every opportunity.

Every few moments, his body would twitch with discomfort as the stabs became more and more frequent. 'Susan. Wake up. I'm in fucking agony. Call the doctor.'

Susan Barber thought she was dreaming at first. But no. Her husband's anguished face looked very real.

'At first, we thought it was pneumonia Mrs Barber.'

The doctor was full of sympathy for Susan as they stood by the hospital bedside. She had called the ambulance when Michael collapsed on the bathroom floor.

Slowly. Ever so slowly. She dialled the emergency services. She didn't want to hurry in case the end was near.

Wouldn't it be great if he died here and now, she thought for a moment.

84

But he was still struggling for life when the ambulance men eventually turned up. Maybe it would be even easier if he died in hospital. Less mess. Less questions. Less suspicion.

In any case, nearby Southend had a perfectly pleasant hospital. Good clean wards and caring nurses. What more could he ask for? But then Michael Barber was hardly in a fit state to appreciate the nurses!

The poison was now definitely beginning to kill Michael Barber. To him, it must have felt as though a psychopath had been let loose inside his body. Travelling to every corner of his system, ruthlessly mutilating every living organ for no apparent reason.

Now, the doctor in the hospital sounded hesitant about the illness. Perhaps he suspected it was poison? Maybe they were trying to put her to the test? Watching her reaction for any signs of fake concern. Had they found traces of poison in his blood stream already?

For just a brief moment, Susan was worried. But then she thought, where are the police if they suspect? She glanced around her. No one was approaching with handcuffs. No one was even looking in her direction. She knew she was still in the clear.

The facade of concern for her husband's well-being should not slip for one moment. She had to keep up the pretence. She must not give them any clues.

The doctor at Southend Hospital looked most concerned. Susan wondered what he was about to say. 'We think it may be a condition called Goodpasture's Syndrome. It's a rare nervous disorder that breaks down the body's internal mechanism.'

Susan was confused. Luckily her confusion helped make her look even more like a heartbroken wife, whose husband was on his deathbed.

It was 1981. The AIDS epidemic had not really begun to take its devastating toll on the western world, otherwise the doctors probably would have suspected he was an HIV victim.

Susan was touched by the doctor's concern. It was so nice of him to be so caring. If only he knew she really did not give a jot.

Susan just hoped and prayed he wasn't such a good doctor that he might find out her husband had been poisoned. Worse still, he might even save Michael's life. That really would not do.

'We recommend he is transferred to a special hospital where they can keep an even closer eye on him.'

She did not care where it was, so long as he hurried up and died.

At the beginning of June, Michael Barber was transferred to the Hammersmith Hospital in West London. It had been less than one month since Susan had laced his gravy with Paraquat poison.

On June 27th, he died a dreadful, painful death. The cause was given as pneumonia and kidney failure.

It was only a small service. Susan, the kids and a handful of friends and relatives.

He would have wanted it that way.

Whether he would have welcomed his wife's lover, Richard, with such open arms was perhaps not so certain.

However, Susan needed him there. He was her support – even though they could not stand too close together in case other people noticed.

Instead, they looked at each other longingly as the coffin trundled slowly into the crematorium oven. The organ music played a timeless hymn in the background and the oak casket slid through the curtain. The final memory of her husband. Burning in a box of wood.

She had insisted on the crematorium. It meant there would be no body to re-examine. No doubting doctor could exhume his corpse and find fresh clues. He was gone forever. No one would find out.

Now she and Richard could go and get drunk and celebrate. The £16,000 pension and the £900 a year allowance for the kids should take care of them for a while. It had all been so easy.

At Hammersmith Hospital, Professor David Evans had a nagging suspicion about the death of Michael Barber. He had carried out a detailed post mortem the day after his death. He even took test samples from the body. Blood, urine, everything he could think of, just in case there were signs of Paraquat. He removed vital organs and ordered them to be preserved in jars and kept in storage.

All the signs were there. It had to be. Why else would a perfectly healthy thirty-five-year-old man collapse and die.

Professor Evans reckoned the tests were a mere formality. Once the results arrived back, he would contact the police and tell them to arrest the wife immediately.

He was stunned when they did come back from the National Poisons Unit. There were definitely no signs of Paraquat poisoning. The Professor could not believe it. But he had to take the word of analysts. Even so, he still felt a nagging doubt.

Something about the case did not add up.

There was nothing he could do about it now. Death was through natural causes – the death certificate said so. He would have to drop the case.

'Aren't you bothered what the neighbours think?' There were times when Richard was shocked by Susan. She just didn't seem to care. She had no pride. He may have been younger than her, but she was the one with the irresponsible streak. The one who was wild and untamed.

It was the day after her husband's funeral, but she couldn't wait a moment longer to have him to herself. She insisted he bring his belongings around and move into the house. He had no choice.

Susan had got away with murder. Now she could enjoy her life for the first time in years. She didn't give a damn what people thought. No one suspected her. It was the perfect crime. Now she wanted her reward – and it came in the shape of Richard. He was the young lover she did all this for. He was the man she wanted in her bed.

Richard, however, was not so keen. It had all started as a casual affair. He'd been swept up by the whole thing.

When they first met at The Plough, he didn't even realise what was on her mind. After all, he was a kid still living at home. She was a happily married mother of three children.

Richard had always lived with his parents. Sheltered from the outside world, he had never even slept with a girl. When his mates in The Plough told him that she had a definite soft spot for him, he thought they were kidding.

When she asked him round one afternoon while Michael was out working a day shift at the nearby Rothmans factory, he went in all innocence – convinced that any fantasies he had about her would not actually come true. She wanted him to fix the fridge. He was more than happy to oblige.

The boys at the pub had already told her he was still a virgin. The idea of seducing an innocent really appealed to her. Richard was even more willing to oblige when she offered to take him to bed.

Six months later, however, he was starting to grow tired of her. She had taught him so much about sex. But now he wanted to try it out with someone new. He didn't want the full time commitment of a live-in relationship – especially with a woman who had just murdered her husband. But Richard was weak and impressionable. That was why she had got him in the first place. He didn't have the courage to tell her what he thought. He just accepted the situation and moved into her house.

It was obvious it would never last.

Professor David Evans was growing more and more fascinated by the Michael Barber case. He kept going back to his findings and re-examining the facts. Just in case he had made a mistake. He was looking for something more that would tell him for certain his suspicions were unfounded. He just would not accept the situation. It kept niggling at him. He knew he had to drop the case from his full-time agenda but that did not mean he had to forget it altogether. However hard he tried, he couldn't come up with an explanation of why Barber actually died.

The inquest might have concluded it was natural causes but Professor Evans knew otherwise. Even if it wasn't poison, it was certainly a fascinating case and he thought it would be intriguing for some of his colleagues to study it.

With the furthering of medical science in mind, he decided to call a conference, the following January, of all the doctors involved in the case – more than six months after the death of Michael Barber.

At least they could swap notes and compare findings. Something that might help save lives in the future.

Susan Barber was bored. She was fed up with being the dominating one in her relationship with Richard. Why couldn't he make a few decisions for a change? Surely he could start acting like a real man rather than a wimp? Maybe it was time to swap him for a more mature model? At least Michael had had a bit of character. Shame, in a way, that he was no longer around.

She laughed at her own ludicrous notions. Michael was the last person she wanted back on this earth.

They were drifting apart. More and more, she was thinking about other attractive men. It was how she felt when she was married to Michael.

It was time to end it – and get out there and start enjoying life once more. Wasn't that exactly what she told herself when Michael was still alive?

Richard was only too happy to go. Back to his parents, four doors away. They might as well have been a world apart.

Susan needed a new man if she was going to satisfy her never ending lust for life. Meeting them was not easy in Westcliff-on-Sea. A small, rather drab Victorian seaside resort, it was filled with pensioners living out their last few years. Hardly the sort of place for a merry widow to find an energetic young lover.

Susan was going crazy with frustration. She needed the comfort and support of a man. But, most of all, she needed the physical pleasures. That was what kept her sane. She thought of sex frequently. She needed to satisfy that demand. But how could she do that in a place like Westcliff?

Strangely enough, she eventually found the answer in citizen band radio. Susan had hardly touched the CB set since Michael's death. Now she had an urge to switch it on. She would find herself a man. First, she had to think up a call sign.

'Nympho' seemed appropriate.

Steel erector Martin Harvey always considered himself fit and healthy, but even he was having trouble keeping up with Susan Barber. They had met in the pub only a few hours earlier but it was clear from the start what Susan was after. Everyone knew what Susan liked to do with men.

'She'll eat you for breakfast mate,' said one helpful soul.

In the pub, she cuddled up to twenty-year-old Martin and told him exactly what she wanted. Richard had gone. She wanted him to share her bed with her, give him her own unique taste in pleasure.

Within seconds of arriving at the house, she had ripped his clothes off and got down to business in front of the electric fire. The first time was pretty traditional but, three hours later, she still had not stopped.

The bathroom. The kitchen. The toilet. The spare bedroom. There was no room left in the house where they had not done it.

Then Susan decided she wanted to try something new. Leaving Martin lying naked on the bed, she walked over to the corner of the room and switched on the CB transmitter.

'Nympho here ...'

She soon found a willing partner. She told him to turn up the volume and listen. She put the microphone on the table by the bed and got back on top of Martin and started to make love to him.

She whispered in his ear not to make a sound. She wanted her CB pal to think she was having sex with him on the airwaves.

She moaned and sighed. Then she turned her head towards the mike and said: 'Can you hear me ... I'm coming ... harder ... harder ... I want you to come too.'

A few days later she was back on the CB again.

'Hello. This is Nympho calling Magic Man. Do you read me ... over?'

Her provocative name would attract the right sort of man.

'Magic Man' turned out to be Rick Search. He had built up quite a rapport with 'Nympho' – now he wanted to meet her in the flesh.

The garage mechanic liked the sound of 'Nympho'. He had that feeling she would live up to her name. He had been surprised, but hardly complained, when she suggested a date. He agreed without hesitation.

Most of the lonely women who broadcast on the CB airwaves tended to be grandmotherly figures just looking for someone to talk to. But 'Nympho' wasn't after a friendly chat. She positively oozed sex down the microphone.

She had decided it was a great way to meet new lovers.

Rick had no doubts what to expect when he called round at her house in Osbourne Road.

He was not disappointed. The magic was definitely there.

Susan was really enjoying the freedom her CB romances allowed her. Most of the men were just interested in one thing – and that suited her. She loved the excitement of meeting men on blind dates. She would wait at the window to her house and watch them arrive. If they were not her type then she would simply pretend to be out.

They'd soon go away. Convinced that 'Nympho' must have been a crackpot who never meant a word of all the sexual innuendo she had spoken over the airwaves.

The merry widow was having the time of her life.

It was now January, 1982.

At Hammersmith Hospital, Professor David Evans had assembled the team of doctors who worked on the strange case of Michael Barber. Before them lay a bizarre collection of the dead man's organs and bodily fluids, which had been pickled and stored away.

The doctors began a minute, piece-by-piece examination of every bit of evidence. They looked at slides that showed Barber's body. They studied the photos of his organs. Then they dissected the actual remains. It was a macabre gathering. But Professor Evans believed it had to be done.

The doctors concluded there were still many unanswered aspects to the case – but there was not enough evidence to re-open it. What baffled them was how Barber could have consumed the Paraquat in the first place. Since 1975, it had been deliberately manufactured with a pungent smell. No one could have taken it without almost immediately vomiting from the awful aroma.

But, as a final gesture, they all agreed that leftover blood and urine samples should be sent to Paraquat manufacturers ICI and the National Poisons Unit.

Some of the medics argued that tests had always proved negative. But Professor Evans just wanted to make doubly sure ...

Two months later, the results came back.

This time they were affirmative. Michael Barber had been poisoned. The original tests had never taken place. All those months earlier, a laboratory technician had wrongly informed Hammersmith Hospital the tests were negative.

In April, 1982, Susan Barber and Richard Collins were arrested in Osbourne Road. On November 8, 1982, at Chelmsford Crown Court, Susan Barber was sent to jail for life after being found guilty of murdering her husband.

Former lover Richard Collins was sentenced to two years for conspiring with Susan Barber to kill her husband.

6

KILLING DADDY

Wet Willie's was the kind of bar you never went into alone. The shoebox-sized saloon was filled with denim-clad drifters and hard nosed bikers with no place to go. 'They were the type of people who would bust your head open for a buck,' according to regular Dick Mills.

Night after night the same crowd of no-hopers would fill the cramped bar playing pool, drinking beer and raising hell. It was the sort of place you read about, but tried to avoid. A room full of renegades existing on incredibly short fuses.

It was situated slap bang in the centre of Daytona's most notorious red light district. The Florida city made famous by the one of the world's most dangerous motorcycle circuits, was a haven for bikers of every race, creed and religion. But, unlike the immensely wealthy speed heroes of the track, most of these enthusiasts had little more to offer life other than a passion for their machines.

The Daytona race was held just once a year – but these people lived their entire existence in the beachside city.

Many of them scraped a living out of manual labour. Others just gave up hope and survived by sleeping rough and stealing a meal every now and again.

Dick Mills was a stocky sort of guy with lots of tattoos up each arm. He was different to most of the crowd. He had tried desperately to get out of the vicious circle of violence and excessive boozing by marrying Connie – a local girl with a good background. Dick had been through a hell of lot in his life.

A Vietnam vet, he witnessed the horrors of war first hand. It was a time that haunted him still, made worse by the realization that the awful carnage he'd seen in South-East Asia was also happening much closer to home. Murders. Rapes. Muggings. They were all everyday occurrences in Daytona.

Dick's first marriage had failed miserably, because he had got caught inside that short-sighted bikers' world. Now he was trying to make amends and start again with a new wife and, he had hoped, a new life.

Connie seemed the perfect kind of girl for Dick. He was gone forty now and knew he wouldn't have many more opportunities to find happiness. When they married in the summer of 1990, it really had seemed the perfect match. But, just four months later, Dick was wondering what had gone wrong. He had dropped his biker image. She wanted them to settle down. Be responsible. Lead a careful life.

It didn't last. There were too many temptations around for Dick to handle.

Connie had kicked him out because the arguments seemed never ending. They rowed about the dishes, the TV, the money. You name it, they battled over it. It all proved too much for either of them to stand.

Now his life was back where it had started. No future. No job. No money.

He slouched into Wet Willie's to drown his sorrows. It was Christmas, 1990. For Dick, that was simply an excuse to get drunk.

Country music blared out from the bar's jukebox in the corner. Two bikers dressed in oil stained denims played a round of pool at a furious rate – spurred on by alcohol and a need to act macho. Three Hell's Angels talked about engine bearings and the inner workings of their Harley Davidsons. Every now and again, prostitutes with hard, gaudy faces walked into the bar, cast a glance at any lonely looking men and then 'home in' to do business. For these girls, it was a damn sight more pleasant inside Wet Willie's than cruising the sidewalks of nearby North Ridgewood Avenue. There, the girls were often raped or attacked after plying for trade with a motorist – who just happened to want to make a woman suffer. They all dressed in either skintight jeans and stilettos or pencil-thin skirts, often made out of slinky leather or rubber. It was a uniform really. They had to attract the eye of every passing male and the glistening shininess of their outfits spelt the message out loud and clear. An advertisement that read: 'I am for sale. Why not buy me?' Then, as a curb crawling driver slowed down to inspect the goods, they would make eye contact. Nine times out of ten that would guarantee success.

Dick Mills wasn't interested in paying for sex that night. For one thing he was skint. And, more importantly, his mind was on other things. His disastrous marriage. His failure in life. His failure as a man.

As he supped at a can of ice cold beer, he was only just aware of the music being played. If a woman had come up and sat right next to him at that moment, he probably wouldn't even have looked up.

He eventually awoke from his problems when one of his all time favourite country songs broke through his stupor. Johnny Paycheck's 'Take This Job And Shove It' had a certain aptness to his own current situation. It brought a wry smile to his face.

He swivelled round on his bar stool towards the jukebox. Dick wanted to see if a real soulmate had put the record on. He was starting to feel sociable again.

There, sitting next to the jukebox, was a blonde woman, all alone.

It was the first time Dick had noticed anyone the entire evening. But then he could not help seeing this particular girl.

She was crying and singing to the droning music all at the same time. She looked up and smiled briefly at Dick.

He smiled back – immediately attracted by her face and her grief.

He examined her for a moment. Even amongst the bikers and the prostitutes, her outfit seemed sexually charged. She was wearing a black leather, tight fitting all-in-one motorcycle jumpsuit. It had a red stripe down each side. Showing up the contours of her body as she sat down at a table on her own.

Aileen Wuornos was heartbroken. She had also just split up with a lover. They had enjoyed such passion together. But now all that was gone.

Every time she thought of the outrageous sex, it made her cry because they would never enjoy each other again. They had parted, split up for good. Now, she realised just how much she needed her lover. She'd been the dominating one, but they both got the same pleasure out of their relationship. If only she had appreciated that at the time.

But then love between two women is often more powerful and possessive than any heterosexual affair.

Dick was perturbed. He had come into Wet Willie's to forget his troubles, not pick up a woman. But the alcohol had gradually begun to ease the pain and now he felt the sort of urges that had nothing whatsoever to do with a broken heart.

He watched the woman by the jukebox closely.

And she knew he was watching her.

As her tears began to subside, she too started to feel something. It was the need to be loved by someone. Anyone. It didn't really matter who.

However, Dick was a shy sort of bloke underneath and he couldn't conjure up the courage to even ask this girl if she wanted a beer. He kept getting up off his stool and then sitting down again – unsure how to make the initial approach.

She was gyrating her body to the music now. Slightly rocking in her seat. Squeezing those leather clad thighs together. Thinking of Tyria Moore, her beautiful blonde lover. Remembering those glorious, hot days when they would spend 24 hours in bed together exploring each other's bodies.

They tried everything together. It was a never-ending world of sexual experimentation. And Tyria never objected. She just wanted to please Aileen all of the time.

Dick couldn't help noticing her gyrations. It was quite exhilarating to watch. This girl had real rhythm. She must be one hell of woman, thought Dick.

At the fifth attempt to move towards her, he actually got up and began the short walk to the table, where she was sitting. He was nervous. He did not like rejection. Even though he was there alone, he found it embarrassing.

Aileen was howling to the music and swigging back bottles of beer at an alarming rate. People in the bar had noticed her all right. But they just looked away, bemused. The sight of a lone woman getting drunk was unusual even in Wet Willie's.

All Dick could see in the dimly lit bar was the slinkiness of her leather suit in the lamplight. He was just a few feet from her when he heard the leather stretch and rub against the plastic seat as she moved in the chair. It was an exciting sound. As he approached the table, he still did not think he could bring himself to talk to her.

'You got a car?' Aileen broke the silence between them. It was a relief to Dick. She had made the first move. Now he felt the confidence to press further.

'Yep. Sure do.'

As he stood by the table next to the jukebox, the music was now loud enough to trigger nosebleeds in the car park outside.

Finally, he sat down opposite her. She smiled wearily. But at least she did not tell him to get lost.

'You wanna lift someplace?'

Dick looked at the zip fastener at the front of her leather outfit. It was undone just enough to show a hint of her breasts, which were squeezed tightly against the hide.

'Hi. My name's Lee Green. What's yours?' said Aileen.

Her real name was just one of many deep and dark secrets she would always keep from Dick.

Within minutes, he had agreed to give her a ride to the Greyhound Bus

96

Station in Daytona. It was the place where Aileen kept her belongings — including a well-used pistol.

As they walked out to the car park, Dick's mind was only on her body, so distinctly outlined by the tight fitting black leather outfit. Even when she abruptly refused his offer to open the car's passenger door for her, he thought nothing of it. She was just some women's libber — not a deadly man hater, he thought.

They drove along North Ridgewood Avenue, past the hookers and the drug dealers on every corner. At one point, while they waited for the lights to change, a tall, black prostitute beckoned to them.

Dick noticed how Aileen stared at the street walker, intensely examining her mini-skirted body. She seemed to know her. But then again maybe not. As they moved off, Aileen turned and watched the girl disappear behind them. Dick didn't think much of it. Just another hooker, he presumed.

Aileen's interest had, of course, been sexual. When she saw that girl's shapely body it had, momentarily, awoken her animal instincts once more. She remembered why she had always preferred women to men. Their bodies were so much more interesting.

Aileen was relieved to get a lift — even from a man. But the fact remained that men had ruined her life a long time before …

It had all begun when she was still in her cradle, 33 years earlier in Rochester, Michigan.

Her mother Diane could not cope with baby Aileen and brother Keith, so she turned them over to her parents for adoption and disappeared. The reason she ran away was simple — her husband had a terrifying temper and used to beat her regularly. Later Leo Pittman's psychopathic tendencies resulted in the sex abuse of one child and the suspected murder of another. Aileen's mother was well rid of that evil man.

The next man to ruin Aileen's life was a brutal teenager, who made her pregnant at just thirteen. He raped her and then denied being the father. Aileen's grandparents swept the entire episode under the carpet and packed her off to a home for unwed mothers, where the baby was born and then taken away.

When Aileen ran away at fourteen, it was no surprise that she ended up supporting herself as a prostitute. With no home and no family to turn to, she had been living under the shadow of death since the day she was born.

Men were the root of all evil as far as Aileen Wuornos was concerned.

Now she was accepting a lift from a strange man in the middle of a dangerous town. She would never learn. 'Pull over. Pull over now.'

The police car megaphone was loud and clear. The patrol car alongside Dick and Aileen was stopping them for a traffic violation, or so Dick presumed.

Aileen was scared. Her fear of cops had steadily increased during the previous 12 months to the point of paranoia. She had a lot to hide. And she wasn't going to stop running now. She wanted to get away.

She felt the cold steel of the pistol inside her overnight bag. In some ways she hoped she would have to use it. Then the end might come more quickly.

Her breathing was uneven now. Aileen was nervous. She watched as the two officers walked around to Dick.

'Tell them to fuck their asses,' she hissed.

Dick thought a more cautious approach might be wiser. He had enough problems at that moment. He didn't want any trouble with the cops.

'Hey. Fuck off cops. Leave us alone.'

Aileen couldn't control herself. She had to get the first words in.

She gripped the pistol hard in her hand as she spoke. But it was still hidden from view inside that bag.

Dick was taken aback. What the hell was she playing at. It was as if she wanted to get them arrested. Why was she doing this?

'Shut the fuck up will you?' he retorted.

Dick was adamant. Aileen turned her head away in fury. No man could tell her to shut up. Men were nothing. They were scuzzbags. They used women and then discarded them like old packets of cigarettes.

They had no right.

Dick somehow managed to smooth over the cops but he was stunned by her aggressive nature.

'She went wild at the sight of them. Completely crazy. I just didn't understand it at the time,' he said later.

But it was only one of the many warnings signs that were to follow.

'Just drive around for a while.'

Aileen recovered her composure. They had only been making a random licence check – nothing more.

Perhaps she wished it had been something more, then she could have fired at them. They would have fired back and, maybe, it would have been the end. Then she could have confessed her sins.

Instead, she had Dick to talk to. He seemed all right, for a man.

They soon discovered their mutual bond – the pain and anguish of broken relationships.

'We're both in the pits of hell. You're blown out over your broken love affair with Ty. I'm blown out over wanting Connie back. We're both manic depressives. Insane in a way,' Dick told her.

He was absolutely right of course. But Aileen didn't want to tell him how correct he really was.

Later he recalled, 'There are two people I've ever met who have met the devil and shaken his hand. One is me. The other is her.'

That night, they drove around Daytona just talking. Talking about the heartache and the misery of losing the one you love. They compared notes. For Aileen it was a weird experience. She was pouring out all her problems to a man. Perhaps the end was already in sight.

It was kind of inevitable that Dick and Aileen would end up in a motel room together. After talking themselves dry, it seemed a reasonable enough thing to do. They were both lonely and unattached. Why not?

As Dick unlocked the door to the scruffy, slightly stale smelling room at the Hawaii Motel, on South Ridgewood, he was just glad of the company. The sex – if it happened – would be a bonus.

This was hardly a glamorous, romantic place. Five pounds a bed for a night, but neither of them had anywhere else to stay.

Aileen was surprisingly relaxed. It had been a long time since she had slept with a man. In fact, when she was with Ty, she pledged never to screw one of those bastards again. But that was over now. So why not? Dick didn't seem like the others. He actually listened to what she had to say without treating her like some idiot dyke. It made a refreshing change. Most of the men she had slept with either paid money for the pleasure or raped her without any remorse. Now she was with a man who seemed genuinely interested in her. Why shouldn't she allow him to sleep with her?

She started to remove her clothes by unzipping the front of her leather all-in-one jump suit. She knew the outfit turned Dick on and really enjoyed watching him watching her. She felt she wanted to give him some real pleasure. Just this once.

Dick was nervous. Aileen had admitted being a lesbian yet she was about to have sex with him. Why? He found her attractive but he could not understand if the feeling was mutual. It was impossible to tell what Aileen was really thinking.

Aileen felt the need. She wanted a man. Usually, a woman was enough. But this time she felt different. She knew that nothing could match the satisfaction a man gave in certain ways.

With Ty it had been good. Incredibly good. They had done everything there was to do. But, just occasionally, she yearned for the full penetration of a man. She still wanted to dominate though. No man would get the better of her and the only way to treat them was to make them do what she wanted.

'Lie down,' she ordered Dick.

He did as he was told and then began a sex session that was led by only one person – Aileen.

What she wanted she got. Like an animal on heat. Sometimes her sexual savagery reached frightening levels. She didn't care about her partner. It was pure luck if he climaxed with her.

But she kept going for hours. Making demand after demand. Determined to get her own way.

Underneath it all, Dick was just another man – and they all had to suffer.

Hours later, the two lovers lay in bed together, thinking …

'I loved her so much. I'll never replace her.'

Aileen was crying tears of love for Ty on Dick's shoulders.

Dick had never experienced such animal passion before. Yet, Aileen still only had one real obsession – her former lesbian lover.

Dick was the last thing on her mind. He was just an object to be used. Ty was different. She was Aileen's life blood. She inspired her to do things. To commit the ultimate crime.

Aileen did that first killing purely and simply for Ty.

It was just a year earlier on December 1, 1989. Aileen – as usual out of work and out of pocket – was hitch-hiking in the Tampa Bay area of Florida. The previous day she had left the home she shared with Tyria desperate to earn some money. She felt an obligation to provide for them both.

'I've gotta find some customers. Otherwise we can't pay the bills,' she told Ty.

With any luck the right sort of guy would pick her up, give her a lift and pay her cash for some fast, impersonal sex.

Electronics repair man Richard Mallory, from the nearby seaside resort of Clearwater knew he faced a few lonely hours on the main US 1 Interstate highway. He didn't hesitate to stop when he spotted Aileen thumbing a lift by the side of the lane. But Aileen did a double-take once inside the car. For fifty-two-year-old Mallory looked just like her father. He would have been about that age as well.

It instantly put her on her guard. After all, he was the man most responsible for her awful life. He was the man who made her wish she had never been born. He was also the person from whom she had inherited the devil.

'You are evil and you will never stop being evil,' her stepparents had told her. Now, she knew why.

As Mallory started to make polite conversation, Aileen grimaced with disgust. Maybe this was her father? Perhaps he was still alive after all?

Mallory had no idea what was going through Aileen's mind.

'You want to fuck me?' Aileen put all those thoughts of her father out of her mind for a moment. She had business to attend to.

Mallory hesitated for a moment. Was this why he had picked Aileen up in the first place? But then how was he to know what she about to offer?

'Pull off towards the forest.' Aileen did not wait for a reply. She was barking orders now.

Mallory just did as he was told.

He was falling for the bait.

They stopped at a wooded area where Mallory parked his 1977 Cadillac.

'Get your clothes off first.' Aileen was in control of another man. She loved it.

Then she saw her brutal father once more. She remembered the cruel beatings he inflicted on their mom. She thought about those two poor little girls whose life he ruined.

He was there. In the car next to her.

She felt a fierce compulsion to reach into her bag for that pistol. She had always carried the weapon with her in case of trouble with clients.

But now she wanted to destroy all memories of her father.

Mallory was angry she had not yet removed her clothes. He shouted abuse at her. An unfortunate thing to do. She wouldn't take that from men. Not any more.

He was transforming into her father. Bullying and accusing her. Treating her like dirt. He showed no respect. She was just a whore to be used and abused.

As he bent down to take off his socks, she pulled the .22 pistol out of the bag and fired.

The first bullet ripped into his back instantly. As blood gushed from the wound, Aileen fired again. This time it tore into his shoulder blade. She heard the crack of the bone as the bullet passed through.

But two bullets weren't enough. She pulled the trigger again. And then again. And then again.

Five open holes were gapping through his back.

Now she had got rid of her cruel father for good. Slumped dead over the steering wheel, just as he should be. An ineffectual lump of meat. She felt no remorse for what she had done. She felt no emotion as she shoved his body under a piece of carpet that lay by the roadside. He was a sick, perverted man. She should know. Getting rid of him was doing the world a favour.

In the trunk she found a suitcase, camera and jewellery. It would be enough for her and Ty to live on for weeks.

Now she had the means to survive.

That evening she used the Cadillac to move Ty and her to a new place to live. Her lover chose not to notice the blood stains on the driver's seat …

Back in the scruffy, seedy Hawaii Motel, Aileen was pouring out her heart to Dick. He was understanding and caring. Only too well aware of the agony caused by a broken love affair.

It was strange really. For underneath it all, Aileen knew that she could not kill again, because she no longer had Ty to look after. It was like a compulsion when they had been together.

She had felt obliged to provide for them both – no matter what. If it meant prostituting herself to make the cash then that was fine. If it meant murdering in cold blood then that was fine. She would have done anything to keep Ty.

Like the previous June when the two lovers yet again ran short of cash. Aileen knew it was time to go out and find a victim.

She again chose her favourite guise as a hitchhiker.

It was so easy to get men if you thumbed a lift. When they gave a ride, they always expected one in return.

This time the venue was the windswept and desolate Interstate 95 and sixty-five-year-old missionary Peter Siems slowed down the moment he saw the leather clad Aileen. His fate was already sealed. The *Christ Is The Answer Crusade* worker was about to meet his maker.

As she got into his Pontiac Sunbird, Aileen became convinced once again that her father was behind the wheel.

The evil man had risen again. She would have to finish the job off once and for all. This time, she would fire seven bullets just to make sure.

Siems, turned his back to her while she undressed. He never saw the hail of bullets that hit his crumpled, elderly body. He was dead by the time the second one tore into his spine.

Less than 30 minutes later, she dumped his body in a wooded area near an abandoned country road and made off in the Pontiac.

Aileen was ecstatic. She loved driving the powerful coupe and couldn't wait to get back to Ty.

She really believed the memory of her father had now been wiped out forever.

It gave her great pleasure to make Ty happy. A nice home. An expensive car. They had it all now.

Aileen wanted to take Ty off to places like Disney World. It was a means of escape from their hopeless existence. A story book environment where they could lose themselves in fantasy.

For almost a month they motored round Florida on a wild spending spree. Going every place they knew. Seeing everything. It was a happy time for Aileen and Ty. But all good things have to come to an end sometime.

It happened in Orange Springs – a sleepy, sun-blasted state town where the major social event of the year was a summer fete for the local church.

So when two women crashed through a fence in Orange Springs and ran off from the scene, they naturally created a lot of interest. And very generously broke the tedium of a few people's lives. Several witnesses, including a local fire chief and his deputy who rushed to the scene of the accident, chased after the two women to see if they were all right as they struggled along a nearby road.

Aileen told them to 'Get lost'.

Police traced the car to missing Siems.

Now, the whole state was hot on the trail of Aileen and Ty.

Dick was growing very fond of Aileen.

To him, she was just a lonely, tragic figure – suffering from the after effects of a broken love affair. He had no idea of her past.

He was so taken with Aileen, he even decided to introduce her to his family at a special get-together. His two daughters had managed to find true marital happiness and he wanted to share his new friendship with them. They were naturally inquisitive to meet the woman who had so completely bowled over their father.

'You see this scar. I got it during a fight with two dykes inside jail.'

Aileen was trying to impress Dick's daughter Reveshia.

Not surprisingly, her story was going down like a lead balloon.

This was the woman her father was so smitten by? Reveshia was horrified. Her sister Tammy was even more stunned when Aileen told her tales of her massive consumption of drugs including LSD, PCP and mushrooms.

The problem was age old: Aileen was becoming more and more drunk. Her defences were down and she was doing the only thing she knew how. She was fighting her way out.

She grew more and more obnoxious as the evening continued.

The more uncomfortable she felt, the more she guzzled down the beers. Dick was forced to go out to the liquor store to get her another crate to sustain her enormous drinking capacity.

It was the last straw for Reveshia.

'Just get her out of my home and don't bring her back.'

Dick obeyed. He knew that Aileen had failed the family test and it was nearly time to finish their romance.

Next morning, at the same motel where they had first made love, Dick was about to prove to Aileen why men cannot ever be trusted.

Having made love to her all night, he was now explaining why they had to finish.

'Here's $25. I'll drop you off wherever you want to go.'

It was Christmas Eve. Aileen had no home, no lover and no one to turn to.

She had committed the ultimate sin over and over again. Now her punishment was beginning.

Aileen headed for the only familiar place left in Daytona – The Last Resort bar. Once a thriving beer-and-wine tavern, it had been redecorated by the hundreds of bikers who swamped there each evening.

Bras and soiled panties hung from the ceiling and in the back yard was the 'Japanese Hanging Garden' – consisting of motorbikes dangling from every tree.

It was an even tougher place than Wet Willie's. But at least Aileen could drown herself in endless bottles of beer without anyone caring.

'Hey man. She's a flat cracker. I'd keep away from her if I were you.'

Two men were leaning at the bar studying Aileen, wondering if there was any point in trying to chat her up.

The 6-foot tall, leather clad barman, Cannonball, warned the men: 'She's a strange one. Be very careful.'

If he had realised how accurate those words were, then he might not have allowed her to sleep on the porch outside, every evening, after closing time.

She had nowhere else to go.

Cannonball knew she was trying to get away from something but Aileen wasn't telling. She just bawled her eyes out each evening before falling asleep in the plastic covered car seat in the corner of the creaky wooden porch.

In Pennsylvania, Tyria Moore was just relieved to get home to her mom. Aileen had been something terrible. She kept thinking about that time she came home and said chillingly, 'I just killed a guy.' Tyria kept telling herself that Aileen was lying. But she knew, deep inside, that it had to be true.

The nationwide TV programme screened the photo fit pictures of her and Aileen – the net was closing.

She was horrified to discover that her ex-lover was the serial killer being hunted in Florida. But she still didn't know what to do until two police officers came knocking at her mom's front door. Soon she was singing to the police to try to help them catch Aileen before she murdered once more.

Sgt Bruce Munster of the Marion County Sheriff's office may have tracked down Moore. But he still hadn't got anywhere near to finding Wuornos.

She was a killer on the loose – liable to strike again at any time. In any place.

It was time to spread the net and begin random surveillance at the sort of Daytona Bars where she might just hang out. One of those bars was The Last Resort.

For more than a week, the two bikers sat and watched Aileen sinking further and further into alcoholic oblivion. They hoped she might leave the bar and lead them to the bodies of some of those men. But she never did. Too sodden with beer to even think about those victims she picked up and slaughtered out there on the highways of Florida.

Instead, she played her two favourite records 'Leather and Lace' and 'Digging Up Bones' on the juke box over and over again.

They were like the two theme tunes to her life, soon coming to an end.

On January 9, 1991, Aileen Wuornos was arrested by the two bikers – plain-clothes policemen – and charged with first-degree murder.

Dick Mills – the man who shared five days of lust with her just a few weeks before – is probably one of the luckiest men alive today …

Aileen Wuornos admitted the murders of Siems and Mallory. She was also accused at the time of publication of the murder of at least five other men and faced the death penalty if found guilty.

7

SISTERS OF MERCY

The screams were blood curdling. Earpiercing yells of pain. Long screeches that echoed into the night.

Then silence. A couple of minutes of blissful silence. Then, another scream. This time even more horrendous. Even more high pitched. Even more agonising.

Five-year-old Charlene Maw and her sister Annette, seven, were lying in their tiny beds too terrified to move.

When they heard their mother let out another anguished cry, they trembled with fear. Too scared to say anything in case he picked on them next.

Then, once more, there was an eerie silence from the kitchen downstairs.

The two sisters hoped and prayed that the beating had finished. That their bullying father had ended his drunken frenzy. They looked at each other across the room, praying that he had given her some respite from the vicious attack.

Maybe he had beaten her so badly she lay unconscious? Possibly even close to death?

The inner feelings of these two little girls were already damaged beyond repair.

On that terrible evening, the quiet that then descended on the ordinary looking semi-detached home in the Yorkshire town of Bradford seemed to indicate the worst was over.

The little girls tried to get back to sleep in preparation for the full day of school that lay just a few hours ahead.

Tears streaked down their cheeks as they listened to the unmistakable sound of footsteps clumping up the stairs.

Their father was stumbling drunkenly to their bedroom one clumsy step at a time. Half way up he tripped and cursed the carpenter who had built the damn thing.

Charlene and Annette were shaking in their beds – terrified that his footsteps would stop outside their room. The door burst open and fifty-year-old Thomas Maw appeared – an ominous shadow in the doorway. Just a black shape filling the entire entrance. The stale stench of cider filled the air as he stood swaying from side to side.

The girls pretended to be asleep. Their faces screwed up tightly in case he made eye-contact. They could feel his eyes boring down on them. Examining their faces for any clues to whether they were actually awake.

Even through his drunken stupor, Thomas Maw knew his young daughters were pretending to be asleep. A lip-curling smile crawled up one side of his face. Just a hint of his back teeth caught the light shining from the hallway.

The first to feel the back of his hand was Annette. He slapped her across the face.

'Get up. Get up you little bitch. I want to show you something.'

Annette could see the hatred in his bloodshot eyes. It scared her. She was confused. Too upset to fight back. Too scared to say 'No'. As he grabbed her nighty, she felt like a rag doll in giant hands. She could feel the force of his grip as he made her stand to attention. She trembled with cold and fear.

Next came Charlene. Having seen her father assault her sister, she was so scared that she got out of bed immediately. Desperate to avoid the sort of brutal back handers she had just watched Annette suffer.

Little brother Bryn, aged three, was the only one who had been genuinely asleep. But then he was a boy and boys do not always feel the full wrath of their father's anger.

'Get downstairs. Now!'

Maw was slurring his words, spittle flying from his mouth. He kept snorting through his nose. Lost for breath and wheezing one moment, shouting and cursing the next. But the message was loud and clear.

'Get down there NOW!'

Annette and Charlene were petrified. Perhaps he had killed their mother and wanted to show them the body as a warning to them all to behave?

The two little girls knew one thing though – they had to get down to that kitchen as fast as possible if they were going to save their mother's life. He would give her another beating if they did not obey. He was always blaming her for their behaviour.

All three little children rushed down the stairway, desperate to see if their mother was all right. Inside the tiny kitchen, pots and pans were scattered everywhere amongst fragments of broken plates on the linoleum floor. And there on the floor, amongst the debris, was Beryl Maw. A clump of her hair was hanging from her scalp where he had tried to tear it off. Her face was red down one side. But she was conscious. Desperately trying to compose herself: so that the children would not see what an awful beating he had inflicted on her.

She could take the punches and the scratches, but when he tried to rip out her hair by its roots, that really drove home the message that she had married a monster. Yet in his more sober moments, Maw would confess that he was jealous of her curly brown locks. It seemed so bizarre for a husband to be envious of his wife's hair. But he actually used to make her keep it short and dyed black. One day she asked him why.

He just screwed up his eyes in fury and shouted: 'It's so bloody curly. I wish I had hair like you.' For the first time in more than 20 years of marriage, Beryl had discovered what drove her husband into blazing temper tantrums – her hair. It was as frightening as it was ludicrous.

Back in that wrecked kitchen that evening, Mrs Maw was just thankful to be alive. She had glimpsed the other side and didn't want to go there yet.

Annette and Charlene rushed to her and hugged her protectively. They were relieved to see she was still conscious, despite being black and blue from her husband's attack.

They held her tightly. But it was difficult for her to return their affection. Just to squeeze her arms around the girls was agony. Everything ached so much. But it was her head that really hurt. It throbbed from ear to ear. It was unbearable. The pain seared left to right, right to left, increasing every time she made any slight movement. When she rubbed her scalp with her hand she felt the gapping wounds where he had ripped whole clumps of hair out by the roots.

Frightened Bryn cowered in the corner of the tiny kitchen. Bemused. Puzzled. He didn't understand. It was one in the morning. Why had they been made to go downstairs in the middle of the night? Were they going some place? He just wanted to go back to his teddy bears and bed. He was confused. But even he could feel the tight atmosphere – it was fused with hatred.

And Thomas Maw certainly knew what it was all about. That was why he had forced his young family to come downstairs. He looked into the eyes of his two daughters. They looked away the moment they caught his glance.

Scared. Appalled by his behaviour. Disgusted at what had happened. How could he do such a thing?

They tried to hug their mother even tighter. But he saw it as an act of defiance that could not go unpunished. Their look of contempt for him was enough to ignite a further onslaught.

The look reminded him of his wife. The woman he had taken solemn vows with twenty years earlier. The same woman he had just spent the previous two hours trying to beat to a pulp.

Without warning, he grabbed Beryl by the hair and pulled her towards him. The children grimaced with horror. He was starting up all over again.

They couldn't stand to look. But they felt that if they turned away he would beat her even more viciously. He wanted them to watch. If they did not, he might finish her off forever.

Charlene couldn't take much more. She could not bear the expression on her mother's face. Alternating from a grimace of excruciating agony to a dull, blank, far-away stare.

She tried to push him away from her mother. He simply swiped her to the floor and warned the other two: 'You're next if you're not careful.'

Then, as if he were a teacher demonstrating to a classroom of pupils, he said: 'This is what I do when your mother disobeys me and this is what I'll do to you.'

The children winced as yet more handfuls of hair were torn from their mother's scalp. He was pulling with such ferocity that her head was being jerked from side to side. As the hair ripped out there was an awful noise, like splitting cardboard.

'Stop Dad. Stop. Please stop,' the girls begged their father. But he was not interested in their pleas. He wanted to make them suffer. Teach them all a lesson – a lesson in obedience.

Then he held his wife's hair with one hand while he smashed her face on the edge of the kitchen sink with the other. Her teeth crunched as they connected with the metal.

The children were screaming now, but he ignored them. Determined to wreak an awful revenge upon the woman he was supposed to adore and cherish.

By the time her head crashed on the sink for the fourth time, Beryl Maw was on the verge of a blackout. She could just make out her three children, standing transfixed by this awful picture of domestic horror.

The pain of watching their faces as he continued unabated, was almost as bad as the physical agony she was enduring. Just to see them being forced to witness this attack was punishment in itself.

She strained to keep her eyes open. Afraid of what he might do to them once she was gone.

Then she lost consciousness.

Thomas Maw had beaten his wife senseless. The provocation? Smiling at him in an off guard moment a few hours earlier.

It was the first time Charlene and her sister Annette had seen their father's brutality — but it was an image that would keep coming back to them over and over again as the years went by.

For once in his life, Thomas Maw was behaving like the true gentleman his wife Beryl had fallen in love with and married nearly twenty years earlier.

They had been out for a meal in an expensive restaurant and she actually felt that perhaps there was some future for them together.

Mrs Maw had endured years of beatings from her husband but somehow never felt the courage to get up and leave it all behind.

There were always so many other considerations. The children. The house. All the things that keep families together through thick and thin.

Now she felt that perhaps it had all been worthwhile. He was making such an effort tonight. He seemed to want to make amends. To win back her love after years of torment. To show that he really cared. But Mrs Maw still had a nagging doubt in the back of her mind.

She had always promised herself she would get up and leave him once the children were old enough to cope. Now, here he was turning on the old charm. The charm that he had used so effectively when they had first met at a dance so long ago. He was a suave airman who had swept her off her seventeen-year-old feet.

They were married just a few weeks later.

But the Thomas Maw she knew then was unrecognisable now.

Even on their wedding anniversary he had managed to get drunk. But at least he was being nice to her. It made a change.

As they drove home from the restaurant she wondered if he really was going to turn over a new leaf. Perhaps he could change back into the man he had once been.

Beryl felt almost relaxed in his company that evening. It was the first time in years she had felt that way.

Thomas Maw was feeling happy too. But his mind was on things other than his marriage as he drove along the busy streets in the town's liveliest late night area.

Mrs Maw then noticed the car was slowing down by the kerbside. She was puzzled. What was wrong? Was the car about to breakdown? She looked over at her husband for a reaction. He didn't even acknowledge her.

No. Thomas Maw had spotted two prostitutes cruising along an empty pavement. His wife may have been sitting right next to him, but he wanted those women. It didn't matter what she thought. She could go to hell if she didn't like it.

He slowed down to proposition them. Beryl Maw could not believe her eyes as her husband rolled down the window and whistled the girls across to him.

'How much?' He asked in a nonchalant manner. The women were almost as surprised as Mrs Maw by his behaviour. After all, how many men stop to pick up a street walker with their wives sitting next to them?

One of them leant over to talk to Maw.

'How dare you.' Beryl was indignant with rage. How could he do this after they had enjoyed such a great night together?

The prostitutes took a step back. They sensed an explosion was about to occur. They even had a sympathetic look on their faces. As if to say: 'How could this man be such a filthy pig?'

Thomas Maw did not see it that way. Women existed to be used and abused. What right had his own wife to stop him picking up a street walker?

He was infuriated that the two women were now walking away. Enraged that his wife had the nerve to decide whether he should pay two compete strangers for sex.

Maw aimed his fist straight at his wife's face. Her nose exploded in a shower of blood. He followed through with other blows to the body.

By the time they arrived home, Beryl Maw had suffered two black eyes, a broken tooth and bruised ribs. Thomas Maw would never change his ways.

'That bloody rabbit has to go.' Thomas Maw was drunk yet again. This time he was throwing his verbal abuse in the direction of Charlene and Annette's pet rabbit. He was furious they had built a hutch for the animal without asking his permission first.

The children grabbed the rabbit out of the hutch and ran into the house. But Thomas Maw had decided that it had to die. Grabbing a knife from the kitchen he charged after the terrified little girls. They stumbled as they raced up the stairs to their room. The rabbit jumped out of their hands – straight into the path of Mr Maw.

He grabbed the white, furry creature and gleefully stuck the knife into its belly, twisting the blade menacingly just to make certain. He did it right in front of the little girls, relishing their distress.

The rabbit was dead. But Maw had another grisly surprise up his sleeve. Three hours later the family sat down to a lunch of rabbit stew. He made them eat up every mouthful.

Maw's cruelty towards animals knew no bounds. They couldn't answer back, so that made them even better victims. He would take awful delight in gassing mice and flies in the kitchen oven, watching them through the window as they contorted and twisted.

Worse was to come. They listened to him kicking a puppy to death in his bedroom – all because it had urinated in the hallway. Only a few days earlier it had been given to them as a present.

Many other awful incidents followed but Thomas Maw surpassed even his appalling standards when the children found a frog in the garden. Snatching the creature out of Annette's hands, he took it into the kitchen and beckoned the children to follow him. They were scared. They knew he was about to do something horrible. They also knew they would get an awful beating if they did not do as they were told.

In the kitchen, Maw took out a straw and told the children to watch carefully. They were puzzled. He never bothered to show them interesting tricks normally. In fact, he hardly ever even acknowledged their existence, calling them 'stupid bastards' most of the time.

But, looking at his smiley, cheery face, they presumed he was about to act like a real father and play a game with them.

Now he had the children's attention, he placed the straw inside the frog's mouth. Still the youngsters were baffled. They could not work out what he was about to do. He was being so friendly towards the frog all the time, stroking it and loving it. They guessed it was going to be something nice and it made them all feel warm and excited inside.

Maw leant down and put the other end of the straw to his lips. His eyes looked up at the children just to make sure they were watching.

They saw the glint then. The expectant look. But they just thought he wanted to make sure they did not miss the trick.

They watched him take a deep breath inwards. Then he blew with all his might. The tiny frog ballooned up, getting bigger and bigger. It began to look like a toy. Not a real, living creature.

Little Bryn began to laugh. Charlene and Annette did not laugh. They knew by now that what their father was doing was cruel and nasty – the work of a madman.

Suddenly the frog exploded like a balloon that's been fed too much air. Bits of its green scaly body flew across the kitchen, hitting the children with a wet sting. They cried with horror, unable to understand what had driven their father to do such an evil thing.

The girls ran to their room and refused to come down for days. Beryl Maw now knew beyond doubt that she was married to a monster.

On March 27, 1989, Thomas Maw poured himself the first of ten pints of cider he was to consume that evening. Sitting in the front room of his home in Ranelagh Avenue, Bradford, he supped thirstily at the pint glass in his hand. He was feeling tense as usual and desperately wanted to feel the rush of alcohol to his brain.

In a place like Bradford, most men go to the pub for a drink. But Maw's ferocious temper had got him banned from every single one in the area. Those landlords had taken the sort of measures Mrs Maw should have taken years earlier.

The rest of his family were nowhere to be seen. They knew better than to hang about when Maw decided to go on a drinking spree. No one except his ever loyal wife would even talk to Maw by now. It had just got too much for the rest of the family. Yet somehow, through all the punches and the slaps, Beryl still loved and adored her beast of a husband. She had already endured so much battering that the pain no longer mattered.

'It was fear and helplessness. I had lost sight of who I was,' she said later.

Then there were his terror tactics – deliberately intended to warn her who was in control. One night she remembered him saying: 'Leave me and one dark night I'll find you and that will be it.'

Mrs Maw believed his every word.

But that night, she sat willingly in the living room with her husband as he downed pint after pint. Her daughters kept warning her to keep away from him. 'He's the devil in disguise mum.'

Annette was by now an attractive twenty-one-year-old and Charlene fast catching up at eighteen. They had their own lives to lead. But they always swore they would not leave her to his mercy. That monster would have to leave the house first.

Beryl made polite, nervous small talk with her husband about the weather and the day's news. It was hardly the level of conversation that a married couple should enjoy. More like a meeting between two complete strangers. But she was so anxious to please even after the awful life she had suffered.

The tense atmosphere took care of that. All the time there was this overwhelming awkwardness. As the minutes passed, she could feel him building up. Getting more and more angry within himself. It was only a matter of time.

But still Mrs Maw sat there, praying and hoping that perhaps they could enjoy a night together. Just the two of them relaxing in the comfort of their own home.

It was something her two daughters would never understand. Why had she let him make her suffer so much? The answer probably lay with them. They were the reason she carried on.

'What do you think of this Margaret Thatcher?' asked Mr Maw. But before his wife had a chance to answer he followed up.

'Bloody *woman* isn't she?'

Maw was spoiling for a fight yet again.

In the kitchen Charlene and Annette could hear the sound of raised voices. They knew it was the first sign of trouble.

Weeks earlier they had promised each other they would not allow his beatings to continue.

'We have got to do something – before it's too late,' said Annette at the time.

Now they had to turn those words into action.

'I've had enough. I'm going in there to tell him what I think of him.'

Annette had cracked. She could take no more. In recent years, he had started taking it out on her as well as their mother.

She was haunted by all the awful incidents. Like the time she had spent five hours doing a drawing for her 'O' level preparations and he ripped it up into tiny pieces – just because she had smiled at him.

He would beat her regularly calling her 'stupid' and 'thick'.

Now he was about to beat her mother yet again. She could not take it anymore. She had to act – now.

Annette wanted to protect her mother. The only way was to confront the beast.

Ironically, as Annette charged through the corridor towards the front room, she strongly resembled her father. Maybe it was the way she was walking, but she reminded her sister of the way their father looked at his worst.

Charlene had no option but to follow her through the house to the front room. She pleaded with Annette to calm down. She genuinely feared their father could turn so nasty it would prove deadly one day. That day might have come.

The two girls stormed in. The diversion at least gave their mother some respite. An interlude in the cruel catalogue of violence. Maw vented his anger in the girls' direction, starting with Charlene.

'Just get out of here, you useless fucking bitch.' Charlene was not going to just soak up the abuse. The time had come. Her mother had put up with too much for too long.

'You're scum,' she shouted back.

115

Maw visibly boiled with anger at that reply. He saw himself as the man of the household. And here was his own daughter calling him names.

For a split second he looked menacingly at both defiant girls standing before him.

'I am not going to take this,' he screamed. Punches rained down on the back of Charlene's head. She had become the first one to feel the full force of his temper.

Maw's eyes were twisted up as he concentrated on thumping her as hard as he could. Harder and harder. He kept crashing his massive fists down on her neck bone. He wanted to crush her body, bludgeon her spirit until it caved in.

Even though they had all been expecting it, it took them all slightly by surprise. He had done it so many times before but on this occasion it seemed worse than ever.

He was delirious with anger. Then Annette joined in.

She tried to jump on her father's back to stop him throwing his punches. It was an impossible task.

'Stop you bastard. Stop.' The screaming was even louder than before. They were fighting back this time. They were not going to let him get away with it. They had soaked up enough punishment. Now it was their turn to attack.

Maw relaxed his vicious onslaught for a moment.

Regathering his energy before starting all over again. Charlene now had the opportunity to grab her sister by the hand and run to the shelter of their bedroom. It had been the only place throughout their childhood where he had not dared to inflict punishment.

Now they prayed he would respect their sanctuary. As they dashed through the house, Charlene could feel the throbbing on her injured neck. Behind them they heard the drunken insults of their father. He was coming after them. He wanted to finish them off for good.

It was like a scene from the worst type of horror movie. He was chasing them. Every moment getting closer and closer.

But this was real life.

As they scrambled up the stairs, Maw lunged at Annette's ankle. He held on tight. She felt herself lose balance. She could not control it. She was falling backwards into his vice-like grasp. Charlene grabbed her arm and a human tug of war was waged on the stairway.

Maw pulled with all his might. Suddenly he lost balance and his daughter aimed a sharp kick to his face. She was free momentarily. But the chase was still on.

The stair carpet came loose and he lost his footing as the girls looked behind them. They were relieved to have escaped his grasp but they knew he would still come after them.

Somehow, he regained his footing and climbed the stairs three at a time. His anger seemed to be giving him fresh impetus in the race to the bedroom.

As Charlene turned to slam the door shut, she felt his weight against the door, forcing it open again. She tried with all her might to keep closing it. But the sheer strength of her father was too much.

For a few desperate seconds they pulled and pushed the door each way until he finally burst through. Now he was in their room. They both had their backs to the paint peeled walls. Terrified of what was about to happen.

'Dad. Let's talk about this.' Charlene was trying to calm him down. A peaceful approach might work. He seemed to hesitate for a moment, responding to his daughter's appeal.

Maybe he could see how dreadful he had been?

Then an umbrella came crashing down towards his head.

Annette saw it now as all out war – and this was no time to start waving the white flag.

Just as the brolly was about to hit dead centre on his crown, Maw grabbed at it and pulled it out of her grasp.

He was in control once more. He had the upper hand and now he was going to teach those daughters of his a lesson they would never forget.

Grabbing Annette by the wrist, he threw a volley of punches at her. Once again, he aimed at the back of the neck. A favourite spot for family battering.

Perhaps he knew the bruises would not show so clearly. Then Mrs Maw appeared at the door. The sight of her husband trying to kill their eldest daughter had inspired her to stoop to his level. She was armed with a huge mirror – ready to use at the earliest opportunity.

She pulled him to the floor and smashed the mirror over his head. The pieces scattered around the room. Maw lay unconscious. The beast had been tamed for a short while.

The three women were drained. Even by their father's appalling standards this was the nearest to death any of them had ever come. For a few seconds none of them said anything as they walked downstairs to recover from their ordeal.

In the kitchen Annette broke the silence.

'Let's kill him before he kills us.' She was shaking from shock. Mrs Maw felt the same way. She nodded in agreement. But Charlene was horrified.

'Don't be so bloody stupid. Let's just leave him where he is and call the police.' She wanted justice, not bloody retribution.

The other two women stopped and thought for a second. They knew in their heart of hearts that Charlene was right, but events clouded their judgement. All they could think about were the beatings, the insults and the terror. Year in, year out at the hands of a sick monster who deserved no mercy. Now they had a chance to do something about it. A chance to avenge incidents like the time he threatened to gas his own children when they annoyed him.

'The Gestapo had it about right. I just wish I had been Himmler then I could have had you lot put down at birth.' Thomas Maw was no joker. He had looked menacingly into his children's eyes as they all sat down one mealtime. He had meant it.

However terrible he had been though, murder, whatever the motives, was wrong. Pure and simple. They knew that. They should look at the situation objectively. Recognise the symptoms and deal with them.

But human emotions are not that easy to contain.

The police should have been called there and then. But something held them back. They wanted to deal with him in their own way. Turn the tables on him. Even if they did call the police, it required a real effort because they had no telephone. It made it more difficult to reach the obvious, sensible decision.

Nevertheless they had to decide what to do before he regained consciousness.

'Go next door and call the police. We've got to get him out of this house.' Both Annette and her mother had come round and seen sense.

The temptation to take the law into their own hands had passed. It would have seemed 'just' to cause him some pain – just as he had done to them for so long. But, underneath it all, they knew the police were the only answer. They could deal with him. Hopefully, the courts would put him away for a very long time.

Charlene was relieved. For a few desperate minutes she had seemed to be the only person in that house who wanted to take the correct course of action. The only way of dealing with a fascist is to become a fascist – unless sense prevails. Finally it had.

Charlene went to put on a coat. She had to hurry.

Upstairs, Maw was stirring.

A hand grabbed Annette around the throat. She hadn't seen it coming.

Maw was going to finish his private war with his own family. His wife and daughters might have decided to treat him like a human being, but he was not going to do them that service in return.

Annette was gasping for breath. He was smiling gleefully at his other daughter and her mother as he held Annette by the throat.

Maybe he had heard about their plans to murder him? Perhaps he had decided to kill them before they managed to do away with him? One thing was for certain. Maw was now trying his hardest to murder Annette.

'Get a knife.' Annette was struggling to spit out the words but Charlene understood what she was saying.

She hesitated, still longing for a peaceful solution. Even as their father stood there trying to choke her sister to death, she hoped he would stop and they could sit down and discuss their problems, instead of turning that night into a life or death struggle.

Charlene hesitated ... but she knew.

There was no time. She had to get the knife.

'For God's sake ... He's killing me!'

Charlene ran to the kitchen and grabbed the nearest knife she could find. She could have picked the huge carving knife on the sideboard, but she chose the small cutlery knife instead.

Annette grabbed it from her and plunged it into Maw's body. She had to be quick. She might not live much longer ...

As the blade sank into his stomach, Annette felt her father let go. She thought she had plunged it deep into his body but as he turned it just snapped in two. It did not even penetrate his outer layer of skin.

Now the monster had switched victims and was punching his wife viciously like a prize fighter desperate to gain an instant knockout.

'A bigger one! Quick!' Annette screamed

Annette was trying desperately to stop her father from killing her mother. She punched him in the back, but it had little effect. It just drove him on to further violence. Charlene went back into the kitchen once more. This time she got the carving knife that would finish off the job.

Annette snatched the knife away from her younger sister like a heroin user grabbing at her fix. But she was more desperate than any drug addict. She had to kill him before he struck first.

She plunged the 7-inch blade into his neck, severing the jugular vein in one quick motion. But he still kept punching, despite blood gushing from the wound all over his wife and daughter. So Annette continued to stab at the neck with all the strength she could muster. Within seconds the monster had crumpled in a heap on the floor.

At last the pain and suffering would be no more.

Annette and Charlene Maw were each jailed for three years when they admitted killing Thomas Maw, before a judge at Leeds Crown Court on Nov 17, 1980. They were originally charged with murder but this was reduced to manslaughter.

A later appeal against their sentence saw Charlene's term cut by six months. Annette's appeal was dismissed.

Charlene was said to have 'played a lesser part' in the killing, according to the appeal court judge, Lord Lane.

He said Annette was the probable organiser of the offence. At the time of their original sentencing, Judge Mr Justice Smith acknowledged that the sisters had been provoked and that their life was 'a sad history'. But he also added, 'It is also a very sad duty I have to perform because you deliberately and unlawfully stabbed and killed him'.

8

DEATH WISH: THE MOTHER WHO STRUCK BACK

Lübeck is a town steeped in tradition. With a fifteenth Century gate and two plump towers, it is so typically German that it used to figure on the 50 mark banknote.

The sheer greyness of the place is daunting when you first walk down its sterile streets.

Block upon block of tidy buildings, never more than ten storeys in height, set a severe backdrop against a population where few people smile and the emphasis is on survival rather than happiness.

On May 4, 1980 residents went about their business in a cold, almost fearful way. Rarely stopping to chat as they performed their chores for the day.

Provincial German towns nearly all share that slightly dead atmosphere in daytime. They only come alive when darkness has fallen and the nightlife takes over to become the life blood of virtually every man under the age of sixty.

There is a commonly held theory about this stark contrast. The Germans work very hard to earn a living. That means they tend to play even harder.

A night on the town in <u>Lübeck</u> was usually a three-stage affair for the typical middle-aged male resident, out with a couple of workmates.

Naturally, food would come first. And that could mean a massive three or even four course meal in one of the town's many restaurants. A dinner consisting of everything from *sauerkraut* to those huge fat sausages. All washed down with vast litre mugs of beer.

Then your typical group would wander to one of the livelier bars in Lübeck where they would regale each other with blustery tales of woe covering a range of topics from soccer to politics.

By about 9.30 p.m. everyone would be well and truly on the way to drink-induced euphoria. This was when the insatiable appetite for sex took over.

They flock to the brothels that are always on the outskirts of town. The townsfolk all know they exist, but they don't want to hear about them or see them. In Lübeck, the brothels attract far more sightseers than those plump twin towers.

Names like The Fun Palace and The LA Club were popular. The Germans have always felt more reassured by brothels with American sounding names. They like that familiar ring to them.

The set-up, though, was always exactly the same: the customers paid a nominal entrance fee. Then they would stroll up to the bar and order a drink. Suddenly, at least six girls, in outfits that usually consisted of skimpy basques, stockings and white stilettos, would appear as if by magic and start flirting outrageously.

For the uninitiated it was a most fulfilling experience because men on their first visit nearly always presumed these girls were only interested in them. They would frequently believe that their good looks and magnetic character had attracted all these single, unattached beauties to swarm around them, like bees in a honey pot. The fact the girls are virtually undressed seemed incidental at the time.

Anyway Marianne Bachmeier and her live-in lover Christian Berthold weren't complaining. They ran one of the most popular bars in Lübeck and it just happened to be the perfect stopping off point for many of those men who were planning an eventual visit to The Fun Palace.

Marianne, aged thirty, with long dark brown hair was a stunning looking woman, more than a capable match for the hundreds of leering, lecherous men who poured into her bar.

She worked in a soft, sensual yet efficient manner. Never offending the customers but at the same time sometimes flirting outrageously with men who caught her eye.

Marianne was a woman who had spent her whole life craving for love and attention. Her fanatical Nazi father was soon replaced by a brutal stepfather who regularly gave her vicious beatings. She hated him so much she couldn't even bring herself to call him anything other than 'Uncle Paul'.

A vicious sex attack by a salesman left an even more indelible mark on her childhood. She was just nine at the time. As she reached her mid-teens, Marianne blossomed into a beautiful young woman. She longed for someone to genuinely love her but far too many men wanted her for entirely the wrong reasons.

It was therefore no surprise that she ended up with Christian. After countless disastrous relationships, two brutal rapes and two pregnancies, Marianne was desperate for someone whose intentions were genuine. She had already worked up an unhealthy dislike and distrust of men. She needed to find someone who could restore her faith in the other sex.

Christian seemed to be a gentle hippy, only interested in love and peace, when the couple first met at an all-night party hosted by an oddball friend called 'Yogi'. Marianne was immediately taken by Christian – and slept with him within hours of that first meeting. They both felt a bond of friendship and love and soon moved in together.

Then she discovered he was a wealthy innkeeper and she actually had some money to spend for the first time in her life. That first bar was in Kiel. It was a great success. They were happy days for Marianne.

Christian sold the business for a fortune. They bought a floating gin palace. But that didn't do so well and that was how they ended up in Lübeck in yet another bar.

Meanwhile, Marianne and Christian's love for each other had turned into a roller coaster of emotional ups and downs. Each often sleeping with someone else as a cry for help when the relationship had seemed to be dissolving.

Somehow they remained together and seven years previously, they had even had a child, Anna, as proof of their love, however tormented it might have been. Now, here was Marianne playing mine perfect host inside the smoky, sweaty bar. Even though she always wore an apron over a sweater or blouse and sexy tight jeans, Marianne still managed to ooze a sensuous appeal – something that some people are born with while others are not.

Just 200 yards away, balding former butcher Klaus Grabowski was definitely not going to join the mass of Lübeck men out on a night of drink and vice.

He was a desperately shy man in his thirties. Sometimes he was so afraid to meet people that he would stay locked up in his tiny one-bedroomed flat in one of those grey town apartment buildings, fearful of the consequences if he should dare to venture out onto the streets.

His fiancé was constantly on at him about his antisocial behaviour. 'You cannot stay cooped up here all your life. You must get out. You have to meet people,' she would tell him. As a result he only saw her once a week. They barely kissed each time they met. She longed to stay the night and make love with him but the urge on Grabowski's part was not there. She never forgot the night she stripped off all her clothing and tried to seduce him. He didn't even get sexually excited. She fled the flat without even bothering to put back on the red tights she had bought especially for the occasion. But she grew to believe this was all a sign of how honourable his intentions towards her really were. But she got sexual urges. How come he didn't? She wondered. They had been engaged to marry for seven years.

She simply had no idea what happened whenever Grabowski did encounter other people in one to one situations ... especially young people.

He had been a popular figure at his corner butcher's shop. There, he had had his regular customers. They all called him Herr Grabowski and treated him as a man of substance. They saw him as a fine butcher whose meat was second to none. They did not see beneath the heavy bearded face that gave him a Rasputin-like appearance. He was just your friendly, rounded butcher, always eager to please.

But that was all in the past. Grabowski had lost his job and his pride with it. He was a broken man who felt degraded by his non status in society.

Grabowski was preparing for bed. He had consumed two bottles of beer and he knew what would happen if he drunk. Those twinges would reawaken the devil that lurked within him. The evil thoughts that most men – according to Marianne Bachmeier – were constantly absorbed by. The intent was always there. It never actually went away for long ...

Back at the bar Marianne too was desperate. She was worn out by the long hours she worked. Always on her feet, it was a gruelling profession. Constantly smiling at the customers, in response to their sexist, rude remarks. Wanting revenge when a drunken man tried to grab her breasts or another beast hung around until the bar emptied because he thought she would be an easy lay.

Luckily, Marianne, Christian and little Anna lived above the bar. At least she could avoid those creepy walks home she had endured when they ran the place in Kiel.

It always bugged her that they had agreed to split the responsibilities of running the bar. He insisted it was more sensible for them to take it in turns to manage the place rather than run it together and both end up working an 80-hour week.

The problem was that it meant they hardly saw each other. One was sleeping while the other was working. It was a recipe for disaster and Marianne knew it. But Christian was not the sleepy laid-back hippy he once was. He had become a jaded, money-conscious businessman desperate for financial success. He felt all the pressures of the world on his shoulders. He became more and more pre-occupied with all his own problems. Giving Marianne and his family less and less attention. It marked the beginnings of a classic relationship breakdown.

The consequences of this attitude were clear for everyone to see. Marianne began to sleep with other people. Her craving for a long lasting genuine love had returned.

Christian was deeply hurt by her indiscretions and took his own sad revenge. He started visiting brothels – the temptations were all so close by.

On one occasion they hurt each other so badly that it was a miracle they managed to stick together. Marianne took it upon herself to travel to Hanover and search out an old boyfriend – the father of her second child, who had eventually been adopted. She tracked him down, but his reaction was to drive her into the countryside, rape her and leave her on a grass verge to find her own way home.

When Marianne arrived back at Christian's bar she poured the entire incident out to him. He was stunned. He had a feeling of anger at the man and betrayal by Marianne for bothering to locate him in the first place. But his emotions came out in the form of severe depression. They began rowing more and more.

One night, he stormed out of the flat and headed for his old haunts in Berlin. Unable to find any of his previous girlfriends, Christian visited one of the city's most notorious brothels.

He had sex for just 50 marks. But the cost to his relationship with Marianne was far higher. On his return to Lübeck, he described the entire experience to her. Every detail about the sex. The way he performed. The way the girl reacted. It was all too much for Marianne. Yet again she had been betrayed. Why did men treat her so badly? What was it in her character that prompted such punishment?

Marianne could not begin to answer those questions, so she did what many victims — especially women — see as the only solution. She retaliated in the most graphic, hurtful way.

'Let's see how he will react if I become the whore,' she thought to herself. 'Will he still want me after that? I want to make him realise how dirty and heartless it is to sell your body. He'll soon find out what it is like to live with a prostitute.'

Just a few hours later, Marianne was walking the streets of Berlin herself, waiting for the first man to come along so she could sell her body to him. She found a man and instantly hated herself for it. But, in her eyes, it just had to be done. It was her own special brand of punishment for the man she longed to continue loving.

Somehow, through all this bruising tit-for-tat behaviour, Christian and Marianne continued to survive, although their friends believed it was now only a matter of time until they split.

On May 4, 1980, little Anna she slept blissfully in her bed in the flat above the bar — unaware of the torment and guilt that constantly enveloped her parents' lives.

As Klaus Grabowski prepared for his own bed that evening, he heard the din of the music coming from the bar. It was eleven p.m. and a couple of drunks were stumbling up the road outside his flat still dreaming of the sex they would like to enjoy with that beautiful barmaid Marianne.

Women like that were the farthest things from Grabowski's mind. His fantasies were far more obscure. They delved the depths of degradation.

His recurring thoughts concerned the sort of sex that would horrify those friendly housewives who'd always made such polite conversation with him at the butcher's shop. No doubt those customers would have grabbed one of those huge, razor sharp meat knives and turned on him if they had even vaguely realised what fantasies flowed consistently through his mind.

As he lay there in his bed, Grabowski conjured up pictures of what he wanted to do. The pain and suffering he wanted to inflict. The screams of fear. The cries of horror. The look on their faces when he fulfilled his sick desires. All the time his face would freeze in an ever-so-slight smile as he came closer and closer to reaching the climax he so longed to get to but knew he could not attain.

Even by his own sordid standards, this particular fantasy was vivid and life like. Grabowski felt as if he were actually there, doing it. He imagined in a frenzy the agony he was causing. And he wanted more and more.

This was a dream he did not want to escape from. He didn't want to leave. He wanted it to go on and on and on. Each time he saw her face, it drove him wild.

The fact that he was thinking up atrocities of such ferocity and brutality that they would be entirely unacceptable in any society did not seem to matter. Grabowski had long since given up any respect for human decency. His life was going nowhere. He had to have something to cling on to. Realizing just one those fantasies was his ultimate aim ...

Marianne was cleaning up the last few glasses after a heavy night. It was almost one a.m. and she was virtually asleep on her feet. Just a few minutes earlier she had pushed the last letching hanger-on out of the front door and started performing the most tedious duty of every evening in the bar — straightening out the premises before retiring for bed.

Christian had decreed that no matter how tired either of them felt, the place had to be spotless for the next day. Marianne knew he was right but on this night she was feeling particularly tired.

Anna had not been sleeping well and it was a strenuous existence. Marianne constantly had to get up early with Anna to prepare her for school at seven a.m. It was often only a few hours after she had gone to sleep.

The past few days had been even worse than usual. Marianne was so tired she had failed on two out of the five previous school days to wake up in time to pack Anna off to classes.

The seven-year-old was delighted. Missing school was a treat. Marianne was worried. She didn't want to end up losing Anna. She was so special to her. She had kept Marianne's life together. Without Anna, her life would fall apart again. She was painfully aware of that fact.

Marianne had given birth to two children before Anna. Both of them were now in care. A pregnancy at sixteen and an unhappy relationship had cost her those children. Anna represented her last chance to prove she was a capable mother. She loved her dearly and that constant threat made her even more special in Marianne's eyes.

Anna was a bubbly bright little girl, street-wise well beyond her years. Everyone liked her. She had a charming, elf-like face with well cut blonde hair. The relatives were convinced she could easily become a model in later years.

She also shared a unique bond of friendship with her mother. They were more like sisters than mother and daughter. Marianne would turn to Anna and vice versa. It was a remarkably close relationship. Some said too close.

But not only did Anna share her entire life with Marianne, she also shared her mother's personality in one, very significant way. Anna had magnetic qualities that attracted people — all sorts of people. Her mother had always longed for love and attention. It came out in a semi-flirtatious sort of way. But it had also led to that incident with the salesman that scarred her for life. She had been just nine-years-old at the time. Marianne just prayed and hoped that nothing similar would happen to her daughter. But she constantly feared the worse. There were always bastards around to prey on the innocent and vulnerable.

By the time Marianne finally fell into bed in the apartment above the bar that night, she was feeling shattered. It had been a hell of a long day.

In the bedroom just a few feet away, Anna slept soundly for once. Completely unaware of what was to come.

Next morning, there was an air of panic in Marianne's household. It was nine a.m. and Anna had not risen in time for school. Christian was only concerned with one thing – the bar. He had to be downstairs to manage the beer deliveries due at any moment. He was furious because Anna was going to miss another day of school. With Marianne's previous problems, they could ill-afford to get a visit from the social welfare people. They would soon misinterpret Anna's recent non-appearances in class.

To make matters worse still, Marianne had an appointment in the centre of town. It was a private thing. She didn't want to discuss it with anyone. Whatever the appointment was, she could not take Anna with her. Marianne was a secretive person at times. It was, no doubt, something to do with her childhood. She would often bottle up her innermost thoughts. Sometimes that could put her under enormous pressure, not to mention the people around her.

It was a private appointment and she had to get there by ten at the latest. She would say no more.

The only person not panicking was Anna. She was looking forward to a day off school.

Marianne was angry with Christian. She had told him she had this appointment. Why didn't he stay behind? They continued arguing. It all seemed perfectly normal to the little seven-year-old.

If they had leaned out of the window of the living room that morning, they all would have seen Klaus Grabowski making his way up the street to go shopping.

He was cycling along the street in quite a rush to make it to the shops before opening time.

Grabowski was well known to his neighbours he might have been fired from his job after a recent prison term but he was still known as the butcher to many locals. But – without exception – they had only seen one side of his character. Certainly they regularly spoke with him. But only to comment on the weather or the price of meat. Never on a personal level. Never prying into his strange mind.

With those cold steely grey eyes perhaps many of them would rather not know. It was this very fact that enabled Klaus to continue living in his sick fantasy world where reality only occasionally interrupted proceedings. It gave him the smoke screen to indulge his evil thoughts. Even his fiancé asked few questions. She just accepted he was a shy, frightened man who needed gentle coaxing not difficult questions that might make him face up to his own inadequacies. That was probably why they only saw each other once a week.

By the time Klaus got to the bread shop a queue had already formed. All the housewives there that morning knew Grabowski. They were grateful for a new face to talk to as they waited. But their children weren't so keen. There was something about him that used to scare a lot of them. In the butcher's shop, they were always catching a glance from him and turning away shyly even when he offered them a sweet from behind the counter.

He had this strange glint in his eye. It used to sparkle flatly when he spotted a mother and her children queueing in the shop. For a moment his eyes would stray to those of one of the children ... just as he chopped those pieces of tender sirloin into manageable pieces. Then they would dart around the faces of everyone inside the shop. Sizing them up as he lunged at his carcases with that huge knife. Some mothers used to wonder how he could cut everything so perfectly when he was looking away from it.

At the flat above the bar, Marianne was rushing out of the front door. As she kissed Anna on the forehead, she told her to behave herself and not to go out of the apartment; an invitation to an inquisitive child, if ever there was one.

Marianne rushed down the stairs to catch a bus she had spotted from the living room window. She did not really have time to think about why she was leaving a seven-year-old girl alone in the home to fend for herself. She had too many other problems on her mind.

Her relationship with Christian was crumbling one moment and passionate the next. She knew it was only a matter of time before they would break up.

Anna, on the other hand, was looking forward to doing exactly what she wanted for a whole day. She was a free spirit with an enquiring mind. She wanted to explore.

After all, this wasn't the first time that she had been left to fend for herself. On the last occasion, she and her best friend Maria had been alone on the streets near their home for hours. And they'd had a great adventure. They met two really nice cats and were invited into an apartment by their owner to help feed them. It had been really fun.

Anna had no pets of her own and, like any young child, she longed to give love and affection to a dog or a cat or some sort of animal. As she and Maria gently stroked the two tabbies they felt tempted to pick them up and take them home.

Then their nice owner had appeared and offered them a chance to feed them.

The two little girls did not hesitate to go back to the man's apartment – all those warnings from their mothers had fallen on deaf ears. Their thoughts were dominated by their affection for these two cats – not the evil intentions of the outside world.

Their naive faith in mankind was still intact. They had not been through the trials and torment suffered by their parents.

Anna and Maria had no need to fear as long as they stuck together. For even the sickest people rarely want their atrocities to be witnessed by anyone else. Their intentions are so degrading that they find it uncomfortable if anyone else is present, whatever their age.

They knew their parents would be angry if they said what they had done, so they promised each other not to tell anyone about their adventure.

But, on this day, Anna was on her own. Maria was at school and Anna needed to find something to do. As she looked out of the window the answer to the problem seemed to be cycling slowly up the street.

As Anna skipped down the stairs to catch up with the friend she had just seen, she just kept thinking about those two sweet little cats. How she wished she had some of her own. Then, on those days when she was left alone, she would not seem so lonely.

On the sidewalk, she soon caught up with her friend. Anna never actually knew his name but that didn't matter. She was more interested in the cats than him.

Klaus Grabowski's eyes glinted the moment he felt the little hand tugging at his sleeve from behind. He instantly recognised Anna from her visit with Maria to his flat some weeks earlier.

He quickly glanced around him to see if anyone had noticed their encounter. No one seemed to be taking the slightest bit of notice. He was hardly able to contain himself. Here was the little girl he was so especially fond of. The little girl who seemed so incredibly attractive. The one he had dreamed about ...

A few minutes later, at his apartment, he was positively shaking with lurid excitement. Here she was. The one he had earmarked. The little girl he wanted.

Anna was stroking the cat, showing the sort of affection Grabowski had longed for as a child but never received.

He was running out of patience. He had got her to his apartment. Now he wanted only one thing.

Only a few hours earlier he had fantasised about the sexual perversity that gave him his only thoughts of pleasure. Now he had a disgusting opportunity to achieve it. Nothing was going to stop him.

Anna was crying now. She did not like the 'game' that Grabowski had insisted on playing. She wanted to go home but he wouldn't let her.

He hated the crying. He wanted to stop it – now. He couldn't stand the noise. It was making him feel vulnerable. But he had to go on punishing her, hurting her. It was wrong but he did not care. He just had to have his way. No grown woman would tolerate such behaviour. This was why he had to have them so young. He hated the way women had always dominated his life. He wanted to punish them for existing. This was his way of getting his own back.

Anna was screaming hysterically now. She knew that this should not be happening. She knew this man was evil. She knew she had to get out of that apartment. But there was no way she could break free. He had a vice like grip on her. Then she fainted.

Grabowski felt the pulse. She hadn't died yet. He went into the bedroom and pulled out a pair of his fiancé's red tights from a drawer.

He used them to strangle the last drop of life out of this poor little innocent child.

Marianne had returned to her apartment. It was lunchtime. There was no sign of Anna. At first she didn't panic. Convinced that she had probably gone around to a friend's home.

One hour later, Marianne telephoned the police in a distressed state. All the memories of her own awful childhood were flooding back. She just kept thinking about that salesman who assaulted her. The horrible stepfather. The neighbour who raped her. It was a terrible world out there. She knew, because all her life she had been a victim.

She could feel that something was terribly wrong. She did not want to think what might have happened.

But, inside herself she knew …

Grabowski was still in a sexual trance. He had the lifeless body of little Anna in his arms and he was placing the corpse into a cardboard box that he had in the kitchen of his cramped apartment.

He didn't flinch as he crumpled the tiny body into the 3-foot square box. For a man who had thrown the carcasses of animals around for a living this was hardly difficult.

It was now late in the afternoon and he needed to dispose of Anna's body quickly and secretly. But Grabowski had one problem – transport. He did not own a car – just a tatty bicycle. He was going to have to use it to carry her body.

Clinically, as if he was carrying a hefty Christmas present, he strapped the box onto the front of the bike and began to ride. At first, the sheer weight made him slightly unsteady. But, as he gained speed, his balance returned. For half an hour he cycled towards the outskirts of the town, constantly looking for the perfect site for a grave.

Grabowski began digging a shallow hole with the shovel he had tied to the back of his bicycle.

He was shaking with fear by now. The reality of the situation was slowly catching up with him and he was beginning to realise what he had done.

As he gently dropped the cardboard box into the ground, he could feel the weight of the body slipping over to one side making it difficult to balance. It must have finally drove home to him the enormity of what he had just done.

He thought for a moment about the lives he had wrecked beyond repair. How one sick moment of sexual satisfaction would ruin so many people's futures. Not to mention the future of Anna Bachmeier.

Grabowski was now suffering the pangs of guilt that should have been there from the beginning. As he cycled back to his flat, he found it impossible to stop his mind wandering back to the look on the face of little Anna as she tried in vain to fight back.

He kept asking himself the same question over and over again. Why? Why? Why? Something deep inside him made his conscience actually prick. The tragedy was that he did not feel it before. Then perhaps Anna would have lived a full life.

Grabowski drove directly to the town's main police station and confessed to his crime.

It was an unusually warm day in Lübeck on Friday, March 6, 1981.

In the tiny courtroom where Klaus Grabowski was on trial for the murder of little Anna Bachmeier, the atmosphere was relaxed.

Outside, the sun was shining. Inside, the defendant had already admitted his guilt. The public gallery was empty except for a group of school children studying German law.

There were few press members covering the event. After all, this was just another in a long catalogue of sex crimes against young children – it was too commonplace to make headline news.

The only person – apart from the judge and the lawyers – remotely interested in the sad proceedings was Marianne Bachmeier. She sat at a table just ten feet from the defendant watching his every response.

There was no dock for this monster. Under German law a defendant is allowed to sit at a table like everyone else – until he is found guilty. Even though Grabowski had already confessed to his atrocities.

By Marianne stood a 4-inch high, framed photograph of the daughter he had butchered. Every few seconds she would look at his face and then down at the face of her pretty little Anna. She had behaved in exactly the same way throughout the trial – which was now into its third day.

Marianne had looked glazed much of the time but it was clear she was listening intently to every awful detail of her daughter's horrible death and the background of the man who had murdered her.

Klaus Grabowski had lived in and around the Lübeck area for most of his rather sad, pathetic life. In the early 1970s he had been twice convicted for the sexual abuse of children. On both occasions he had lured innocent little girls into his home and brutally assaulted them leaving them psychologically and physically scarred for life.

While serving his sentence, Grabowski had himself been sexually abused and beaten up by fellow prisoners.

Traditionally, child sex offenders are the most hated inhabitants inside prison. Wardens would turn their heads the other way, whenever Grabowski found himself facing an angry mob.

By 1976, he was desperate to get out of jail. The beatings were proving unbearable and he knew that no one would help him. After all, he was a pervert and a threat society.

Then Grabowski volunteered to be castrated to secure an early release from prison. It was his only chance. In a short operation, he permitted his sexual urges to be destroyed for ever – or so all the experts had believed.

To lose his manhood seemed a small price to pay for the escape from the daily abuse of his fellow prisoners. But life on the outside proved tough for Grabowski. He never got his old job back as a butcher and his world seemed hopeless. He wanted to find someone to love but there was no love within. The old, sick urges seemed to have subsided. But he wanted more out of life.

Grabowski had no sexual feelings whatsoever, but he was fully aware what they felt like because he had once had them. Now his life would be empty forever – unless he could plan a way to get those responses back.

The answer lay in hormone treatment. The very thought of those sexual feelings returning motivated him to seek help.

In 1979, just a few months before he made helpless Anna his victim, Grabowski tricked his way into getting help from an urologist. He persuaded the medic to give him, the necessary hormone treatment to help him get those deadly urges back.

He did not admit that he had been castrated because of the sex offences he had committed. Instead he persuaded the doctor to help on the grounds that he was simply an exhibitionist.

But now, he assured the physician, he was cured and he wanted his sex life back. The doctor didn't bother to check his record.

On the day he murdered Anna, Grabowski's hormone levels were as high as that of a normal man.

Marianne listened to all this evidence impassively. She was stunned by revelation after revelation but she had no right in a court of law to stand up and air her opinions. She had to bottle up her feelings of anger, disgust and sadness. Being repressed had long since become a way of life for Marianne.

And then there was the guilt. How could she have left her daughter alone? Why didn't she just take her with her into town? If only she could turn the clock back. But it was too late.

All this was a dreadful repetition of her own tragic life. She had so desperately hoped things would turn out differently for Anna.

Her best friend, pretty blonde lawyer Brigitte Muller-Horn recalled how: 'Anna's death was more important to her than her own death. In a way, she died with Anna. Anna was a very bright and clever child. More like a small adult than a little girl. She was her mother's confidante and friend. Marianne talked to Anna about problems like she could talk to no one else. She was closer to her than she had ever been to anyone else in her entire life.'

All these thoughts and much more were rushed through Marianne's mind as she continued her courtroom vigil.

Just one hour earlier, Marianne had visited her daughter's grave in the vast, impersonal cemetery in the centre of Lübeck. She had kneeled at the tiny white cross and begged forgiveness. She felt the weight of guilt about Anna's death. There were so many ifs. If only she had not gone out to that appointment. If only they had never sold the bar in Kiel. If only she had woken up on time to send Anna to school. The list was endless.

Back in the court Grabowski was centre stage.

Marianne looked into straight into his cold, almost dead eyes but he turned away. Now her mind returned to the murder scene.

'He had his hands around her throat. I heard her scream ...'

At that moment Marianne fumbled under the green coat on her lap. She pulled out a small Beretta pistol, aimed at Grabowski's back and squeezed the trigger six times.

She watched coldly as his body jerked from the hail of bullets that hit him. No one could do anything to help the former butcher as he slumped to the floor. He died instantly.

She then calmly threw the gun aside, sending it skidding across the floor of the stunned courtroom. Marianne stood up to allow police to escort her from the building.

When she visited Lübeck Cemetery to select Anna's last resting place, the undertaker asked her: 'Would you like to select a single or a double grave?'

Without hesitation, Marianne replied: 'A double. It is for Anna and me. Soon I will be with her anyway.'

Marianne had chosen the courts of justice, to exact an ancient retribution: an eye for an eye.

She had avenged her daughter's death in a fashion that no one in the entire world could fail to sympathise with.

In March, 1983, Marianne Bachmeier was sentenced to six years imprisonment after being found guilty of the murder of Klaus Grabowski. Immediately after her sentence was pronounced she was allowed free, pending an appeal, after which her sentence was reduced to two years suspended. She is now happily re-married and living in a cottage on the Baltic coast.

9

BLIND RAGE

Her hair was thick, lustrous and so dark it might have been spun on the same loom as the night. Her shoulders and back were slender. Her legs were turned to one side, covered up to mid-thigh by sheer black stockings. The curve of her calves was distinct and, under different circumstances, might well have been considered sexually appealing.

The shapely legs, the full hips, the trim waist, the full breasts — all were fully exposed. But it was her face that gave it all away.

The matt grey eyes stared blankly into the moonlight. The rain pelted on to her face then ran down her breasts, exposed by the ripped-open blue nurse's uniform that partially covered her lilywhite body. Her pubic hair was soaked by the rain, her underwear long since removed. At the back of her head was a small hole rimmed with a black burn mark — the only evidence of assault.

There was no one else at Broat's Farm. Just a corpse in the muddy yard as the rain slammed hard against the ground on that bitterly cold December evening.

The body of nurse Jayne Smith lay there uncovered. It was an undignified death for anyone. The apparent victim of a horrific sexual assault. Something that no woman could ever wish on her worst enemy.

A tiny beam of light from the farmhouse illuminated the lower half of the corpse, highlighting the tops of her thighs and glistening against her drenched stockings.

The whole scene seemed staged. As if some movie director would emerge from the shadows and shout 'Cut' so the actress could get up and walk back to her trailer for a fresh application of make-up. But the body did not stir. And the film crew never materialised.

A car came around the corner into the entrance to the farm. As the headlights panned across the yard, they momentarily picked out the body. The car jerked to a sudden halt. The driver scrambled out, leaving the door swinging on its hinges, and slid through the muddy yard to the crumpled body of Jayne Smith.

Before he even reached her body, William Smith knew she was dead. There was no movement. The body was twisted slightly out of shape. His wife of just seven months lay, lifeless, in front of him. For a few moments, he just blinked. Unable to absorb the awfulness of what had happened. He squeezed his eyes tightly shut in the hope that when he opened them again, she would be gone – back inside their farmhouse, making him supper lovingly. Smiling at him lovingly. Being a good wife lovingly.

She was still there. Abused and dead.

William knelt in the puddle beside her body, immune to the icy wind that swept up from the North Yorkshire moors. He took her hand in his. Desperate for one last response before she was taken from him for ever.

He felt her fingers. The nails. The softness of the skin that had been so very much alive just a few hours before.

He squeezed her hand tightly. The cold clamminess did not matter. At least he was here. With her. Showing how much he really loved and cared for her.

He moved his hand further down into her palm, pressing tight. Something was missing. But in the emotional turmoil that had occurred during the past few minutes, he could not make out what it was.

He moved his hand up towards her fingers once more. Despite the tears that welled up in his eyes and throbbing pain of tension in his head, he kept feeling her hand. Why this? He had to know. He had to know.

He looked down at the limp discoloured fingers. And he realized with a jolt what was missing.

Her wedding ring.

Somehow his numb fingers punched in the three numbers.

'You've got to help me.'

After a few seconds, a WPC came on the line. She sensed it immediately. She could tell that this was genuine.

'My wife has been murdered at home. I have just got in.'

His voice was straining all the time. It was almost impossible to say that word. *Murdered*. It thumped the truth home to him.

He wasn't sure if he could continue with the call. What was the point? Nothing was going to bring Jayne back. No amount of sympathy. No miracle cure. She had gone forever.

William was a pragmatic man. As a child, he had always been taught to bottle up his emotions and never cry in public. 'Men don't do that sort of thing son,' his father once told him. But now he wanted to shed floods of tears. Let his emotions loose on the phone to a complete stranger. What would his folks have said to that?

He had to continue. He took a deep breath.

'She's laid in the yard. There is blood all over.'

Blood. Just one word. It was there. It was real. His voice was really choking now. He just didn't know if he could go through with it.

She was dead. There was no future without her. How could he carry on?

Another deep breath gave him just enough courage.

'Her clothes have been removed and she looks as though she has been raped and murdered.'

He slammed the phone down after spitting out the words. It was the first contact he had had with anyone since the discovery. Now he knew it really was actually happening. The nightmare had begun.

Yet just seven months earlier, this dreadful episode wouldn't have seemed possible to twenty-eight-year-old Jayne Wilford and farmer William Smith, seven years her senior.

Their wedding had been beautiful. Held at a church in the heart of the North Yorkshire Moors, it had seemed like a scene out of Wuthering Heights. Farmers and their families gathered for a really happy occasion in a picturesque setting.

Although it was May, 1988, it could easily have been any time this century. Time does not seem to catch up with anything in that part of the world. Relatives and friends were convinced the happy couple would be together till they died. They had that feeling about them.

They seemed to go so well together.

William, a shy, bearded, hard working man of the land. Jayne, the caring, outgoing nurse who looked forward to having a family by the man she first fell for when she was still at school.

They say opposites attract each other to make the perfect marriages. In their case, it looked like being true.

Yet it could all have been so very different for William.

Just over a year earlier, he had been due to marry another, older woman when Jayne stepped back into his life.

Yvonne Sleightholme had wanted William from the first moment she clapped eyes on him, at a rugby club disco on New Year's Eve, 1979. Beneath her rather staid clothes and practical hairstyle, lurked a ruthlessly determined woman.

William had always been a bit of a slow starter, so she had to make the running in every sense of the word.

At first, William was happy to be led by Yvonne. She was a brittle, strong Yorkshire lass. Always planning every moment they had together. Nothing was too much for Yvonne. She enjoyed running his life for him.

It meant she could take control. She decided who they did and did not see. Which of his friends were in and which were out.

Yvonne had big plans for them. Including marriage.

William didn't even think about it at first. His world stopped at the gates to Broat's Farm. He just let her carry on with the arrangements. He kept meaning to take a step back and consider it all, but it was a busy time on the farm and he never got the chance. He just wanted a peaceful life. Married or not. It didn't make a whole lot of difference to him.

After eighteen months of courtship, he did not mind the idea of a wedding. He was approaching his thirties. Most people in those parts took the plunge by then.

Gradually, however, it dawned on him that marriage to Yvonne might not be such a good idea. She was brilliant at running his life. But surely there had to be more to love than just that? True, she had moved into his farm and it was nice to have a woman around. But marriage?

He took her out one day and quietly, but tactfully, told her it was over between them.

She was stunned. She had been about to book the wedding arrangements. How could he turn around and dump her without any warning? There wasn't even anyone else.

Regular churchgoer Yvonne saw in William someone she genuinely felt she could love and cherish for the rest of her life. Someone who was soft, gentle and considerate. Someone completely malleable. She was not going to let him go that easily.

A few weeks later, she insisted they meet for one last time.

William agreed because he did not want to hurt her feelings. He soon began to wish he hadn't.

'I've got leukaemia – and it's all your fault.' Yvonne was shouting, close to tears, at William. 'It's got worse since you finished with me. You've got to do something.'

William was speechless. Here was the woman he had cleanly and kindly tried to finish a relationship with, insisting that he had sentenced her to death by not continuing their affair.

He didn't expect a lot out of life. But why was she saying these things? It wasn't his fault, surely? But William was a trusting sort of bloke and Yvonne Sleightholme convinced him it was all his fault. Riddled with guilt, he agreed to carry on their courtship. He could not bear to see anyone so ill. Perhaps there was a chance she might recover now, he thought.

Miraculously, all traces of the illness disappeared within weeks of them getting back together. And William even began to think that maybe they did belong to each other. Perhaps fate had meant them to get together again? She was a good woman after all.

So William was hardly surprised when Yvonne began making new arrangements for a wedding.

This time, she told herself, he won't get away.

'I want this wedding,' she said. 'It is going to happen. It is going to be the most beautiful day of my life.'

Yvonne was in her element. Being a doctor's receptionist was clearly taking second place to her latest career – organising her forthcoming marriage.

The date was set six months ahead to give her ample time to sort out the church, the dress, the reception, the honeymoon. It was all very time consuming and Yvonne did so love to organise ...

Meanwhile, William carried on working hard at the farm, rarely having time to go out except to attend the countless fittings for his morning suit and to see the vicar to discuss the ceremony.

On one rare, fateful trip into the nearby town of Salton, he bumped into his old friend Jayne Wilford.

They had once been very close. But both had drifted off into different directions after she had reached her twenties. William often thought about what had happened to Jayne. But she always seemed to have a new boyfriend on her arm whenever he saw her. She seemed to have outgrown him or so he presumed.

Jayne had heard about the wedding plans and wanted to give him her congratulations. There was, of course, another motive for seeking him out. She also thought a lot about William.

'You know. I always reckoned that one day we would get married. It has always been one of my secret dreams.'

William was shocked but at the same time, pleased. It was exactly what he hoped she would say. There had always been something special between them. They might have drifted apart years before, but there was always a feeling that destiny might play a hand in bringing them together once more.

Jayne wasn't just trying to steal another woman's husband-to-be. She had a chilling message to deliver to the man she really loved more than anyone else.

'I think you are being conned into a relationship that you know is not right for you.'

William listened intently. In the back of his mind these were the very things he feared about his impending marriage to Yvonne.

Jayne went on, 'You are being dragged into a relationship by someone who is lying and scheming.'

William nodded his head in agreement. He knew that every word she was saying was true. Yet how could he break off his relationship with Yvonne? He was well aware of the hurt he would cause.

For a few weeks, William was in a complete quandary. Every time he started to tell Yvonne that it was off, she would over-ride the conversation with her prattle about the arrangements for the wedding.

William then did something he had never contemplated ever doing in his life. He slept with both Jayne and Yvonne at the same time. He was unable to break the news to Yvonne. It was a remarkable sham. And he hated himself for it. It tormented him.

Betrayal did not come easily to William. Some men cheat all their lives, but William had never done it. Now the strain of keeping up a relationship with two women at the same time was tearing him apart emotionally. He could not stand it. He knew it was wrong. And it was impossible to know if Yvonne realised. She just seemed so wrapped up in those damned wedding arrangements.

Yvonne's family were delighted their daughter had at last found happiness. She had lived at home on their farm for so long they had been worried she might remain a spinster for life. William seemed such a lovely character.

It was all yet more pressure on him. Making it more and more difficult to come clean. Yvonne had long since moved into his farm, making herself busy putting her own inimitable female stamp on the decor. Choosing new curtains, kitchen equipment and other essentials that had always been missing when William lived there alone.

He was guilty of cowardice and he knew it. By letting her continue to think he was willing to marry, he was just getting deeper and deeper into trouble.

Jayne kept urging him. Aware of what it must be like for the other woman. She was just as uncomfortable with this blatant deception. She kept thinking how she would have felt if the situations were reversed.

Then it happened. The one thing no one ever plans for, but everyone dreads just before a wedding. Yvonne became pregnant. She became distraught because she might not fit into the wedding dress. For days she told no one her secret. Fearful of the shame it might bring on them, but especially worried about that dress. In North Yorkshire, they still frowned upon children conceived outside marriage.

All the tension had tragic consequences because, within a few days, she had miscarried. No one knew about the baby except her doctor.

Meanwhile, William was wracked with guilt about his affair with Jayne. He decided he had to tell her the truth.

'I've found someone else. I just don't think it would be right to carry on. Let's finish it for good this time.'

He was trying to be honourable. He had confessed his deception and now he just wanted them to finish peacefully. He knew he had done wrong. But he was coming clean. Telling the truth was the only way he knew. He felt it had gone on for quite long enough.

Yvonne was devastated. The hurt was immeasurable. She was still in love with him. She was just weeks from marrying him. What could she tell their relatives and friends?

But, perhaps worse of all, she had just lost his baby – and he hadn't even known she was pregnant. She needed his love and support through her difficult time. She didn't want to hear that the man she was about to marry had fallen in love with another woman.

'I have just miscarried our baby.'

William didn't know what to do. This was turning into an even more difficult situation. After her last attempt to keep him through lies, he didn't even know if she were telling the truth.

He felt awful, but no amount of sympathy would bring them back together yet again. He still couldn't marry her.

'I no longer have any desire for you. Don't you understand?'

It was hurting William almost as much as it was hurting her. But it had to be said.

'We have both tried so hard but it hasn't worked out. I want to be free to find out how I truly feel about Jayne.'

William's words were so carefully put – even at such a crucial moment. Yvonne knew she could do nothing but accept that it was over, though underneath the polite, civilised conversation, she was nurturing a resentment and hatred that would bring horrific consequences.

Just a few months later Jayne Milford moved into Broat's Farm.

The ghost of Yvonne Sleightholme had not yet been finally laid to rest. Unable to accept that it was completely over, she hadn't removed any of her belongings at first. It was as if she was convinced that William and Jayne would part and she could just carry on where she left off.

When she did eventually turn up, three months later, to gather her things, the atmosphere was strained and difficult. The three of them hardly uttered a word.

She soon left. Drove away from the farm, out of their lives forever. They hoped.

The voice at the other end of the phone line was menacing and cold.

'I'm going to kill you bitch ...'

There was a click and the line went dead.

Jayne Smith had just returned with new husband William after their honeymoon.

Everyone gets cranky calls some times. But the voice seemed familiar.

No. It couldn't be her, thought Jayne. It was all over long ago. No one could harbour such intense resentment surely? When she told William, he dismissed it in much the same way. The Smiths were a happy, trusting couple. They didn't really see the bad side of anyone. They didn't want to.

'Quick. Quick. There's a fire in the barn.' William rushed out into the yard. For almost half-an-hour he bravely dampened down the blaze with water and blankets.

It could have turned into a major catastrophe.

Strange really. He could not work out how on earth it had happened. Then he started to think that maybe it had been started deliberately. Perhaps *she* was responsible. Then again, no one would go to those lengths. Would they?

'This is it.' I've bloody well had enough of this nonsense. I'm going to see the police.'

It was not often that William Smith lost his temper. But this time she had gone too far.

In his hand he held a wreath with a chilling message, 'Jayne. I'll always remember you.'

William was outraged.

'She's sick in the head. She's got to be stopped.'

Domestic disputes don't come high on the police's list of priorities. Nevertheless, under pressure, they agreed to visit Yvonne to see if she was behind the incidents. But they were not that interested. As far as they were concerned, there were real villains to be caught – not lovelorn spinsters.

And when they interviewed Yvonne she really switched on the charm. The two officers came away from her family's farm convinced she was far from a danger to the Smiths. In fact, she seemed like a very nice, responsible sort of person. Hardly the type to carry out a vicious hate campaign. And, even if she was behind some of the incidents, a jilted woman making a pest, of herself was hardly an unusual occurrence. Let the dust settle and she'll soon give up, the police assured William and Jayne.

Shortly after the wreath incident, Yvonne decided enough was in fact enough – she had to clear her head and try to start afresh.

The first stage in this self-induced rehabilitation was to travel across the nearby border into Scotland, hire a holiday cottage and forget about all her problems. She even got herself a new boyfriend.

In ambulance driver Anthony Berry, she had at last found a new man – whom she felt fond of. At least he satisfied her physically, if not entirely socially. Hidden away in the border country, they could make love until the cows came home. She could put William and all her troubles behind her.

It would be a wonderful break for them both, she told friends. But, inside, the resentment and hatred was still bubbled. She was obsessed with the man who had spurned her. Every time she looked at her lover next to her, she saw William. Every time she walked in hand with him through the fields, she saw William.

It was no use pretending. She would have to get him back. Punish that witch Jayne for humiliating her. For making her the laughing stock of all her sneering relatives. For making William turn his back on her when she needed him most.

But, by December 14, Yvonne was like a different person. They had been on holiday for over a week and it was as if all the cares of the world had been lifted from her shoulders. She was beaming with delight. Looking radiant. And best of all she was feeling really passionate.

She had been out for a very long drive alone and now she was back at the cottage, demanding sex from Anthony. Anywhere. She just had to have it — then and there.

He began by probing her mouth deeply with his tongue. Then she allowed him to stroke her body gently. She shut her eyes and savoured the waves of pleasure that coursed through her agile body.

She wanted to imagine it was William, not Anthony, exploring her body. She could see his face, above her, satisfying her, kissing her, loving her. It made the actual sex more enjoyable.

As Yvonne lay there enjoying endless pleasures, she cast her mind back to less than 24 hours earlier. It was a vivid recollection and it made her feel even more aroused.

She had laid patiently in wait for William to leave the farm for his regular game of five-a-side football. After all those years together, how could she forget his soccer. Every Tuesday, without fail, he would go off, leaving his ever-so-sweet little wife all alone at the farm to fend for herself. Alone and vulnerable.

From her vantage point just off the road by the corner, Yvonne knew he would have to pass. She watched silently as his car drove down towards the village. Even though she was not close enough to actually see his face through the car window, she felt a sense of excitement just to know she had been near to him once more.

Soon, she would have him back. He would be hers once more.

She waited patiently in her car. Just in case he returned. He might have forgotten a boot or a sock. She could not be too careful. After ten minutes, she knew he had gone for hours.

She got out of the car and took a deep breath. The wind from the moors whistled furiously around her. The rain was stinging her face as it lashed across the road in front of her. Sometimes the ice cold water would sweep up into a virtual whirlwind before landing with a smack on the tarmac of the road.

It was pitch dark except for the two room lights that shone out from the farm house. The luminous eyes of a fox glanced right in front of Yvonne. The creature scuttled back into the thick undergrowth by the side of the lane. She paused for a moment. Then smiled a knowing sort of smile. A look that said nothing would scare her that night. She glanced up at the farmhouse as a silhouette crossed a window. Sweet little Jayne was in.

As Yvonne walked through the muddy yard towards the front door, she felt a surge of tension go through her body. She was hyped up. Stiff with expectation. She felt that resentment and hatred return once more. It was driving her on all the time. Telling her to continue ...

She was breathing quite heavily now. In through her nose, out through her mouth. All the time exercising the muscles of her fingers. Twirling them as if she were about to play the piano. Making sure they were loosened and responsive.

Just two steps from the door, she pushed her hand under her anorak and felt the warm glossy veneer of the wooden handle of the rifle. She pulled it out. It was quite heavy and it took both hands to ease out.

Now she had it pointing downwards with her right hand on the trigger. Her other hand covered the upper end of the barrel. She pressed the doorbell with the end of the rifle. It was a cold calculating movement.

Yvonne narrowed her eyes and squinted at the door as she waited for it to open. The gun now trained dead centre on the entrance.

Jayne was not the sort of person to worry about strangers calling at the house at night-time. She had typical country trust – the belief in people's better natures. She could not imagine anyone wishing her harm – even after all that fuss with Yvonne.

Jayne had only just got home from her night shift at the old people's home where she worked as a nurse. There had not even been time to change out of her uniform.

As she pulled open the door, her pretty face filled with surprise at first, rather than fear. It was a symptom of that momentary feeling of disbelief that always occurs when something completely out of the ordinary happens.

She looked straight at Yvonne. Then at the gun. Then stood there. Unable to react.

But Yvonne soon broke the silence.

She marched Jayne over to the farmyard. Prodding her constantly with the gun to keep her moving in the direction she wanted. Jayne knew precisely what all this was about.

Yvonne's bitterness had known no limits. Jayne had overestimated the woman's better nature.

They stood there, buffeted by the torrential rain. No conversation between them. Just a rifle barrel for communication purposes. Pointing right into the back of Jayne's head. It was the waiting that was the worst. Waiting for Yvonne to take control and pull the trigger.

She hesitated – not because she was scared. She just enjoyed the suffering. She wanted to see the pain she was causing. She felt the urge to flex her fingers once more. She held the weapon tight in her grasp, remembering everything she had learnt on the rifle range years before. She didn't want to mess it up. Clean and quick. And oh-so-beautiful.

Yvonne felt the central muscle on her finger squeezing tightly on the trigger. She felt the barrel quiver as the bullet raced into Jayne's head. In a split second it was over.

Yvonne did not panic. She looked at the crumpled body on the muddy yard and realised there was ample time to avoid being accused of this murder. But first, she had to guarantee that he alone would know that she had done it.

She pulled Jayne's limp left hand off the ground and tried to pull off her wedding band. It would not budge. The torrential rain had swollen her finger. Yvonne could do nothing. For a moment, she panicked. The murder had been too easy. But trying to remove her wedding ring was part of her obsession. She had to get it off – no matter what.

She had to know that Jayne would go to her grave without that ring.

She was Mrs William Smith, not Jayne. That scheming bitch had no rights to him in the first place. She had stolen him from her. Now she was denying her the right to remove that ring.

Yvonne would not give up. She struggled to get the ring off. Finally, she managed to twist and turn it enough to pull it up and off her finger.

Elated at her achievement, she now began to consider her next move. People would think it was her. She had to do something to divert attention away from the obvious. That meant making sure it looked like the work of a man.

She crouched down over the body and ripped open the buttoned front of Jayne's nursing tunic. At first, the well-sewn buttons would not give. But, with one almighty yank, they began to pop apart. She stood up and studied her work. It did not look at all convincing. It had to look like the real thing. Not some feeble attempt at pretending it was rape.

Once again, she bent down. All the time the rain was sweeping across her, sometimes hitting her straight in the face. But she knew there was still more work to be done.

She pulled the dress down off her shoulders and arms. Not stopping for a moment to consider the beauty of the person whose life she had just destroyed. She undid the bra and, flexing those fingers like a concert pianist once more, she squeezed the breasts as hard as possible to leave the sort of marks that would be a clear indication of a sexual motive. Men must do that when they rape women, she presumed.

Yvonne was in her element. She loved the organisation side of it. Getting the scene right meant methodical thought, and she had ample supplies of that.

Next, she removed Jayne's pants, nearly slipping in the thick mud as she did so. She pulled them over Jayne's thighs and down the calves towards her slender ankles revealing drenched black stockings.

It was almost over. But not quite. This was supposed to be a sex attack and one vital detail was missing. She stuffed the sodden pants into her pocket and then lent down, flexing those fingers for the last time …

Yvonne was close to climaxing as Anthony continued heaving himself up and down on top of her.

Her mind had wandered back from the exquisite events of just 20 hours earlier. It seemed like a fantasy. The only reality was that William would soon be hers once more.

After a sensible period of time, she could see the man she really loved again. Then they could marry. Meanwhile Anthony would do. He was a good lover. Anxious to please. Keen to listen.

She felt as though she were in some warm cocoon. Safe in the knowledge that she had committed the killing and she had done everything to put the police off her scent.

The two police officers were charming. They just wanted to have a few brief words with Yvonne. Anthony let them in immediately.

He was completely unaware of what his lover had done. Yvonne seemed shocked by the news.

'It can't be true. How awful.'

Yvonne burst into tears when the officers told her. She was clearly distressed and upset. They had been warned to expect her to be hard nosed and unfeeling about Jayne. But here she was crying profusely. It hardly seemed the reaction of suspected murderess.

The officers said she certainly did not seem to behave like a suspect.

And William's mother could not believe that Yvonne would do such a thing.

After all, she received a delightful Christmas card from her the day after Jayne's death.

Inside was a handwritten note. It said: 'I have a lovely boyfriend.

'He has been with me for quite some time now ... through all the worrying times.'

It seemed to convince everyone that she had put all thoughts of ever marrying William firmly out of her mind. Yvonne posted it just a few hours before she went to Broat's Farm.

She had been very, very meticulous.

William Smith was distraught.

His life was in ruins. He did not know if Yvonne had murdered his wife or not. He was too numb to care about anything except Jayne.

As he hurried along the busy High Street, he knew he had to do one last thing before they buried his darling, beautiful wife.

He frantically looked up and down the road. It was difficult to concentrate in such a bereaved state. But, after a few minutes, he was certain he had found the right shop.

He walked in hesitantly – just in case he was wrong.

But the jeweller recognised him instantly.

'You sold me a ring ...'

William started to explain but the man remembered him immediately.

Detective Superintendent Geoff Cash had at last got a breakthrough in the case. Everyone said it must be Yvonne Sleightholme, but the attack seemed to have been carried out by a man with a sexual motive. Then, his officers discovered that she had not been at that cottage in the Scottish borders on the night of the killing.

Then they had found blood stains, matching the victim's group, in Yvonne's car.

Inside the funeral parlour, William Smith walked towards the open coffin – to see his wife for the last time.

She now looked – in death – almost as near to perfection as she had whilst alive.

In a few minutes, they would be taking her away to the funeral ceremony. But for those last few precious moments, he looked at her, remembering all the good times. The wedding. The happy home they shared together. The smiles. The plans.

William lent over the coffin and gently placed the gold ring on Jayne's finger. Now they had become one again. Not even she could take that from them ...

On May 10, 1991, Yvonne Sleightholme was jailed for life at Leeds Crown Court.

Shortly after her arrest for the murder of Jayne Smith she was diagnosed as having gone blind following the trauma of the incident.

Judge Mr Justice Waite told Sleightholme: 'When your fiancé broke off the engagement and married another woman you wrought upon the newly married couple a terrible revenge.

'You planned in cold fury and executed with ruthless precision the killing of your rival.'

10

VICTIMS OF THE NAZIS

The house was simple. Plain bricks. Sloping roof. Nothing too elaborate. It was a bungalow with an abundance of windows but not much character. Set back off the road, its stark, square, modern look made it more in keeping with the suburbs of Los Angeles, than an isolated part of mid-Wales.

It rained a lot in the tiny hamlet of Pant Perthog. The grey clouds and harsh gusts of wind were a permanent feature of life for the handful of residents, yet the climate only helped to emphasize the beauty of the terrain. Lush, rolling hills strewn with acres of ancient woodlands surrounded the village. It was a picture postcard spot where little had changed for over a century.

Just 50 yards to the rear of the bungalow lay the real reason it had been built in the first place. The River Dovey twisted and turned as it snaked a path through the Welsh countryside. Splitting fields in two. Creating bushy river banks amongst little clumps of trees. Providing an excuse for a scattering of those curved, grey stone bridges built so lovingly by the Victorians.

Most properties in the area had their own names like Pear Tree Cottage or Alamo. But the bungalow that Wanda Chantler lived in had no name. Its very existence was enough for her. It was her *home*.

She would have been happy to hide herself away in that house from the world outside. She had no interest in other people. Just eternal gratitude for being alive and well after a life steeped in tragedy.

Wanda and her husband Alan had deliberately chosen the isolated area of Machynlleth as their home because they wanted the peace and solitude that had always eluded them. They really needed the quietness. Both of them had, for too long, been influenced by events that were out of their control. They did not want that any more. They wanted to be in charge of their own destiny.

Wanda had lovingly planned every detail of the construction of the house with her husband Alan 20 years earlier. It became their sanctuary. Their own little piece of paradise in an evil world. An escape from the unspeakable atrocities that occurred every day somewhere on the globe. A place where they could bring up their two sons without worry.

And that is what they did. As a family, they became a self-contained unit. Just the four of them. They didn't bother the world and it didn't bother them. They loved to explore the countryside on long rambling walks. Sometimes they would travel to the coast and enjoy a picnic on deserted beaches facing the Atlantic.

But then they made a mistake. A big mistake. After the kids had grown up, they made the heart-wrenching decision to sell the bungalow and head off to Australia to be with one of their sons. It had seemed like the perfect opportunity to come out of their shell-like existence in Pant Perthog and to start to rediscover the outside world. Their plans had failed miserably. Outside of that tiny retreat, they found that nothing had changed.

The same evil forces dominated. The same problems existed. The same wars ravaged on. It was all a bitter disappointment to the Chantlers. They had really hoped and prayed that the new, modern world might be more welcoming. But it was not to be.

Australia wasn't right for them. The idea of sun, sand and sea just did not appeal. The gentle waves of the mid-Wales coastline were a far nicer proposition than the giant surf of Bondi Beach. They felt out of place in an alien world where nearly everyone was under forty.

Wanda, fifty-seven years old, was a highly articulate woman. She always appeared a little dishevelled in a friendly sort of way. She had an intense, introvert manner much of the time. Always slightly on her guard but basically full of good intentions. A trained physiotherapist and a linguist with nine languages to her credit, she found Australia a shallow place. She had little in common with the people she met. She longed to look once more at those lush pastures of Pant Perthog.

Her favourite hobby was painting. She just wanted to have an opportunity

154

to use her water colours to once more re-create that stunning scenery. Back at the bungalow, she used to spend hours lovingly producing her own interpretations of the surrounding countryside. She could lose herself in the paintings. Forget about those painful memories. Only think about the beautiful things in life and put them on canvas.

Alan, just turned sixty, felt just as uncomfortable as his wife in the so-called 'New World' of Australia. Bespectacled and still with a reasonable head of hair, he was an average looking character. He knew full well how happy Wanda would be to come back to mid-Wales. It meant so much to them both. They were convinced they would feel an immense warmness the moment they arrived once more in the area. They kept wondering why on earth they had sold up their dream to take on a nightmare? It was for the love of the children of course. But they had both grown up by now. They had their own lives to lead. Wanda and Alan needed to get on without them. It would all be so much easier back where they belonged.

So, it was no surprise when Wanda and Alan decided to leave Australia and return to mid-Wales in the late 1970s.

They were so relieved when they arrived back in the area. So delighted to see all those old familiar sights. So enchanted by the slow pace of life. So pleased by the easy going nature of the people. Nothing appeared to have changed.

Everyone welcomed them back to Pant Perthog as if they had never been away in the first place. That pleasant feeling of warm security began to return as they settled back in the area.

It was so much nicer than Australia. There was a post office and a little shop in the village. Nothing more, nothing less. It was definitely meant to be.

They loved to be able to wander up and down the lanes without that fear of the unknown. The fear they had been haunted by more than 30 years earlier. The fear that returned when they went to live in Australia.

As far as Wanda was concerned, only one thing was still missing. She longed to have that bungalow back. She was desperate to live once again in the place she had been so happy. On the journey back to mid-Wales she kept telling Alan how wonderful it would be to buy the house once again. It held so many cherished memories. He was just as keen, but he feared it might not be as easy as all that.

Wanda's dream really kept her going. She imagined herself back there with all the happy memories of the children.

New owners Roger and Josie Hartland were delighted when they bought the bungalow from the Chantlers. They saw it as their home for the rest of their lives. In much the same way as the Chantlers once had done, they envisaged staying there for ever.

There was something about the area. It was so pure and simple. There were so few complications … until Wanda Chantler returned.

It had been a dream come true for the Hartlands when they bought the place. Roger, forty-eight, had decided he wanted to quit the rat-race and leave his job as an industrial chemist in the Midlands. He couldn't stand the relentless high-pressure existence. Pant Perthog seemed the perfect location and his young wife was just as convinced they were doing the right thing.

They loved the Chantlers' taste. They admired the way they had managed to make a very plain looking house incredibly warm and cosy inside. It had a vital, airy atmosphere. Something that instantly attracted Roger and Josie when they were looking for a home to retire to.

They even felt grateful to the Chantlers for creating such a perfect home and fully appreciated just how heart breaking it had been for them to move out. They tried to reassure them on their move to Australia to join their son.

'It's supposed to be a lovely place. You'll soon settle there.'

But the Chantlers' obvious reluctance to move put a sad edge on the whole. proceedings. It seemed such a wrench. However, it also showed how much the Chantlers cared – and that was, in a strange sort of way, most reassuring for Roger and Josie. They would have hated to have bought a house from a couple who did not feel any attachment to the place they were leaving. It wouldn't have been the same.

In the end, it was quite a relief when they did actually move in and the Chantlers set off. As they bade farewell to the old couple on their long journey to the other side of the world Roger and Josie presumed that would be the last they would ever see of them.

So when Wanda turned up on their doorstep some three years later, it came as something of a surprise. She still seemed the same gentle, caring creature they had first met. She explained to them how the move to Australia hadn't worked out. The Hartlands felt genuinely sorry for Wanda. She seemed so distressed by it all. They offered her a friendly cup of tea while she poured out all her problems. All the time they were aware that she seemed to want to say something, but kept straying from the point.

They talked about the woods, the river, the trees, the children, the happy memories. But all it did was make Wanda even more sad. Then she changed the whole course of the conversation.

'Would you sell us back the house. We so dearly want it back.'

The Hartlands were stunned. They entirely understood her sentiments ut they told her firmly how happy they were there and that they could not leave it. They felt awful about the whole situation. They could see from Wanda's response that she really had lived in hope of returning to the place of her dreams.

Most people would have respected the Hartland's decision and left it at that but Wanda would not be that easily deterred. It was the only place where she could put her nightmare to rest. She had to have the bungalow back. It was her only chance to lead a normal life again. If she didn't get it the past would haunt her forever.

All her awful visions were returning. It was as if the occupiers had come back to capture and torture her. The Hartlands were becoming like an army of occupation. They were ordering her not to do something. They wanted to stop her from stepping back inside her mental retreat, preventing her from fleeing the evil forces that had plagued her for more than 40 years.

The shock of their refusal to sell the bungalow threw Wanda back into an awful period of her life. It reopened the wounds that all began in 1939 ...

She was just seventeen years old. Her shoulders were broad but perfectly shaped. Her hair was fair and well-conditioned. Her bone structure was strong and her expression was permanently confident. The picture of an attractive girl on the edge of womanhood.

When her father sent her from their home in Western Russia to law school in Berlin, it seemed a natural step for such an exceptionally talented scholar. The first few months there had been a real eye-opener. Being on her own at such a young age had its problems. She overcame them with her looks. They were her passport to a good time. Berlin was a debauched but exciting place in those days. The sense of danger on the streets was always prevalent, but that made it all the more intriguing if you lived there. There were soldiers on every corner but they didn't bother her except to make fresh remarks about her legs. The bars and cafes of Berlin were wonderful. Packed with artists and writers, oblivious to the repressive regime they lived under.

It was an experience of a lifetime for Wanda. She was learning so much. More than she could ever have hoped for back in Russia. And at the end of her three year stay, she would return home as a trained lawyer. It was an achievement that would really mean something to her family. Maybe she could work abroad? That would be even more fun. The world was at her feet. There was so much she could do with her life, so many possible avenues to go down. She could do whatever she wanted. Nobody and nothing could stop her. Or so she thought ...

At first, she did not even notice the street violence involving the soldiers with their swastika armbands. Her mind was focussed on her ambition to succeed. Everything else took second place.

'Outside now!'

The German soldiers did not waste time with explanations.

They were rounding up every name on a list – and Wanda was one of them. She did not know where she was being taken or why. But the look of fear etched on the others' faces told her enough.

They were all students. Young, highly articulate people. None of it made sense. They weren't the enemies of the Germans. They were just studying in Berlin. What was behind all this?

Maybe it was all just a mistake and in a few hours they would be released. But the hours soon turned into days and the days into weeks.

They wanted to know her name, her age, her qualifications. They were particularly interested in her intelligence. They fired question after question at her. How many languages do you speak? What are your qualifications? What is your father's profession? It went on and on and it was becoming very clear that they had something in mind for Wanda. Something awful was about to happen. It would not have been so bad if she knew what it was. The uncertainty was causing the most pain. She was well aware the time would come when they would take her away to some dreadful place.

She thought of escape. But the opportunity never arose.

Soon Wanda was transferred to a prison unlike any she had ever heard about before. It was more like a farm. There were lots of children. Well, very young adults. Nearly all girls. Everyone was relatively free compared to the previous compound. But that very liberty unnerved her. There was something strange about the place. On the surface it seemed like a school in the country or a holiday camp. Underneath, however, you could taste the misery. Students played on the grass in front of the building, but none of them were smiling. And always in the background were the guards with their stiff uniforms and menacing rifles.

All the girls had a certain attractiveness. They had good figures, exquisite faces – and they all shared the same blank look of fear. None of them seemed to know why they were there.

One younger girl – she must have been about fourteen – was crying on the shoulders of another. But Wanda didn't know why. It was an uncertainty which would haunt her for the rest of her life.

The guards were young as well, with many still in their teens. Most of them looked typically German. Well built. Blond hair. Big jackboots. It was the real adults who seemed the most terrifying. There were doctors and nurses everywhere bustling around the place.

One day Wanda was subjected to a physical examination the like of which she had never before experienced in her entire life. She thought it was going to be a straightforward medical. It turned out to be an horrific encounter. Something she would never forget. The doctors examined each of the girls in turn with clinical inquisitiveness. Probing every orifice. The pain when one male doctor roughly examined her made Wanda wince. Then they checked her general health, her strength and fitness. Still Wanda was bemused. Why were all these doctors examining her? What were they planning? She was blissfully unaware that anyone who failed those first medicals went straight to the death camps.

They lived in ignorance for weeks. They were well fed, given many books to read, encouraged to learn and subjected to numerous tests.

Wanda soon realised the doctors were pleased with her. They would say words like 'perfect' and 'beautifully formed' as though they were describing animals rather than human beings.

Then one morning, Wanda was ordered to see the camp's chief physician. She wondered what it was about. She had passed the tests. What more could they possibly want to do to her?

When she walked into the room, there, standing with the doctor, was a tall, well-built German with blond hair and chiselled features like a cardboard cut-out

He examined Wanda with his sharp crystalline eyes. Looking up and down her body as she stood there. At first, they said nothing. She was just ordered to stay still and not speak – just allow this total stranger to cast his eyes all over her body.

The doctor turned to the man and said, 'What do you think.'

That word 'perfect' was used yet again.

It was at last starting to dawn on Wanda why she was there. The doctors. The man. The questions. She was terrified. All the nightmare scenarios she had considered were now coming true.

She had been nurtured and fed at that farm in order to create the perfect baby for the perfect race. She was to become a surrogate mother for the Aryan race – Hitler's consuming obsession.

She was a virgin faced with conveyor belt sex on demand. No emotion. No love.

Wanda was taken into an adjoining room. In the corner was a mattress. She was forced to strip off her clothes …

Forty years later in Pant Perthog, Wanda was reliving that dreadful nightmare. She couldn't get the sex farm out of her mind. Of course, she had thought about it every day for the whole of her life. No one could forget what had happened. But before, she had control over those feelings. Now, she was consumed with out and out anger. The Hartland's were standing in her way. Punishing her. Hadn't she already had punishment enough? She couldn't allow it. She had to do something.

They had become Nazi guards. Their refusal to sell the house was as much an atrocity to her as the behaviour of those blond Aryan brutes.

Wanda's husband Alan was beside himself with worry. He could see his wife's obsession growing at an alarming rate. He tried to explain that there were other places to live. But nowhere except the bungalow would do for Wanda.

The Hartland's would have to suffer for the torture they had inflicted on her.

Wanda's first step was to enrol at the local gun club. The Aberystwyth Rifle Club was the sort of place that is frequented mainly by men. Set in the heart of the Welsh countryside, it was primarily used by genuine enthusiasts and responsible farmers trying to keep in their aim.

When Wanda first showed up to learn skills with a gun, there were a few raised eyebrows, but the members soon became used to seeing the grandmotherly figure cocking a weapon to her shoulder and firing off round after round of bullets.

She rapidly gained a reputation as a very fine shot. No one asked her why she wanted to learn in the first place. They aren't like that in mid-Wales. Mind your own business, ask no questions and life will stay easy. Her aim became deadlier by the day.

Josie Hartland was close to tears as she screwed up the letter that had just come through the post box of their house. She was worried by the threats. What made it worse was the fact they both knew exactly who had written it. Wanda Chantler.

It was the third letter to have arrived in a couple of weeks. Each one had become more elaborate. More sinister. And now it mentioned treasure hidden under the bath.

Wanda Chantler was becoming increasingly withdrawn. She and her husband had found a place to live at nearby Garth Owen. But it wasn't the same as the bungalow. The countryside didn't look or sound the same. It was more built up. More noisy. Less private.

Living there made Wanda even more obsessed with moving back to the bungalow. She hated meeting people in the street near their new home. They just didn't seem so friendly.

Wanda felt less and less inclined to go out. Apart from her trips to the rifle club she rarely left the house. Alan Chantler was becoming increasingly worried about his wife's health and mental state. All she could talk about was the bungalow. How she had to have it back. He kept telling her to forget it. But she would have none of it.

She started to convince herself that she had left some hidden treasure under the bath. A lot of gold trinkets and an assortment of other things. Losing the house was bad enough, but the treasure was legally hers. She was the rightful owner. No one should be allowed to take that away from her. She kept asking the Hartlands, and they said it did not exist. But she knew it was there. She knew it.

Wanda began to write another letter. This time it was to the local paper. The venom soon flowed. Her targets were the Hartlands. If she could not persuade them to give up her house – the house she created and made into what it was today – then she would hound them until they hated the very sight of it.

'You have got to do something. The woman is deranged.'

Roger Hartland had had enough of the threats. His wife was in tears when he had got home that day. It was an outrage that anyone could make such vicious comments about someone they hardly knew.

Something had to be done, so he turned to the police.

Crime was almost non-existent in Pant Perthog. Nothing much ever happened. And that made it all the more difficult for the police to respond rapidly to any problem that might arise. The officers were sympathetic. But how could anyone take a grandmother's threats seriously? There was no possibility of her carrying them out.

Roger Hartland was convinced otherwise. He believed that Wanda Chantler's threats had the ring of authenticity about them. That was why they were so frightening.

'Just give us a call if you have any more problems.'

The policeman was merely doing his duty, but no more. This sort of thing never happened in a place like Pant Perthog, after all. Why should it start now?

Alan Chantler also knew otherwise. He was well aware of Wanda's obsessive nature, after nearly 40 years of marriage. After all, they had first met when he and his fellow allied troops arrived at the sex farm in 1945 and liberated the inhabitants. It was an emotionally draining job. But it had one reward – he met Wanda.

Within a short time, they had married and moved to Britain. Those past horrors seemed to have been put behind them. Wanda never really spoke much about the farm. She bottled it all up. Thinking constantly about it but never telling her closest friend. It had to come out sooner or later.

Alan was well aware his wife was on the verge of a nervous breakdown. She had become agoraphobic – refusing to leave their new home for anything other than rifle club training.

Reluctantly, he went to the police and got her shotgun licence revoked before any tragedy could occur. Instinctively, he knew she was heading in that direction. He could feel each second ticking away before his wife's inevitable explosion. He was convinced it was only a matter of time before something awful happened. The threats, the letters. She had even been around to the Hartlands to try to frighten them into selling the house.

Wanda's main topic of conversation at home was the treasure under the bath. Alan knew it didn't exist but he also knew that in his wife's mind it was the only piece of reality she could still cling to.

The Hartlands were as bad as the SS in her eyes. Maybe they even came from Germany, she thought.

In Wanda's mind, the sex farm and the Hartlands were rapidly becoming synonymous with each other. Maybe they took their orders from the camp commandant? Perhaps they had been sent here to hunt her down and take her back?

One sunny Monday, June 16, 1980, Wanda Chantler plunged into the abyss of insanity.

At Garth Owen, Wanda was in a better mood than she had been for weeks. Alan was delighted by this improvement in his wife's health and decided to leave her for a few hours to do the shopping.

The moment he left the house, she scurried to the wardrobe to get dressed. She felt good inside herself. There was a job to be done. She had an objective for the first time in months. It gave her a fresh appetite for life. Maybe that had been the problem all along? She needed to have something to achieve. Life had to have its goals otherwise what was the point in existing?

Josie Hartland was feeling in the same sort of mood over at Pant Perthog. She was getting on with the household chores like washing and cleaning the kitchen and all the other essential work of the day. She enjoyed keeping the bungalow clean and fresh.

The weather made her feel happy as well. It was so rare to get a really nice day in these parts.

The last few weeks had been blissfully clear of problems from that woman. It seemed they had heard the last of her.

Wanda pulled her car up about 50 yards from the entrance to the bungalow, just out of sight of the actual property. She opened the boot, took out two air pistols and tucked them over each hip cowboy fashion.

Then she lifted out the double-barrelled shotgun. It was much heavier than the pistols. But then it was also far more lethal.

Lastly, she took out that treasured painting of the landscape surrounding the bungalow – one of the pictures she had toiled over so lovingly all those years before.

She looked an incongruous sight with the thick leather belt strapped around her waist over a very tweedy, country outfit. If it were not for the guns, she would have looked like a typical country squire's wife out for a walk in the country.

It was quite difficult to carry the shotgun and the painting. But Wanda managed. The determination was there. She could achieve anything that day.

She had to get away from the Nazis. Get them out of her life for ever. Destroy them before they destroyed her.

As she walked up to the front door, her mind kept flashing back to the sex farm. The experiments, the examinations, the clinical rape. This time she would rid herself of those memories once and for all.

She would have her revenge. *And* her treasure under the bath. *And* her bungalow.

She thought she was back in Germany. It all seemed so clear.

'I have a present for you.'

The Hartlands were stunned when they opened the front door to see Wanda standing, armed like some sort of elderly, female Rambo, on the step.

'It's a painting I did of the area. I thought you would like it.'

'You've got to come quickly. She's got three guns …'

The Hartlands' telephone call to Alan Chantler was still remarkably calm, considering the arsenal of weapons she had on her.

She waited on the doorstep.

Roger Hartland went to open the front door to tell her that Mr Chantler was on his way. Wanda aimed the shotgun straight at the entrance. As it opened, Roger saw the barrel pointing right at him for a split second before it went off.

The sheer force of the shot sent him to the ground in a crumpled heap.

Inside, Josie Hartland was grappling for the phone. Dialling 999. She just hoped the operator would answer quickly. She got through, but was told to wait for a police officer to come on the line. Seconds passed while she waited for the answer. Still there was no one at the other end of the line. When would they come? Hurry. Hurry. Hurry.

Wanda was now in the bungalow, seeking, out her tormentors. She entered the kitchen quietly to see Josie cowering in a corner of the room with the phone, frantically shouting down the receiver in the desperate hope someone would help her.

But all she had in fact done was lead Wanda to her. Wanda stood for a moment and stared at Josie before cocking her gun.

The two shots hit her full on. But she was still alive. Still struggling for breath.

Wanda calmly reloaded the shotgun and fired another shot. One was enough to finish off the enemy. They were so weak when you confronted them. Cowards squirming pathetically in a corner. She hadn't even used up all her rounds.

On 24 October, 1980, Wanda Chantler admitted the manslaughter of the Hartlands and was sent to Broadmoor Hospital without limit of time.

Sentencing her, Mr Justice Hodgson, said: 'Nobody could possibly have heard what we have here without feeling the most terrible compassion. In a sense, you are as much a victim of your Nazi experiences as the Hartlands were victims of that same horror.'

11

FREE TRIP TO GOD

A strange silence shrouded the grounds of the Lainz General Hospital. It was as if there was no air. Nothing moved. None of the many trees swayed. No one walked in the grounds. The grey, crumbling façade of the main building contrasted with the pretty apple blossoms dotted throughout the five acres of grassland surrounding the hospital.

Huge ferns cast great shadows on the ornate 150-year-old mansion that had long ago been converted into a centre for the sick and elderly. There was so little sign of life from the outside. So much silence. So much expectation.

The vast gothic windows appeared almost black from the outside. The five storey property looked far taller than it really was. It could have been ten or even fifteen storeys. It had that sort of imposing effect when people visited.

Atop the main frontage were gargoyles — a set of six of them staring intently down on all who entered. A piece of masonry just next to their footage had once crashed down in front of a group of elderly patients. Perhaps it was time for them to leave?

The place exerted a strange emotional pull on anyone who happened to be passing. The sheer enormity of the building. Its long, drawn out features. The lichen encrusted statues built into virtually every corner. The once pale stonework darkened by a century and a half of grime. Up one side, clumps of ivy clung desperately to powdery mortar.

165

If it had ever been given the maintenance it deserved, then the Lainz could have maintained its original splendour. It had all the classic ingredients to be pronounced a building of great historical value, but the general public tended to keep well away. A place full of the dying and the elderly was hardly going to become a tourist attraction. There was something about it that made the locals suspicious. An aura of death hung constantly around it. Poor souls waiting out their last days in morbid, hopeless circumstances.

When people drove past, it would catch their eye. But only for a second. You wouldn't want to stare too long. All the same, the people of Vienna knew the Lainz General Hospital well. It regularly starred in their news bulletins and featured in the newspapers. But that did not stop it becoming a place to avoid.

Inside, however, it was full of typical, prim Austrian efficiency. The high-ceilinged rooms helped the light pour into every corner. It was clean but the paintwork had certainly seen better days. The walls and corridors had a slightly off white sheen with the occasional damp stain here and there, like a record of all the residents who had come and gone over the years.

The worst thing, though, was the silence.

Of course there were noises. Elevators opening and closing. Trolleys being pushed along the shiny, patent floors. But there was no hum of people. No friendly voices. No childish laughter.

It was like a barrier that hit everyone who entered that place. First they would be struck by the emptiness in the grounds, then they would be taken completely aback by the lack of voices inside. It was not as if there were no people around. There were nurses, auxiliaries, and porters everywhere. Scurrying up and down the corridors on endless errands. But no one stopped and smiled. No one uttered a word. And where were the patients? That eerie silence was the biggest reminder of all. Where were the patients?

A cold, bleak darkness fell on the Lainz General Hospital one day in February 1989. As the day shift staff moved off to their homes in the nearby suburbs they were replaced by the night workers. The men and women whose lives somehow adapted to those strange nocturnal habits. Many of them held together whole families despite the fact they were starting work when most people are thinking about bed.

By midnight at the Lainz, that daytime silence had been completely replaced by an even more sinister atmosphere. Now the sounds of the elevators, the trolleys, and the errands had long gone. But nothing had taken their place. Every now and again a cough or a splutter broke it. But the sound proof doors would smother it, like a hand over the mouth. No one but the chosen few could possibly know what was going on.

You could walk each and every corridor in the hospital and learn nothing about the patients. They might as well not have existed. And since 80% of the residents of the Lainz were over seventy years of age it was unclear if anyone really cared.

Most of the doctors had long gone. They tended to work a five-day week like any good office worker. Few of them ever appeared at weekends. Sickness could wait. If it was an emergency one of the housemen could cope – even though he (or she) may have only just medically qualified. It seemed ironic that the most dire cases ended up being dealt with by the least experienced doctors.

And that attitude was starting to drift through to the nurses. Fewer and fewer of them wanted to work those gruelling night shifts. They were happy to hand over control of the wards to the teams of lowly paid auxiliaries – the men and women who wanted to be nurses but failed to pass (or take) the necessary exams. It was not really the right way to run things, but the system prevailed at the Lainz and no one really seemed to care.

The silence grew.

Auxiliary nurse Waltraud Wagner was more than happy to take on the additional responsibilities. The fewer bossy nurses patrolling her ward at the hospital the better. The night shifts were bad enough but if you ended up with some Sgt Major breathing down your neck it would have been intolerable.

In fact, Waltraud rather enjoyed her job as a result. She had much more power and influence than she could reasonably have expected and she was allowed to just get on with her work on the ward – known as Pavilion 5.

Back home, husband Willi hardly inspired her. He demanded food and sex – in that order – most evenings BEFORE she left for work. But she really did not feel in the mood at that sort of time. Her favourite moments for passion came late at night or really early in the morning – but Willi was never around then.

Still, Waltraud understood her husband's frustrations. After all, she was his wife and they had once enjoyed a good sex life. It was just so difficult to explain to Willi. As far as he was concerned, the moment she put on that nursing uniform it was an invitation to lust. But it was nearly always at the wrong time. In any case, she couldn't go to work with a crumpled, messy uniform.

So, over time, as the grind of a night shift life became ingrained in her system, Waltraud found other ways of satisfying herself.

Julia Drapal had been quite a ballerina star in her day. During the 1950s she had performed at the Vienna Royal Ballet time and time again. Kings, Queens, Presidents – they had all seen her dance.

In Austria, she was as famous as Margot Fonteyn had been in Britain. Julia had been a very privileged person during that period. Chauffeur driven limousines would take her and her husband everywhere. They dined out at the most expensive restaurants. They travelled the world. It was a marvellous time. And it was those very memories that were now keeping Julia alive.

Her frail body had failed her once too often in the previous few years and now she had become a patient at the Lainz General Hospital. She hated it there. But there had been little choice in the matter. The doctors had told her husband she needed full-time medical care. He could no longer cope. She had to be looked after. But, like anyone who once received the adulation of millions, Julia was not an easy person to deal with. She had been used to people attending to her every whim. Now she was just another number on a clipboard at the end of her cast iron bed. Her hatred for the hospital and all it represented manifested itself in her attitude towards the staff. In short, she was a cantankerous woman. Given to bursts of insults and bad temper.

Sometimes she would push the nurses away when they tried to tend to her. On other occasions she would try to degrade them by referring to them as 'common people.'

Julia was not exactly the most popular patient on Pavilion 5.

'Time for mouthwash.'

No elderly patient had the energy to refuse when Waltraud Wagner issued orders. Some of the old men rather liked her dominant, strong-willed manner. With her large, round eyes, she certainly looked an attractive proposition to some of those patients. Her uniform always seemed to hug her body in just the right places and those black, regulation stockings – well …

But not many of those old men would ever consider actually getting fresh with Waltraud to her face. However, that didn't stop them fantasising about what she might do to them if ever she caught them.

And Waltraud knew full well that some of the men on Pavilion 5 had crude thoughts about her. She didn't mind. In fact, she found it quite flattering. But she did get annoyed when they occasionally tried to molest her.

There was the time the old gentleman in bed number twelve complained of having trouble passing water. When Waltraud arrived at his bedside, he insisted she hold his penis while he tried to urinate. For a few moments,

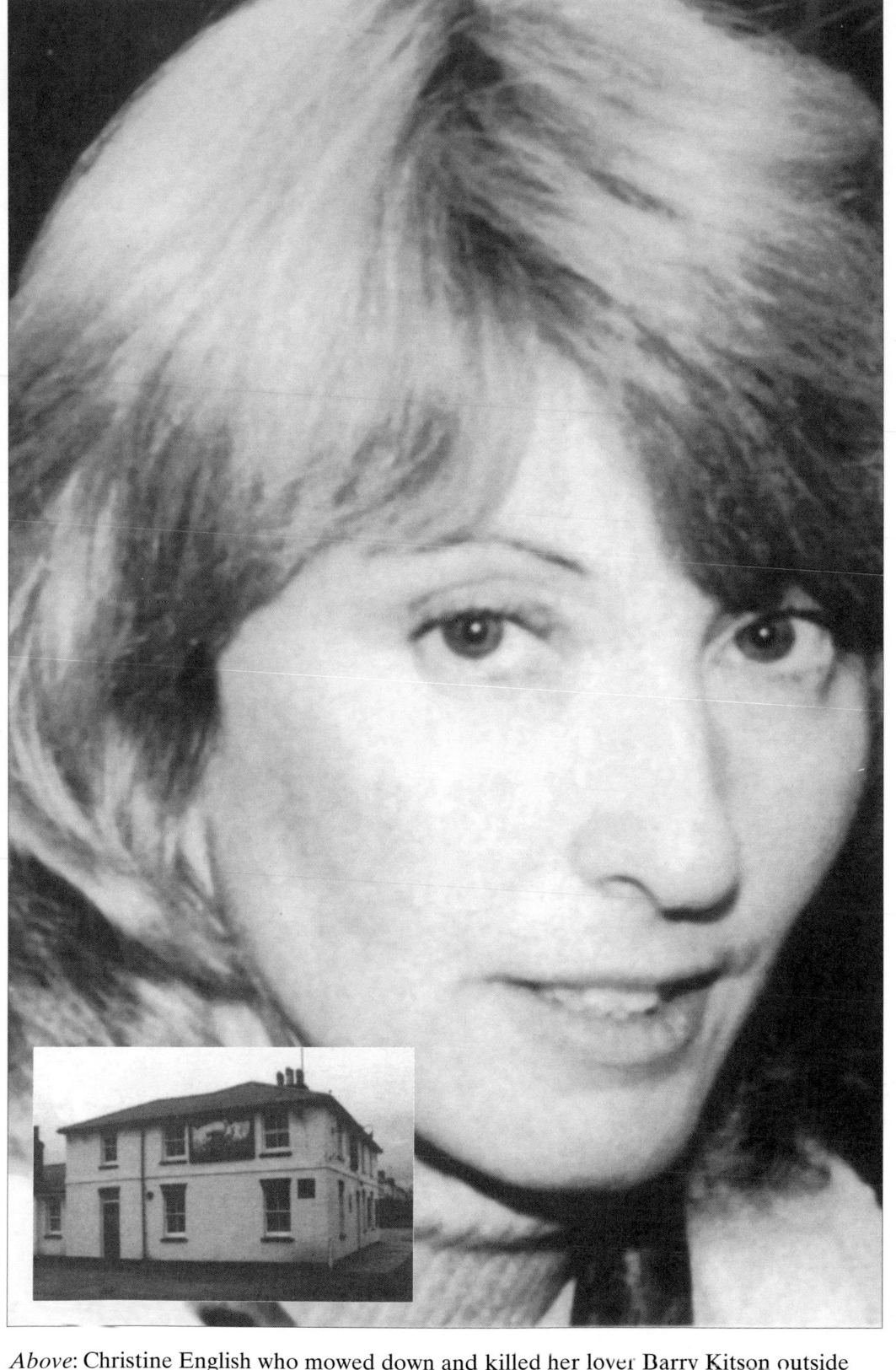

Above: Christine English who mowed down and killed her lover Barry Kitson outside the Live And Let Live pub in Colchester (*inset*).

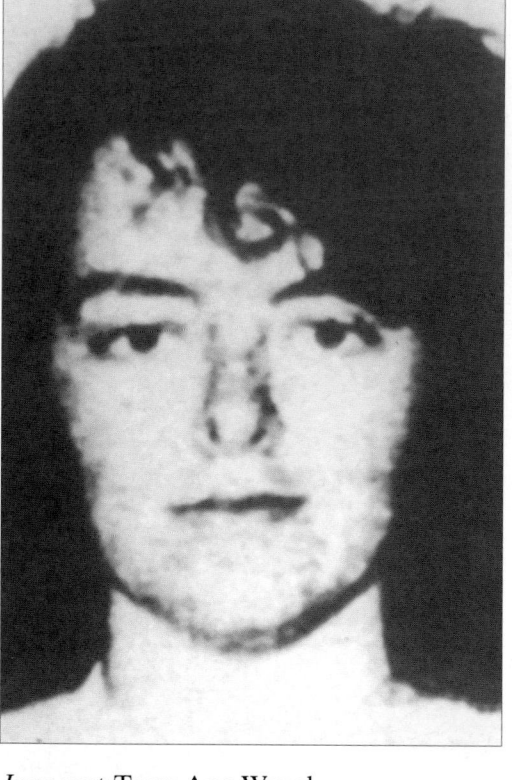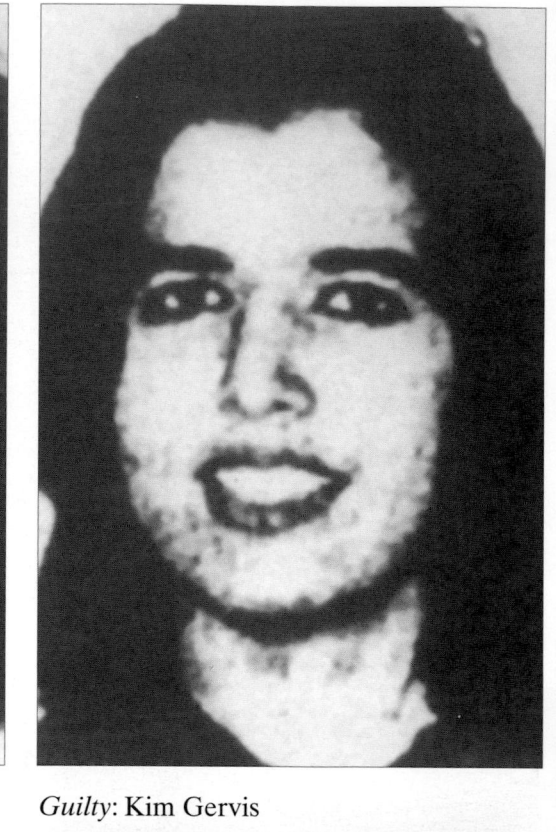

Innocent: Tracy Ann Waugh

Guilty: Kim Gervis

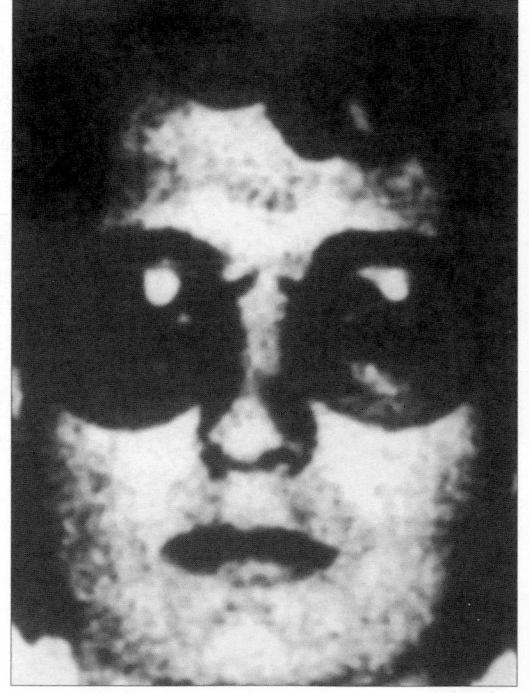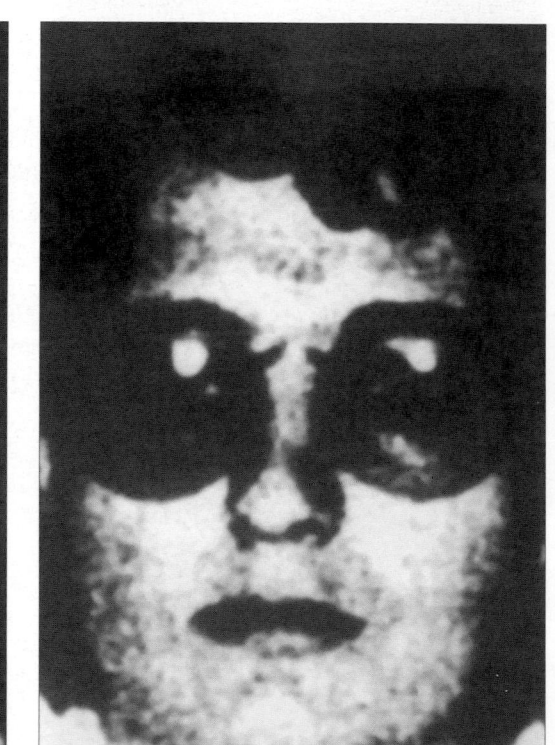

Guilty: Lisa Ptaschinski

Guilty: Tracy Wigginton

Above: The four accused women in the lesbian vampire trial.

Above: Lesbian vampire victim Edward Baldock.

Above: Teacher Pamela Smart used 16-year-old pupil William Flynn (*right*) to coldly kill her husband Gregory Smart.

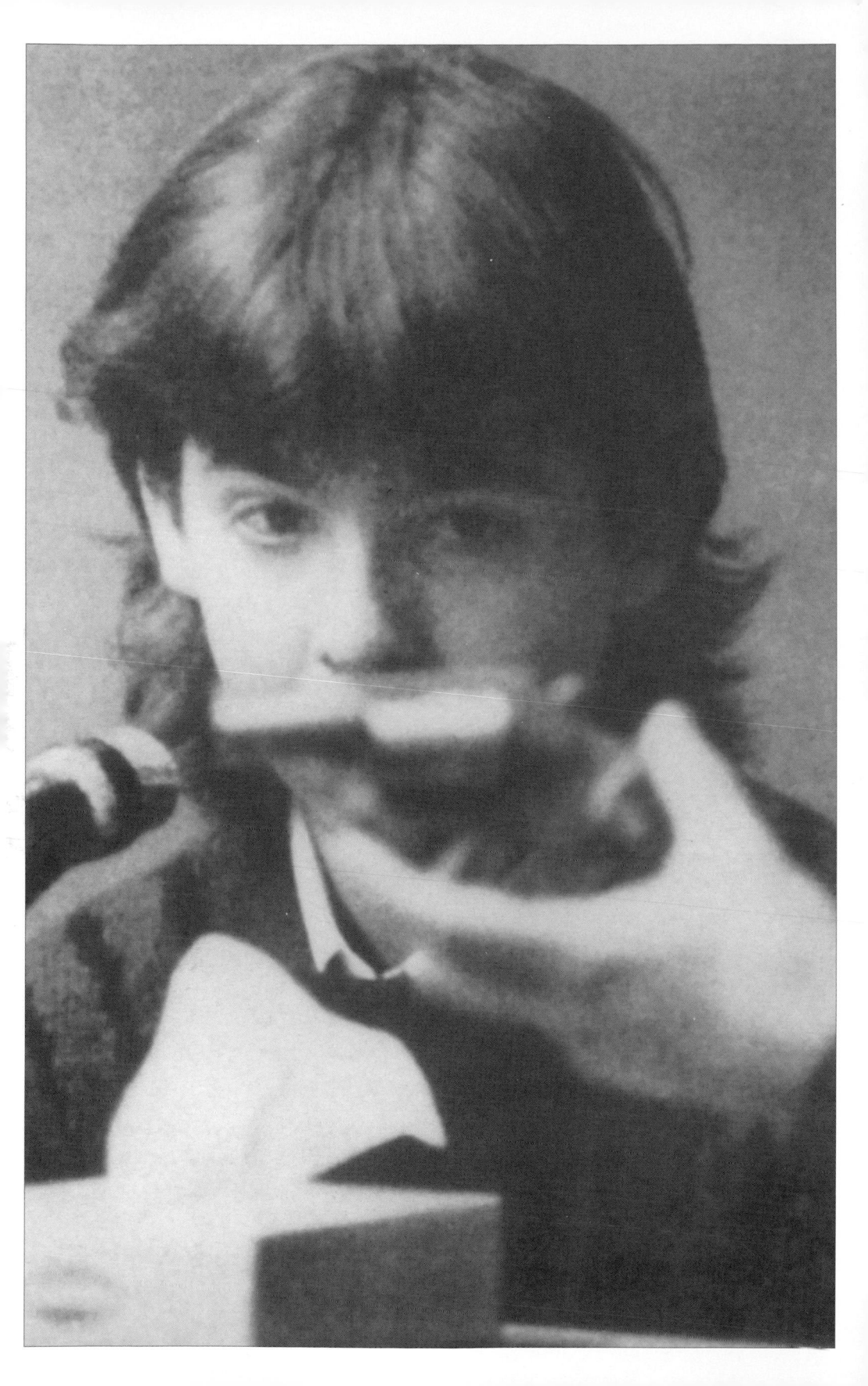

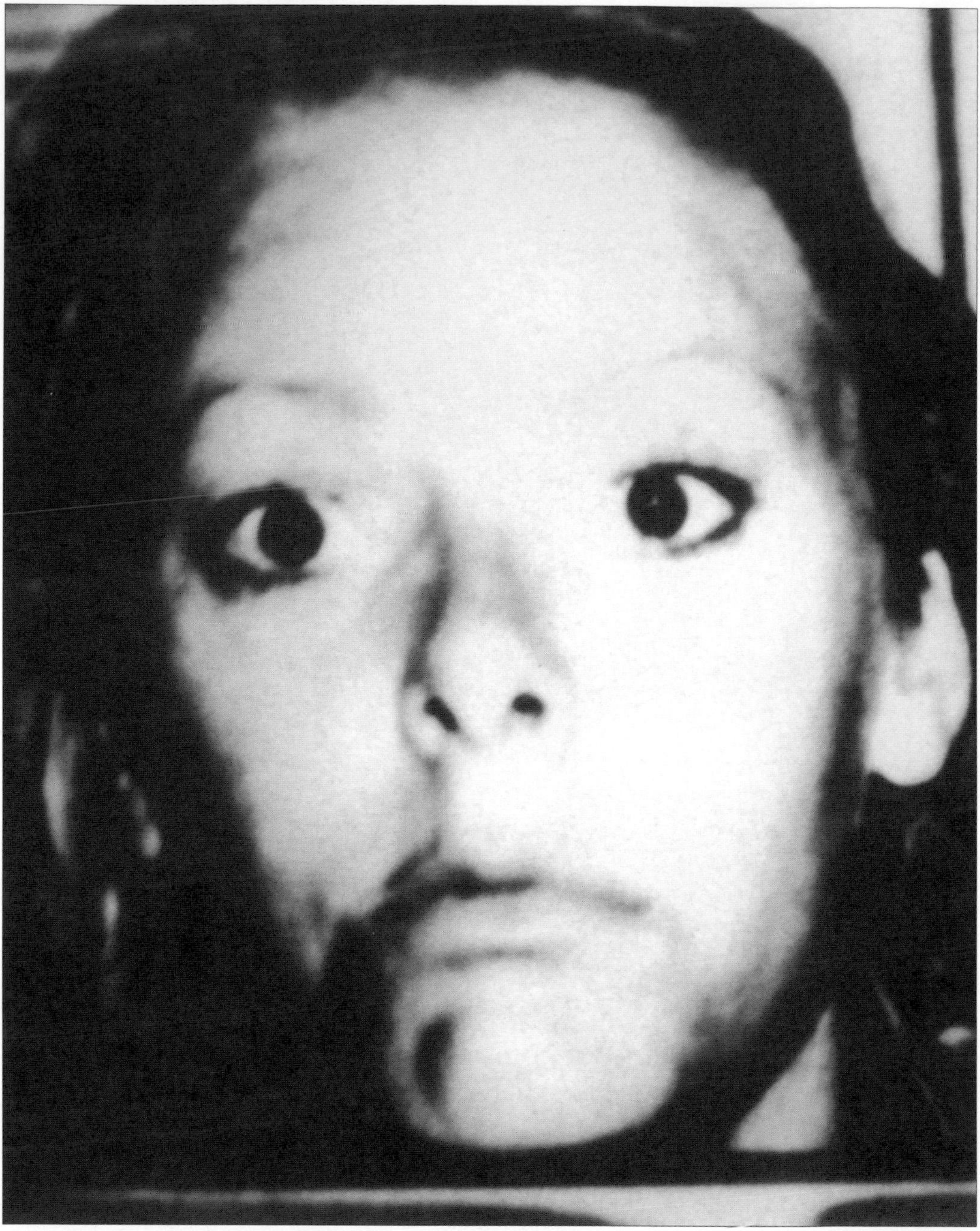

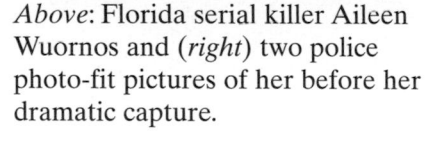

Above: Florida serial killer Aileen Wuornos and (*right*) two police photo-fit pictures of her before her dramatic capture.

Far right: Some of Wuornos' alleged victims.

Charles Carskaddon

Douglas Giddens

Troy Buress

Gino Antonio

Peter Siems

Charles Humphreys

David Spears

Richard Mallory

Above: Poison Pie Killer Susan Barber.

Waltraud obliged until she realised what that dirty old man was really up to. Some of the other auxiliaries used to gossip about seducing the patients.

'I'd marry one of those old sods if they promised to leave me all their money,' said one of Waltraud's colleagues.

She was appalled.

'Oh. I could never do it with an old guy. I don't mind what they are thinking about me but to let them touch me. Uggh. Now if they were under fifty that would be a different matter ...'

Waltraud had her own strange set of standards in life and they were just as inconsistent as everyone else's.

'Come on now Julia. It is mouthwash time.'

Time to get down to business. Julia Drapal was a bloody annoying patient. Only a few days earlier the old boot had called her a 'common slut' when she had tried to change her bedclothes.

She had decided then and there that Julia definitely needed a mouthwash but she needed a colleague to help her administrate the 'treatment'.

Irene Leidolf tended to work closely with Waltraud because they were two of the youngest auxiliaries on Pavilion 5. At twenty-seven, Irene was also a fairly attractive sight compared with many of the other thick set auxiliaries, most of whom were in their late forties and early fifties. She was much shyer than Waltraud though. She rarely joined in with the gossipy chats they frequently all enjoyed on the ward. But Waltraud liked her because she did as she was told. Irene never questioned any order.

'Come on Irene. Help me give her the mouthwash.' It was midnight in Pavilion 5, but quite a few of the elderly patients were awake. They watched as the two burly nurses approached Julia's bedside.

It was not a pleasant sight.

Those frail and withered people were about to witness what they lived in fear of receiving themselves – the dreaded mouthwash treatment. No one knew why it was administered. But they were well aware that it always brought things to an abrupt ending.

Waltraud put a heavily stained plastic glass filled with water to Julia's lips. They would not open.

'Come on Julia. It's mouthwash time. You know you must have your mouthwash. Now come on. Open up.' Julia was having none of it. She had watched enough beds empty in the previous few months to know that this was not a treatment she wished to receive.

'Right. Hold her down!' Waltraud barked at her younger colleague Irene.

'Come on. We must get this one done.'

She always referred to the patients as if they were more like cows in line for a branding than human beings. Waltraud pinched Julia's nose closed with her thumb and her index finger.

Suddenly a look of complete horror glazed across the old lady's face. Her gaunt cheeks and sagging neckline seemed to stiffen with anxiety. Her eyes were wide open now. Desperately searching for someone to intervene. She tried to move her arms up to ward off the nurse but Irene had both her wrists locked tight.

'Now. You will take the mouthwash won't you Julia.' There was absolutely no doubt in Waltraud's voice. She knew exactly what she was doing and that made it all the more terrifying for her victim.

As the water slithered down Julia's throat, she tried to cough it back up. For a split second she succeeded in arresting the flow. But the effort proved too much to sustain and her lungs surrendered to the cascade of water that was now pouring down her gullet.

Julia's eyes tried to catch Waltraud. They tried to appeal to her to stop. But Waltraud had deliberately blanked her expression. She was staring at the wall behind the bed. She did not want any emotion to impinge on the horrifying reality.

The only noise that could now be heard was the slight gurgle when Waltraud forced too much water too quickly down her patient's throat. She responded by slowing down slightly. It was imperative that the water filled those lungs to bursting point. It would not be long now. It would not be long.

Irene Leidolf stood there holding down this frail old lady without really giving any thought to what she was doing. She had a family to feed and she wasn't going to put her job on the line by refusing to help Waltraud. In any case, Julia's time had come. It was as simple as that. Her attitude was no different to the guards at Auschwitz. It came as second nature to follow orders. Why question them and upset the apple cart. Life had to go on ... for some.

Waltraud had by now emptied the entire contents of that glass of water down Julia's throat. She released her hold on her tiny, limp nose.

'There. That wasn't so bad was it?'

If Julia had had the energy to speak she would have cursed Waltraud to a thousand deaths. Instead, she knew her own demise was imminent.

As Waltraud walked back towards her desk she turned to Irene and said: 'There. That's another one who has got a free trip to God.'

Coughing and spluttering, Julia could feel the darkness setting in. The pain in her lungs was so great it was as if someone had forced an iron bar down their entire length. Her arms were no longer being held down by Irene, but they might as well have been. There was no strength left in them. Her head slumped to one side and she stared out along the ward to where Waltraud and Irene were sitting. They seemed to be sharing a private joke. Maybe they were talking about her? She realised with a jolt of finality, that she would never be able to find out.

The pain in her lungs was awful. A stabbing sensation had taken over now. Breathing seemed like a great labour, something unnatural to her body. She just wanted the agony to end.

As the last few minutes of her life ticked away, her thoughts of fighting and her sense of survival were all but fading. Julia had lost her last battle, and cursed her last nurse.

'It's one of the patients. I think she's dead.'

Some hours had passed since Waltraud had administered her mouthwash treatment. Now Waltraud was telling the duty doctor that his services were required.

'I'll be there in about 30 minutes. There's hardly any point in rushing.'

Pronouncing a patient dead was not exactly classified as an emergency in a hospital like the Lainz. In any case, water in the lungs was a common contributory cause of death amongst the elderly. The doctor would not even raise an eyebrow at the discovery of the liquid. Waltraud knew. She had done it so many times before.

Waltraud then casually drew the curtains around Julia's bedside. Ironically, it was that very action which told the other patients they had lost another resident. If those curtains had never been drawn, probably they would never have known. But now it was being advertised in vivid detail. Another desperately needed bed for another hopeless case. For most of the patients who entered Pavilion 5 had little or no chance of survival. Waltraud Wagner and her colleagues would see to that.

Waltraud was troubled by one aspect of this deadly scenario – why did she enjoy it so much? Each time she snuffed the life out of yet another Pavilion 5 patient it prompted a surge of satisfaction. A feeling that made her immensely proud. Maybe it was something to do with the power it gave her? Or perhaps she actually felt like a true angel of mercy – putting all those bleak, worn lives to rest for ever?

The afterglow would stay with her for hours after a killing. She would arrive home at her flat at six in the morning elated by the horrendous act she had just committed.

'How was work darling?' her husband would ask innocently through his sleepy haze.

'Oh. Fine', she would reply. Waltraud could hardly describe her working night as an auxiliary nurse as 'wonderful' to her husband, but that was precisely how she felt. A radiance would illuminate her soul.

It was at moments like that she would give her husband the sex he had craved for most the previous nights. Often, Waltraud would not bother taking her uniform off – she knew he liked it that way.

Unbuttoning the front of her tunic and exposing her breasts would be enough for him to know what she wanted.

'It's so easy. And they'll never know we did it.' Waltraud Wagner was enjoying a rare evening out at a local beer cellar with her co-conspirators Irene Leidolf, Maria Gruber and Stephanie Mayen.

The four women had decided they deserved a night on the town – after all they had managed to murder nearly fifty patients over the previous 5 years. The truth was they had stopped counting long ago. The numbers really began to increase after Waltraud devised her mouthwash treatment. That was so much easier than injecting huge amounts of insulin.

Stephanie was far older than the other three and seemed to fit the role of a ferocious, bulky auxiliary far better than her younger colleagues.

Yet, ironically, she was the more hesitant member of this self-professed chapter of the Angels of Death. Maria – a heavy set women in her early fifties – was appalled when she first realised what was happening. But then Waltraud started to convince her they were doing all these elderly, infirm patients a favour.

'In any case. Some of them are so bloody annoying they deserve it.'

Chilling words from the ringleader. But the other women were not about to argue with her. They were all in this together.

In that lively basement beer cellar that night, the four women were off duty for once. There would be no distant cries in the night. No incontinent old men. No senile dementia. For once, they were together outside work – and they were determined to have a good time.

When Irene and Waltraud caught the eye of two businessmen types in the far corner of the cellar, they returned their glances provocatively. These women were out to enjoy themselves after many months toiling in the killing fields of Lainz General Hospital.

The beer and wine flowed freely as did the talk that evening. As usual Waltraud was the one holding court. She craved for attention wherever she was. In the hospital she loved the fear she induced among the more timid patients. She relished in her display of power over them. She could decide whether they lived or died. It was an amazing feeling.

It was exactly the same in that bar cellar. She wanted to be the one in charge. She would love to look at all their attentive faces lapping up every word she uttered. She knew she had them under her spell.

She decided to put them all to a little test. A way to see just how loyal they really were.

'None of you ever say much about what we have done. Why not? Are you not proud of the fact we have put those awful sick, elderly people out of their misery?'

The other women said nothing. They did not know how to respond. Doing it was one thing. But facing the reality of their actions by talking about it openly outside work seemed too much to contemplate.

Still they were silent. For a moment that same eerie silence that haunted the corridors of the Lainz had returned. It was a significant silence though. For it showed how little these women had even questioned their own killing instincts. They had stifled the life out of all those countless patients – and yet they could not even contemplate talking about it. Waltraud was appalled.

'Come on. What do you really think about what we have done? Tell me.'

No response. They really did not know what to say. Here they were being confronted with the facts but they were afraid to speak – much more afraid than they were to kill.

'Let's talk about something else.'

At last, a reaction. Stephanie at least made her feelings clear. She may have helped murder a lot of innocent people but she certainly did not feel it made for good dinner table gossip.

'But we have killed all these people. You must feel something about it? Don't you love the power we have? The influence?'

It was time to change the subject. Waltraud had just discovered that her co-conspirators were nothing more than sheep. Nothing more than Nazi troops doing their duty. They had no feelings.

But someone nearby had heard every word of their conversation – and he was about to try and end their murderous reign of terror.

Dr Franz Pesendorfer was horrified by what he had just heard. Sitting near the group of auxiliary nurses had just revealed one of the biggest mass murders in post-war Europe. The doctor went straight to the police.

Waltraud was a little surprised by the recent changes at Pavilion 5. Some of the newest patients seemed to be rather young – in their sixties and even one in his fifties. This was supposed to be a geriatric ward after all.

She sensed something was not quite right but she just could not be sure what it was. Her basic instincts told her to be careful. She decided the killing had to stop for the time being. It was not as if they were making any money out of the slaughter of the innocent.

It was purely a way to relieve some patients of their agony and get rid of others who had annoyed them by being rude. That was cold blooded murder. No real motive other than the inbuilt sense of power that came with every killing. Anyway, Waltraud decided she should slow down – just in case. Just in case someone had told on her.

The 'younger' patient was indeed an unhappy resident at the Lainz. He hated every second of his stay in that smelly, rotten Pavilion 5 ward. All the nursing staff had quickly grown to dislike him about as much as he loathed them. By a strange twist of fate, if he had been a little older and Waltraud had not been on her guard, then he would definitely have been a candidate for the mouthwash treatment.

In fact, he was a very miserable undercover policeman, planted inside the ward after Dr Pesendorfer had tipped off the Vienna Detectives Bureau following the conversation he had overheard at the beer cellar.

At first the detectives had been scathing about the good doctor's fears. But the hospital administrator had friends in high places so they were forced to respond. 'Old people do tend to die.'

The detective who originally dealt with the case was just a bit cynical. He could not believe that a few women auxiliaries would cold bloodedly murder all these people.

'How can we prove it?'

There was only one way. They would have to be caught in the act.

But Waltraud was on her guard. She knew like all good criminals that something was not right on Pavilion 5 – and she would not risk another kill while the situation prevailed.

Meanwhile, the undercover policeman got more and more depressed. Sleeping in a ward surrounded by dozens of coughing, farting, snoring, groaning old people was not his idea of a plum assignment.

It was hardly surprising when the Vienna Detectives Bureau called off the case following six weeks without so much as a hint of a killing. The good Dr Pesendorfer was stunned that the police were pulling out.

'But you are just allowing them to carry on.'

The policeman was sympathetic to the doctor's plight but he reckoned there were some real criminals out there who needed catching.

Waltraud knew it. She had suspected there was something odd about him from the start. When the news swept around the hospital that an undercover policeman had been a patient on Pavilion 5, it came as no great surprise.

But now he was gone. His tail firmly between his legs. None the wiser for his awful stay in that depressing ward.

It was time to begin the killing again. She felt the urge. She had earmarked the most likely patients. The ones who had annoyed and insulted her. The pathetic ones who were ready to curl up and die. It was so easy really. The fully trained nurses were never around. They did not care what the auxiliaries did. It had got to the point where no one ever questioned the right of those under-trained assistants to administer drugs and hand out other treatment. That was why Waltraud and her friends had got away with it for so long.

As Waltraud pressed her thumb down on the syringe, she watched the huge dose of insulin rushing into a patient's sickly vein. The elderly women had asked for pain relief so why shouldn't Waltraud give her the ultimate cure – death?

She had grown a little bored of administering the mouthwash. In any case, if there were any spies left on the ward they would be more likely to notice two nurses holding down a patient than the giving of an injection. 'Nurse. Nurse. Has this patient been given any insulin in the past three hours?'

Waltraud looked the young doctor straight in the face.

'No doctor. Not a thing.'

She gave the medic one lingering glance up and down. He is quite a fine looking man, she thought to herself. The welfare of patients was never near the top of Waltraud's list of priorities.

She much preferred to let her mind wander in a world of sexual fantasy. It was so much less depressing. That same elderly women who had been given a huge dose of insulin just an hour before, was close to death – and Waltraud knew it only too well.

Now this rather handsome young doctor was asking awkward questions. How annoying of him, thought Waltraud Wagner. Why doesn't he just let her die? It would seem the sensible course of action.

In any case, in a few more minutes she would be dead – and no one would be any the wiser. Waltraud's mission of murder was on course once more. She had regained the taste for killing after a brief interruption. It was a good feeling. She would have to try to step up the rate. She found herself needing a fix more and more often.

The doctor, however, had other plans for Waltraud. He was very unhappy about that elderly woman's death. He suspected she had been administered an illicit dose of insulin.

Waltraud presumed he was just a fussy medic trying to cover his own inefficiencies.

'They know. They are on to us.'

Waltraud dismissed the alarm bells ringing in her colleagues' voices when they cornered her a few hours later.

'Don't worry. That doctor thinks he will be accused of not looking after his patient properly.'

Though the other women were not convinced, they had no choice but to accept what Waltraud told them. She held the key to their fate.

Meanwhile the good Dr Pesendorfer had got involved once more. He had never dropped his initial suspicions about the women. Now he was hoping that this new case might be just the breakthrough he had been hoping for.

'I know they have murdered a lot of patients. We cannot let this continue. We must stop them.'

They were the same words he had first uttered two months earlier after overhearing their beer cellar chat. But this time he felt certain they would be brought to justice. He hated the very notion of knowing that five women who had murdered tens if not hundreds of patients still had the free run of the hospital. It was a scandalous situation he was determined to end.

When the autopsy on the elderly woman revealed her body to be riddled with insulin the police were called back into the Lainz General Hospital and Waltraud Wagner and her three accomplices were arrested.

Wagner, Leidolf, Mayen and Gruber were jailed for their roles in the murder and attempted murder of forty-two patients at Lainz following their trial in Vienna in March, 1991.

Wagner collapsed in court as she was jailed for life. She had confessed to 10 killings, been found guilty of 15 cases of murder, 17 cases of attempted murder and 2 cases of inflicting bodily harm.

Leidolf was also given life for five cases of murder and two cases of attempted murder.

Mayen was jailed for 20 years for a case of manslaughter and seven cases of attempted murder. She too collapsed in the dock and had to be taken out on a stretcher.

Gruber was sentenced to 15 years for two cases of attempted murder.

Wagner had claimed during the trial that she was 'relieving the pain of patients.'

The Judge told her: 'These patients were gasping for breath for up to half a day before they died. You cannot call that pain relief.'

Wagner did not reply.

12

THE FIRST DAY OF THE REST OF MY LIFE

They looked every inch the happy couple.

She was blonde, slightly round-faced. With her long hair swept back off her forehead, maybe she more resembled a member of the swinging sixties than the 1990s, but there was a definite attractiveness about her. Despite being just twenty-nine she also had a certain homeliness that comes with being a young mother. It was a pleasant enough combination.

He was tall and dark with a neatly trimmed moustache. Well built. Even slightly cumbersome. He often looked less than his thirty-five years. And the only real clue to his profession were his hands. He had large, stubby fingers with incredibly short nails – a sure sign of his work as a labourer.

Paul and Pamela Sainsbury hardly warranted a second glance inside the crowded Carinas Nightclub, in the picturesque seaside town of Sidmouth, in Devon. As the soul music throbbed relentlessly from the huge speakers that hung on every wall, the scene resembled a cattle market. For it was the in place for anyone under forty. Groups of men and women would swarm into Carinas on a Saturday night looking for fun and excitement. Many of them were also looking for sex.

Gangs of young men would patrol the disco floor looking for suitable girls to ask for a dance, many of whom had their own secret code that would pronounce their availability. If they were looking to be picked up, they would stay huddled in little groups near the dance floor, sipping slowly on their rum and blackcurrants in the hope that some white knight would ask them for a dance and maybe even offer them a refill.

Other groups of women, intent on just enjoying each other's company, would go straight out onto the dance floor and put their handbags on the floor between them as they danced to the music. It was their special way of saying 'We are not available.' Sometimes they would dance for hours, perfectly happy not to attract the company of any males. Meanwhile, those predatory guys would be filling themselves up with lager – the staple diet of 90% of all men in that club on most nights.

All this meant that by about eleven p.m., there were always quite a lot of inebriated people in Carinas – and this particular evening was no exception.

Paul Sainsbury may have had his pretty wife Pam for company but that didn't stop him supping a lot of pints that night. It was his idea of a good night out. In any case, Carinas meant something really special to them – it was the place where they first met 8 years earlier. It held a lot of sweet memories for Paul. It reminded him how lucky he was to have Pam. How fortunate he was that she was the mother of his two children.

Yes, Paul really did appear to have a domestic set up that was the envy of many of his friends. And, as he sat with Pam and a few of their local pals at a table near the dance floor, he was no doubt able to reflect on that good fortune. For many of his male friends were still reduced to trying to pick up women in Carinas or any other club for that matter. It was something he did not need to concern himself about. He had Pam. He really loved Pam. She was his life and soul. She was the perfect reflection of his inner self. She understood his weaknesses and nurtured his strengths. They were good together.

Pam, meanwhile, was delighted to be at the nightclub. It was a rare excursion out of the house for her. These days she hardly ever seemed to get out. Maybe, she thought to herself that evening, maybe I should try it more often.

It was difficult to converse above the throbbing beat of the disco, so Pam and Paul found themselves looking around the club, inspecting the vast crowd – many of whom they knew. After all, Sidmouth is one of those sort of places. Most people know each other, even if it is only by sight. And a lot of the men and women gathered at Carinas that night had virtually grown up together. They had gone to the same schools. They had drunk at the same bars and they often went out with the same women (or men).

Pam was slightly different though. She had not grown up in the Victorian town that looked out over one of the prettiest coastlines in Britain. She had been just another holidaymaker when she had visited the town in the early 1980s. But the moment she set eyes on Paul she had known she wanted to be with him – and now Sidmouth was her only home.

But, not being a local had its compensations. It meant that people were more curious about Pam. She had a certain mystique about her and she spoke with a much posher accent than her rough and tumble West Country husband. Many of her neighbours had been really impressed when they heard Pam had been at an expensive private school. In fact she had even been a prefect. But Paul had put all that high-class nonsense firmly behind her. She was his wife now – and he didn't want to even think about the rich and exclusive world she came from.

He didn't like all that sort of talk one bit. Some of his friends reckoned it was because he had a chip on his shoulder about being 'common'. Paul just insisted all that 'rich folk talk' got on his nerves.

Like any reasonably attractive woman, Pam enjoyed flattery and attention. It was nice to be appreciated. Unfortunately, she rarely had an opportunity to meet that many new friends these days. That made her visit to Carinas all the more enjoyable. She was actually able to come into contact with other people.

She had specially washed and ironed her favourite white dress for that evening. It was not often she had the chance to wear it. As she sipped slowly on her own non-alcoholic drink, she was aware of occasional looks from some of the men who passed by their table. At first, she did not look up as she felt a touch embarrassed. But there seemed to be so many single men out there.

Across the table, Paul was studying the women in much the same way the men were examining his wife. Some of them looked really cracking, he thought to himself. If only I was single again. Paul especially liked the ones in their early twenties who tended to favour short, skintight skirts combined with dangerously high stiletto heeled shoes. A new one seemed to drift past his table every other second. Where did all this talent come from?

Ironically, it was only when the numbers of single, pretty girls started to disperse that Paul noticed a man standing nearby leaning against a pillar ever so casually. He seemed to be looking over this way. But then again perhaps he wasn't.

For a few moments, Paul ignored the man. But when he glanced back in his direction he was still there. What was he looking at? Paul turned to face his wife and momentarily caught sight of her eyes. They were definitely pointed in the direction of that man. What the hell was happening?

Pam had only given the man the briefest of glances after she had felt his gaze penetrating her. He was quite a good looking fellow but that was irrelevant. She wondered if perhaps he was a friend of Paul's. It was only natural that she should respond for a split second. But it was at that precise moment, Paul caught her looking at the other man.

'Why are you looking at that man? Do you know him?'

Paul sounded agitated.

Pam was taken aback. She was lost for words. 'You know him don't you?' he said

Paul was convincing himself there was a reason behind his wife's glance at that man.

'Don't be silly. I thought he was a friend of yours.' Paul took another huge gulp of his lager and then got up. Pam was puzzled. No. Surely he wouldn't. But he did. At that moment, he swayed, slightly drunkenly over towards the man.

'Hey. Why are you looking at my wife? Take your bloody eyes off her.'

Pam was now deeply embarrassed. She could not believe Paul would do such a thing. The other man said nothing and tried to walk away. But Paul was having none of it. Pam had seen this happen so many times before. Why couldn't her husband control his obsessive jealousy?

'Come on you. Out with it. How well do you know her?'

Pam and Paul's friends were now fidgeting nervously. They'd seen it all before. But no one got up to do something about his behaviour. Everybody at that table knew how violent Paul could be. None of them wanted to take him on. But, ultimately, it was Pam who would have to take some sort of action – and she would pay dearly for it later.

'Don't be so daft Paul. I've never seen him before in my life.'

'Liar. Fucking liar. I bet you've shagged him proper!'

'That's enough Paul. Come on. Home. This is ridiculous.'

'I told you woman. Don't use those long words on me. Don't try and make me feel common.'

As the stranger disappeared into the crowded dance floor, Paul struggled to free himself of his wife's grasp. He hadn't finished his entertainment for that night by any means.

'You fucking slut. How dare you ...'

The crunching sound of his fist sinking into her cheek was horrendous. Pam felt her teeth wobble as he connected with her face.

She crumpled to the floor, desperately holding her chin in place with her left hand. Too stunned to move. Too frightened to breath. Too terrified to utter a word. Then she heard it coming. A whoosh of air as his right hobnailed boot smashed straight into her shin as she lay there still trying to recover from his first flurry of punches. The crack was so loud it might well have broken the bone.

'Get your fucking clothes off you whore. You're just like a dog.'

That word 'dog' filled Pam with more pain and fear than the physical assault that had just occurred. It meant only one thing. He was going to degrade her like he had done so often before. She really did not know if she could take it again.

'Come on. Get those fucking clothes off now' Pam's favourite white dress that she had so lovingly washed and pressed just a few hours earlier was now ripped down the front exposing one of her breasts – brutally uncovered by her monster husband.

He walked over to the wardrobe next to their bed. It could mean only one thing. She felt the dread of expectation sinking through her mind and body. She knew the worst was still to come.

She had no choice. She was a prisoner in that bedroom yet again. She would have to do as he ordered. She had no option.

'I want everything off. Everything.'

Pam felt like a scared fox being pursued by one large, brutal hound. She scrambled along the floor and into the corner of the room and tried to sit up against the wall. But the pain was so severe, she could hardly move the leg he had so callously kicked just moments earlier. There was no escape.

Pam had already started to give up. She was going to surrender once again. She started to remove her dress. In the end it was easier to rip it off. It took less time – that meant he would get it all over more quickly.

But getting her panties off was more difficult. Every time she tried to half get up to pull them off, she felt overcome by dizziness. But Paul Sainsbury was in no mood to be patient. His animalistic urges were taking full priority. He looked down at the pathetic creature who was his wife and grabbed one of her ankles before yanking the panties off. She could smell the awful stench of stale lager wafting from his lips. His eyes looked almost dead with alcohol as he staggered back to the wardrobe and pulled out various items.

'Come on dog. Come on. Behave like a dog. Be treated like one. You love it don't you? Don't you?' Pam knew her husband was expecting her to reply. But her jaw and cheekbone were still vibrating from the throbbing pain inflicted by his punches minutes before.

'Come on. Say it. You dog.'

Pam looked up pathetically towards her towering brute of a husband.

'Woof. Woof.'

She could hardly spit the words out the hurt was so bad. But Paul was satisfied … for the moment at least. He had lots more plans in store for his wife.

'Don't get up dog. I am going to take you for walkies.'

WENSLEY CLARKSON

Paul then produced from behind his back a collar and lead. Pam had seen it all before. She knew what to expect as he leant down and fixed the studded choker around her neck.

'You're a bitch and I am going to teach you a lesson. Dogs need training.'

Pam's brain was so scrambled by the onslaught that she had all but given up. That was the way he liked it. She just accepted her punishment – and provided him with the pleasure he so sickly craved.

Now she was on all fours being led around the bedroom by the lead. Every time she slowed down, he pulled viciously at the choker. She could feel her throat being pulled in. It was a bit like the sensation of drowning. She would snatch a few breaths and then he would yank viciously at the collar causing her neck to wrench.

Her husband had also now stripped naked. But he had only just begun. He was about to force his wife to perform some of the most degrading sex acts imaginable but first he wanted to make absolutely sure she really did feel like a dog.

'Come on eat. Eat I said.'

Paul Sainsbury put the dog bowl down on the floor by his wife's head. She did not know what was in the bowl. But just the smell of it made her feel nauseous. It could have been anything but it looked awful. Brown, splodgy pieces of something that filled the entire beige coloured bowl.

'Eat. I said Eat.'

Pam crooked her neck downwards towards the bowl. She had no choice. If she did not eat it, he would beat her until she did. She may as well get it all over and done with as quickly as possible. This was a regularly recurring nightmare in the sad life of Pamela Sainsbury.

As her tongue probed the dark mess just in front of her tear swollen eyes, she shut her mind out and began to eat.

Two hours had passed since that first punch. Now, at last, he had collapsed on the bed in a drunken stupor. She had endured pain and penetration in virtually every orifice in her body. The spirit had been drained out of her but the frustration she was feeling was building up.

Pam struggled to get up off the floor. She fell back down at first. The dizziness brought on by her beating was so severe she could hardly balance herself. His cruelty towards her had known no bounds. She felt as if she had been raped, tortured and sodomised by a brutal attacker – not her own husband.

But through that haze of horror she felt a deep anger from within. Never again. Never again. Never again.

As she pulled at the leather studded choker that was still tightly wrapped around her neck, she felt a surge of disgust, fury and contempt for that animal lying there just a few feet away.

Throwing the collar and lead across the bedroom, she put on her dressing gown and sat for a few moments at the end of their double bed. This had happened over and over again. How could she just let him carry on? How many more times would she allow him to turn sex from an act of love into an act of aggression? Pamela Sainsbury had finally snapped. She was going to do something about it.

She washed her face and tried to straighten out her bedraggled appearance. Now was the time. She went to the tool cupboard at the bottom of the stairs of their modest three-bedroomed council house. She found Paul's work tool bag. In it was a long length of plumb line.

Back in the bedroom, Pam stopped and looked at the snoring hulk of a man who lay in their bed. He seemed so peaceful lying there. She had to make herself remember the disgusting degradation he had just put her through. This was the time to act. After 8 years of abuse it had to be stopped.

Pam tied one end of the plumb line onto the headboard of their bed. Then she carefully and gently wrapped the rope fully around her husband's neck. He still couldn't feel a thing. The line was not tight – yet. He stirred at that moment. She thought perhaps she had disturbed him but it was only the restless sleep of a man pickled in alcohol.

Pam tightly wrapped both her small hands around the rope as if she were about to pull in a tug of war. She stood by the side of the bed with the rope coming towards her from her husband's neck. She took one last glance at his face. He was the man she had given up her entire life to be with. The man she had produced a family with. The man who actually probably really did love her in his own twisted, perverted way.

For a moment, she wondered if this really was the right thing to do. Perhaps he would change? Maybe there was a chance they could start all over again?

Pam knew there and then that would never happen. She had been through all this before. He had made promises and broken them all immediately. He wanted to love her to death. Now she had to kill him to avoid her own demise. There was no choice. With one huge heave, she pulled frantically at the rope. She could feel the strain on the headboard. It creaked as she tightened her grip. She also felt the rope burning into her palms as she pulled with all her strength.

Then he woke up. The very thing she most dreaded. He had shaken out of his drunken slumber as the rope dug deeply into his windpipe. She saw his eyes upon her. They were appealing, terrified eyes. The exact same look she had given him so often during the course of her beatings and abuse. Now he was suffering. He was experiencing the terror and the fear.

The moment his eyes opened she pulled even harder on the rope. It was as if his sheer agony was inciting her to accelerate the process of death. She could not stop herself now.

The colour was draining out of his face rapidly. She could see the pupils of his eyes begin to dilate. His fingers had long since given up trying to grasp the rope away from his neck. His hands and arms had flopped down by the side of the bed. Pam somehow seemed to have found even more inner strength. The power she was generating was increasing. Nothing would allow her to let go of that rope until her job was complete.

The burning sensation caused by the rope digging into her hands had been replaced by deep set cuts in her skin. But she did not flinch. The pupils of his eyes had now completely dilated. There was just a flickering of white, nothing else. The eyelids were wide open though. It was as if they had been jammed open by some exterior force. Pam was glad his eyes were still open. It meant he had seen everything until the bitter end. That was important. That suffering had to continue for as long as possible. With one last surge of energy, Pam gave one final tug. But it was clear her husband was already well and truly dead. She relaxed her grip. Then his body seemed to convulse. Perhaps he was still alive? Maybe she had not completed the death sentence?

It seemed like an electric shock was running through his body for a split second. Pam was startled. She tried to regain her grip on that rope again. But by the time she had pulled it tight once more, her husband's body was still and limp. There was no life left inside him.

Now she had to remove him from the bed. He had bludgeoned her body and mind for the last time. She had to be practical for a moment. She did not want her children, Lindsay and Terry to find their father like this.

Then Pam looked over at that wardrobe. It had become like an evil dungeon where he kept the whips, the collars, the leads and the other awful, perverted equipment that he had forced her to wear over the previous 8 years.

Yes. He belonged in the wardrobe. There amongst the sick strands of leather and studs. Pam would make sure he was very comfortable there.

She untied the rope from the bed head and then noticed how deeply cut her hands had become. She went to wash down her hands before preparing to haul that dead piece of meat across the bedroom floor.

By the time she managed to push his body into that wardrobe, it was almost three a.m. But it could have been any time of the day or night to Pam. She was caught up in the web of a fantasy that had become a reality. Had she really just killed her husband? Did she actually strangle the life out of him? Then, as if looking for some kind of reassurance, she glanced at the calendar by the side of their double bed – the bed where it had all just happened. And she wrote, words that soothed her tortured self, justified her actions, made sense of what had happened:

THIS IS THE FIRST DAY
OF THE REST OF MY LIFE.

It was September 1, 1990 and Pamela Sainsbury's life had in fact begun all over again.

'He beat me up last night. Almost broke my leg. I told him to get out otherwise I'd call the police.'

Pam was very convincing as she told one of her husband's relatives why he was not at home.

'I think he's gone up north. I don't care anyway. I never want to see him ever again.' Only she realised that fact had already been guaranteed. None of the Sainsbury family or friends seemed that surprised. Some of them had witnessed his awful fit of jealousy at Carinas Nightclub a few days earlier. Paul was a brutal sort. Good riddance.

But while Paul Sainsbury had definitely gone for ever, he still presented something of a problem for his wife. Where could she put his body?

It was four days since his death and his lifeless remains were still stuffed in amongst his sex manuals and bondage equipment.

Pam decided that she had to do something. And once again, she was on her own. She could not afford to risk telling anyone.

Pam made one last check to see if the children were fast asleep. She crept into their bedroom and looked at their angelic faces for a few moments. It reassured her that all the horrors she had suffered had been worthwhile. Just to see them soundly sleeping was enough to convince her she had done the right thing. They were her flesh and blood and she wanted them to have the happiest lives possible. She would make sure of that.

Now that the house was quiet, she had to sort out the problem of Paul. She had to dispose of that body. But how? He was simply too heavy to carry out of the house in one piece. Pam removed a foot long tenon saw and a razor sharp carving knife from the kitchen and took them upstairs. She braced herself as she went to open the wardrobe — that evil mini-dungeon of horrors had got its just dessert now. The Master. The animal who inflicted such pain and anguish on Pam was now rotting amongst his own perverted possessions.

His stiff corpse fell out into the bedroom as she unlocked the double doors. The stench of death wafted out that instant. His naked body had turned a bluey-grey colour.

Pam held her breath for a moment. Some of the contents of his seized up bowels were still in that wardrobe. It was a grisly sight for anyone to suffer. But Pam quickly recovered her composure. She had a job of work to do. She was not going to let him beat her — even in death. She would never again allow him the satisfaction of appalling her. She wanted to get away with the killing. She wanted to free herself from his evil spell. He was not going to force her into submission now — or ever again.

Pam rolled the heavy corpse of her husband over onto some plastic sheeting she had laid out on the floor of the bedroom. It was time to begin.

At first, it seemed really difficult to saw the arm at the shoulder blade. The instrument just did not want to embed itself in the skin. Then Pam pressed down hard so that the razor sharp instrument sliced a niche in the soft bluey flesh. At last she could really get going.

Once she had conquered a certain technique with regard to the sawing, it was all relatively easy. Within a minute or two, the arm had been almost separated from the rest of the body. Pam gave it a slight tug and heard the final strands of flesh tearing as she pulled it off and laid it in a black dustbin liner. The only thing that surprised her was the weight. It was heavy. There was no way one could gingerly remove it. It definitely required a certain amount of strength and that made the whole process feel ever more real and graphic. Pam had envisaged it being much easier.

After depositing both arms in the plastic bag alongside the body, she moved down the corpse to begin work on the legs. They were even harder. Initially, she tried to cut them from where the thighs meet the stomach but that proved impossible. With a heave, she rolled the body over and began slicing through the hip bone.

More than an hour later, Pam had completed removing the arms and legs from the torso. But there was still the matter of the head. She looked down at the cold, lifeless form on her bedroom floor and wondered if it really was Paul. Maybe he would come walking through that door at any moment? She sat crouched there on the plastic sheeting alongside what remained of her husband in a sort of trance.

How can I be sure? How can I be certain he really is dead if I dispose of the body?

These questions were really troubling Pam. So long as his body had been rotting in that wardrobe she felt reassured that he was definitely dead. But now she was about to get rid of the body for ever. There would be nothing left of Paul – nothing to show her he really was dead.

She lent down and started to saw through his neck. By the time she had separated the head from the torso she had decided: she was going to keep his head. She wanted to always be absolutely sure he was actually dead.

It was way past midnight by the time Pam had hauled the two huge dustbin bags down to the back door. She hoped no one would see her when she began digging a hole near the vegetable patch at the end of the garden.

She took a shovel out of the garden shed and found what looked like a suitable spot and began digging. Well, she tried to dig. But the ground was as hard as a rock. There had been little rain for weeks and the earth was solid. No matter how much she crashed that shovel into the ground, only a few small clumps of earth moved.

She tried another part of the garden but it was much the same story. There was no way she could dig holes deep enough to bury those bags. Now she was getting worried that the neighbours in Le Locle Close might see her out in the garden late at night and begin to wonder. No one had stirred yet. But if she made much more noise they were certain to get disturbed and then they would see what she was up to.

Pam returned to the kitchen, distraught. The remains of her husband in those two plastic bags were just sitting there by the back door. *You can't get rid of me,* they said in Paul's mocking voice, *I've beaten you.*

What could she do? He was not going to win. He just couldn't! She would think of another way of disposal. Pam walked back down to the bottom of the garden and pushed her husband's wheelbarrow towards the back door. She struggled to load one bag at a time onto the wheelbarrow. The tension and turmoil of the previous few days was catching up with her. But any weakness was overcome when she thought about the driving force behind her actions. The quest to start a new life. That was enough to keep her going.

Pam was about to take an enormous risk but she had to get rid of the body. She weaved her way down the path to the back wall and ground to a halt. Then she summoned all her strength to heave the bag over the wall and into the bushes that backed onto their house. It was thick bracken and a hedge that belonged to a field that never seemed to be used for anything in particular.

Pam repeated the operation with the next body bag. She had got rid of the body the best way she could. She had got it off the premises – that was the most important thing.

Back in the kitchen, there was one bag remaining. It was smaller than the others. Round. Shaped like a large football. That would stay at home, with pride of place in her cupboard, a perpetual reminder that he would not, could not, return.

The music was throbbing away as usual in Carinas Nightclub. But there was one big difference for Pamela Sainsbury. She was not living in fear of a severe beating the moment she got home.

For this was her first visit without her husband to the nightspot that marked the beginning and the end of her 8 years of horror at the hands of a monster. As she relaxed near the busy bar with a girlfriend, she reflected on how – just a few weeks earlier – her life had all been so different.

She had stuck rigidly to that promise she made to herself the night Paul died. Every day she would look at the words written on her calendar: THIS IS THE FIRST DAY OF THE REST OF MY LIFE.

Now she was living the rest of that life and it was proving far more enjoyable than she would ever have believed. She could even afford to laugh and smile at men who caught her eye across the dance floor without facing that inevitable degradation. Soon she would feel confident enough to start going out with men again. Enjoying the company of, hopefully, gentler males than the sicko she had married.

But to start with she would keep them all at a bit of distance. It was going to take time to adjust back into the real world. For not only had she faced brutality beyond belief at the hands of Paul, but he had also forced her to spend most of her time trapped in that tiny house in much the same way the hostages were kept locked up in faceless parts of Beruit. She needed to adjust to normal, decent, hard-working people. But her girl friends were proving a real mainstay.

They felt sorry for Pam. Abandoned by her bullying husband, she had been left to bring up the kids alone. She deserved to get out and have some fun occasionally.

By the time Pam and her friends left Carinas, they felt she was well on the road to recovery. But there was something nagging at her. A feeling that perhaps, just perhaps *he* was still around. Still watching over her. Still waiting for her to get home so he could batter her once again. Everywhere she looked there were reminders of him. This was his home town after all. It was an awful feeling. Just the slightest chance that he might not be dead. It sent a shiver of fear through her body.

There was only one solution. The moment Pam got home that evening she rushed through the hallway and pulled open the door to the tiny meter cupboard under the stairs.

It was OK. There was the shape of his head pressing through the plastic bags she had tightly wrapped around it. She knew then that he was definitely dead. She had to keep his head as a constant reminder of her freedom. She stood there in the darkened hall for a few seconds and just stared straight at the grisly stump. She knew that no one must know what bizarre lengths she had gone to. But just so long as she knew, then it would be all right.

As the months passed by, Pamela gradually rediscovered her life once more. She learnt to enjoy herself. She started to date other men. She became a happier, more content person. And every time she felt any doubts or guilt about what she had done, she would return to that meter cupboard and make sure he was still there. The only really distressing aspect that still remained was the seclusion she felt whenever she faced his head there under the stairs. It was the only time she felt all alone in the world. She so desperately wanted to tell someone what had happened. Suppressing the truth was not easy. There had been many times over the previous months when she had sat down in the kitchen of that same house — just a few feet from where Paul's lifeless face stood in the darkness — with a girlfriend and wondered to herself if she should talk about what happened on that awful night. Each time, she would hold herself back at the last moment, suddenly aware that it would be crazy to expect anyone not to tell the authorities.

But by the summer of 1991, Pam was reaching breaking point. She had to tell someone. She could not bottle it up any longer. She had managed to convince herself that by admitting it all to a friend it would then wipe out any of the remaining guilt once and for all. They say confession wipes the slate clean. Pam believed that her new life was perfect in all but one respect. It was time to tell.

'I am so relieved I've told you. It's so good to tell someone.'

Pam's girlfriend did not know how to respond. She was shocked and horrified by what she had just been told. Unfortunately for Pam, she had chosen the wrong friend to confide in.

'We'd like to talk to you about your missing husband.' The uniformed policeman standing on the front door of Pam's house seemed gentle enough in his approach. But she knew why he was there.

'Just give me a few minutes. I need to organise a babysitter for the kids.'

The officer was happy to wait while Pam went back inside the house. It gave Pam a chance to seek reassurance just one more time. She opened that meter cupboard door for the last time and looked in at him. It was enough. She knew for sure he was dead. He would never return. Now she felt a sense of relief that the police had come. It was perhaps the missing piece of the jigsaw. The one aspect that weighed on her mind. She had to confess to guarantee he never came back. Now the police were there she knew for certain he had gone. Calmly, she lifted the head of her dead husband and dropped it into her rubbish bin for the dustmen to take the next morning ...

On Friday, December 14, 1991, Pamela Sainsbury was placed on 2 years probation after admitting the manslaughter of her husband Paul. She also pleaded guilty to a second charge of obstructing the coroner in his duty by concealing the body.

Plymouth Crown Court judge Mr Justice Auld told her: 'For many years you suffered regular and increasing violence and other forms of extreme sadism and sexual degradation at his hands. There is no right sentence in a case such as this. On one hand it is my duty to mark the serious crime of manslaughter which you have committed. However, I am prepared in the exceptional circumstances of this case to make a probation order for two years.'

The head of Paul Sainsbury was never recovered by police.

13

BAMBI

Even in her jogging pants Lawrencia Bembenek looked stunning. Everything about her was just right. Her face was beautifully structured. Her flowing chestnut-brown hair styled perfectly. Her breasts firm and ample but not too large. Her bottom curved, yet delicate. The perfect all-American twenty-two-year-old dream.

But it was her eyes, her eyes that really clinched it. Huge dark brown seas of sensuality. Always wide open. Always happy. Always looking straight at you. Like the eyes of tentative deer. They had it all and they landed Lawrencia with a nickname that was going to stick for the rest of her life – Bambi. Somehow it summed her up. She had an endearing air of innocence about her, a vulnerability that was incredibly attractive. But there was also an animal cunning – a natural instinct to survive.

She certainly had an extraordinary effect on policeman Fred Schultz. He had met Bambi just a few days earlier at a bar in their home town of Milwaukee. They had struck up a brief and pleasant enough conversation – but no more. Bambi was no easy pick-up for recently divorced older men like Schultz. She did not mind talking to him but that was as far as it would go.

'How about coming jogging with me tomorrow?' Bambi was taken aback. She had been expecting all the usual lines about coming back to my place but this guy was asking her for a jog. That shy, somewhat icy veneer had been knocked off balance. This was not what she expected. Maybe this guy was genuine?

'Sure. Why not? What time do you want to meet?' Bambi could not believe herself. What was she doing agreeing to go for a jog with a man she did not even know? But there was something about him. He seemed honest. He seemed to really care. In any case, he could hardly attack her while they were jogging.

So they agreed to a date – If that is the way to describe running on the streets of Milwaukee. It was hardly a romantic setting for two would be lovers, but it seemed appropriate at the time.

The actual jogging part of that first meeting was not exactly informative. As they huffed and puffed their way around a vast park on the edge of the city, there was little energy left for actual conversation. That would come later. For now they were testing each other's physical limitations without even touching. And Bambi was proving the fitter of the two.

She soon found herself racing yards ahead of the thirty-two-year-old detective. But he did not care one tiny bit. Being beaten by a woman did not bother Fred Schultz. He was enjoying a completely different aspect of their race through the park. He loved watching her slim and shapely body movements ahead of him. Her buttocks seemed so firm through the skintight material of her figure-hugging sweat pants.

Fred reckoned he could pant behind that body for the rest of his life. And maybe beyond.

When they finally came to a halt, he could not take his eyes off her hot, glistening face. Watching the beads of sweat gently roll down her forehead, past those gorgeous eyes onto the perfectly formed cheeks then cascading onto those moist lips before her tongue darted out and licked them away.

Fred Schultz was smitten. He did not even know her full name yet. But this had to be the woman for him. She just had to be.

Then it happened. That spark of coincidence that marks the start of any successful relationship. As Bambi and Fred sat down in a cafe to chat she asked him that classic question.

'What do you do Fred?'

'Oh. I'm a cop. What's your line?'

Bambi stopped in her tracks. For a moment Fred thought it was that old familiar sign of a woman who doesn't like cops. Maybe her father's in jail? Perhaps she's had a run in with the police? It happened so often he just took it for granted. He had hoped and prayed this woman might be different but now it seemed that he was facing the usual anti-police sentiments.

But just the opposite was true.

She sipped her coffee, licked the froth away with her tongue and smiled. 'I used to be a cop too.'

And with those words, Bambi instantly sealed the fate of a relationship that would lead to marriage and so much more besides.

The wedding was a simple affair. They had little money but it cost nothing to choose the most romantic date of the year for the ceremony – Valentine's Day, 1981.

Fred had been married before. With an ex-wife Christine and two sons to support, he did not have a lot of spare change at the end of each month. The $363.50 mortgage plus $330 in child support soaked up almost half his detective's take-home salary. It was tough. And Bambi wasn't in the big earnings league either. Working as an aerobics instructor by day and a Playboy Bunny by night, she was struggling to pay off mounting debts.

But they had each other – and that was what mattered most.

Bambi regularly blew her lid about the money Fred was shelling out to Christine and the kids. Here she was marrying an older, successful man but they could hardly afford the rent on a modest one-bedroomed apartment while Christine lived a few blocks away in a lovely detached house. It just did not seem right. But Fred had obligations to keep – and he was a man of his word.

Still, it continued to really grate at Bambi. She could not get it out of her head. Even as they hosted a special gathering of close friends at a dinner party on the evening of the wedding, her mind kept wandering back to it.

'You know. It would pay to have Christine blown away.'

Judy Zess stopped chewing the piece of a chicken in her mouth for a moment. She could not believe what she just heard her old friend and former room-mate Bambi say.

This was the eve of her wedding and she was threatening to 'blow away' her new husband's first wife. What on earth did she mean? It was hardly a healthy start to the marriage. Judy Zess never forgot those few, sinister words. They would one day have a prophetic significance.

Fred Schultz, however, was deliriously happy. He had found himself a beautiful bride to restart his life with. After years of marital grief with Christine, he truly believed he had found the girl of his dreams. Someone he could spend forever with.

He was so besotted, he ignored the sneers of some of his colleagues at work. They remembered Bambi as someone quite different from the pretty, sensual creature he had fallen in love with. They recalled her as being the 'dope head' girl cop who did not charge a pal when she was caught smoking cannabis. In their eyes, she was trouble – and she had shamed her unit by sympathising with druggies. In fact, they suspected she even smoked marijuana herself. That was one of the reasons they fired her back in 1980.

Bambi had a lot of enemies inside the Milwaukee Police Department:

'She was too darned pretty to be a cop in the first place.'

'Her type should never have joined the force.' Bambi certainly provoked opinions. She was a person of extremes after all. You either loved her or hated her and Schultz loved her to death. But his fellow colleagues hated her with a vengeance.

Nevertheless, there was one aspect of Bambi that her husband deeply detested – her job at the local Playboy Club. Fred did not care that on a good couple of nights, Bambi could earn the entire month's rent on their modest apartment. He may have been permanently broke but no wife of his was going to work in *that* place.

Bambi sort of understood her new husband's feelings but she also knew they were financially hard pressed. In any case, she had a great body. Why not show if off a little and get paid for the pleasure?

'Those guys pay me a $50 tip just so they can look at my body.' Bambi was very matter of fact about it. She would never, ever even consider selling her body for sex. But dressing up in a slinky leotard with a fake bunny tail stuck on her bottom did not seem so bad. In any case, she was proud of her fit, lean body. She knew she had good breasts and gorgeous hips. She did not mind wiggling the right parts if necessary. It was all harmless stuff.

But Fred was adamant. He did not like the idea of all those guys lusting after her – and it was hardly the right sort of career for a policeman's wife. So, after much cajoling, Bambi handed in her bunny's tail and waved goodbye to those, sleazy, risky nights at the Playboy Club. The trouble was that it gave her more time to herself. More time to think. More time to brood. More time to get angry. More time to get vicious.

Fred was working longer and longer hours in his job as a busy crime detective on the streets of Milwaukee. Crime was rife in most neighbourhoods in that gritty, busy city. And that meant Fred and his colleagues really had their work cut out for them.

It also meant a lot of lonely nights at home in front of the television set for Bambi. She could not concentrate on most programmes. Her thoughts were filled with vengeance. Here she was in this tiny, cramped apartment while *that woman* had a beautiful house. Why? Why was Bambi suffering when she was the one who had just got married?

The only TV shows that diverted her attention were the bleak crime movies. The grisly murders that keep viewers gripped to their seats in terror. They did not scare Bambi. They just made her start to wonder ... The evening of May 27, 1981, was hot and steamy in Milwaukee. But that did not affect Christine Schultz and her two sons Sean, eleven, and Shannon, seven. The children were comfortably tucked up in the air conditioned bedroom of the family's well-maintained detached home in one of the city's better Southside suburbs.

As thirty-year-old Christine kissed them gently goodnight and left the bedroom, her thoughts could not have been further from the happiness of her ex-husband and his new, young wife. She could only recall the unhappy years with Fred. The arguing. The fighting. The tears. Now, at last she could get on with her new life. A new lover and even the chance of a fresh, happier marriage eventually.

She watched her boys as they drifted into sleep. Life would come good for them, she was sure of it. A thunderous roar broke overhead as a huge airliner made its descent to the nearby airport at Mitchell Field, but they slept through it, safe in a cocoon of dreams.

Christine quietly tip-toed out of their room and headed towards the bedroom she once shared with Fred. A peaceful night in front of the television. She could think of nothing nicer.

Settled into the comfy double divan, she propped herself up with three pillows and immersed herself in one of her favourite shows – M*A*S*H*. Christine laughed out loud at the hilarious adventures of Radar and all the rest of the gang who starred in the top rating programme. She loved the show's harsh, cynical humour. The reality of it appealed to her. But the real world outside was about to swallow her up forever.

It was 2.20 a.m. when little Sean stirred from his deep slumber. At first he thought he was dreaming. He could feel something cold, almost damp, pressing over his face and mouth. Then he felt a choking sensation as if a cord were tightening around his neck.

This was no dream. This was the ultimate nightmare. For a split second, he kept his eyes tightly closed. Hoping that if he did so then it would all go away. But he was having trouble breathing now and his throat felt as if it were about to explode. He had to open his eyes. There was no other possible means of escape.

So he did, and there was terror in its truest form. No goblins, no wicked witches, no make-believe video that sent shivers down your spine but you could laugh at later. Just a leather gloved hand clasping, pressing down on his face. Then another hand, fumbling for a second then pulling a cord tight around his neck. Sean's first scream was muffled. Then his assailant loosened the pressure momentarily so that the noose around his neck could be pulled even tighter.

Just one more breath Sean told himself as his world began to go blurry at the edges through lack of oxygen. He let out an ear-piercing shriek. It was his only chance. His last one. Sean put his entire little body and spirit into that yell and it had the desired effect. The intruder ran out of the room.

What was happening?

The two boys lay there too afraid to move at first. They just did not know what to do. Maybe they should just go back to sleep and then they would wake up in the morning to find it never really happened?

Boom. Boom.

It sounded like a firecracker going off in their mother's bedroom. The boys froze with fear. The reality of that attack moments earlier had now dawned on them utterly and completely. They ran to the bedroom. The bedroom where once they had rushed to sleep with their mother and father whenever they had a bad dream. Now they were about to encounter the worst type of nightmare – reality.

But their protective instincts towards their mother were paramount in their minds at that moment. As they dashed across the hallway they encountered the worst piece of evidence imaginable as a tall, shadowy figure pushed past them towards the stairs and the front door.

They found her face down on the bed. A sight no person should ever have to witness, let alone two small children. There in that bedroom they faced the aftermath of murder – and the victim was their mother.

A clothesline was tied around one hand. She had obviously put up a struggle. In her right shoulder was a gaping gunshot wound, flesh ripped away to the bone. But it was the blue bandanna gagging her mouth that was the most startling sight. It seemed to contort her face into a thousand lines of fear. Thankfully, her eyes were closed so neither of those innocent children had to see the horror etched permanently within.

But how can a child react to such a horrendous scene? They are not emotionally mature enough to know how to cope. Why should they be prepared by their parents for such a terrifying situation? No one expects it to happen to them.

Sean aged 10 years in those first few seconds as he stood in front of his mother's bloodied body. He tried desperately to stop the blood spreading from Christine's shoulder wound. Thank goodness he did not try to move her body because then he would have seen the full extent of that wound – caused by a single .38 bullet shot at point blank range in her back. It had glanced off her shoulder blade and gone through her heart. She never stood a chance. But it was better this way. At least Sean did not have to look at the graphic nature of the bullet's journey through his mother's body.

As Shannon stood by watching in a terrified trance, Sean struggled vainly to stop the blood from draining out of Christine's body. So often she had been the one to dab his cuts and bruises. She had kissed them better when they hurt like hell. She had covered the cuts with plaster to stop them dripping blood. She had loved and cared for him whatever the circumstances.

Now he was bravely trying to return the previous 11 years of love and attention. But no matter how hard he tried, there was nothing he could do to save her. There was no ebbing life to preserve. She had gone before they even reached the room.

A few minutes later, the shaking, quivering youngster called his mother's boyfriend, policeman Stu Honeck, who lived around the corner.

The cops arrived within minutes.

'It's just not fair Mike. I can hardly afford the price of a pair of shoes.'

Fred Schultz was complaining to his partner, Det. Michael Durfee, about that alimony yet again. Day in day out, the same old story. It was getting too much.

They were filing a burglary report when Fred picked up the ringing phone at their desk. Within moments, his face went white. His eyes began to well up with tears and then he dropped the telephone and left it hanging there.

Fred had just been told that his ex-wife – the mother of his two young sons – had been brutally murdered. He was in a daze. He did not know what to do. He just sat there slumped on his desk, his head in his hands sobbing. There was nothing his partner or anyone else could say. But he did have Bambi to turn to. She was still there. She would support him. She would help him cope. He had to turn to somebody.

Peep. Peep. Peep. Peep ...

The line at their home was engaged. What was Bambi doing on the telephone at 2.40 in the morning? Fred was puzzled. He needed her support. Her love. And she was on the phone. Why?

Finally he got through.

'Laurie, wake up! Chris has been shot. She's dead. I'll call you back when I can.'

Bambi said later she thought it was all a dream when Fred called her. But in fact, she was the instigator of the worst nightmare of all.

'He was a big guy with browny red type of hair and a pony tail.'

Sean had somehow regained enough composure to describe to detectives what the intruder looked like – less than an hour after the awful incident occurred.

The youngster told them he was wearing a baggy, green army jacket and black, police-type shoes. And a green jogging suit. And the gun, the gun had a silver pearl handle.

At least the detectives had something to go on.

'I'm sorry Fred but I got to see if your gun has been fired recently.'

Fred Schultz was stunned. His ex-wife had been murdered just a few hours earlier and now his partner Mike Durfee was at his front door suggesting that his own gun might have been used in the killing.

'What the fuck is this?' he screamed.

Mike gulped, he had to do it – but the despair on his friend's face …

All he could manage in response was, 'it's just a formality.'

Bambi watched coolly as her husband and his partner carefully checked the gun. Durfee found dust on the hammer and sniffed for any tell-tale signs of gunpowder odour. There was nothing. This weapon had not been used for quite some time.

'Look Fred. What can I say? It had to be checked.' Fred nodded slowly. Deep down, he understood the reasons behind his partner's visit. In fact, he felt fairly relieved because he knew who they would all be pointing the finger of suspicion at – his beautiful new young wife.

Bambi did not bat an eyelid. She looked as sexy and seductive as ever when they finally climbed into bed together to try and snatch a few hours sleep.

Policemen have a well known coldness when it comes to death. They encounter it so frequently that they soon become emotionally divorced from the reality of all the normal responses it provokes.

'It's just a body. It's not someone you know and love so it means nothing.'

An everyday occurrence. If it starts getting to you it's time to get out. But sometimes, inevitably, there are occasions when it hits home. The death of Christine Schultz should have been one of those occasions. Yet, bizarrely, Fred had recovered his composure completely by the time he was summoned to the city morgue to formally identify his ex-wife's body.

The cop and his pretty young ex-cop wife walked into the cold, sterile room as if they had been there a thousand times before. And they had. But surely this time it was different? They were about to see the brutally slain corpse of the woman who bore him two children. It had to be a difficult moment for any person – surely?

'Hey Laurie look at the size of this wound will you?'

Bambi was astonished. Whatever her true feelings towards the woman who lay on that morgue slab, she hardly felt in the mood to start passing medical comments on the size of the wounds.

But Fred was insistent.

'Come on Laurie. You saw enough stiffs when you were in the force.' As it happened Bambi had not been 'in the force' for very long and she managed to avoid seeing too many 'stiffs'. But that was irrelevant. She felt reluctant to go near that corpse. She did not want to face the reality of the situation. It frightened her.

Still Fred persisted. For a good few minutes he stood examining the fatal wound that had rubbed out his ex-wife's life.

'Wow! That's some wound.'

Bambi could not take this gruesome verbal post mortem another moment longer. She left Fred alone with his ex-wife for the one and only time.

Cops investigating Christine's tragic slaying were baffled. All their enquiries kept leading them to Bambi. She had told so many people of her dislike for Christine. The threats were commonplace, the envy an open secret. But so far they had not a shred of evidence.

Even Fred began to wonder. He took a pretty active role in the investigation. Some of his more cynical colleagues suggested it was to hide his own guilt. But it was becoming more and more apparent to Fred that Bambi certainly had the motive, if not the means.

There were no witnesses to place Bambi outside of that apartment on that night in May. But she had access to the off-duty gun Fred kept at home and the keys to the house where his ex-wife lived. There was no sign of forced entry by the murderer.

Then the cops got a break – of sorts. They found a reddish brown wig in the toilet system at Bambi's apartment block. A brown synthetic hair recovered from Christine Schultz's leg was very similar to the fibres from that wig. Then they discovered a hair recovered from the gag in Christine's mouth was not unlike Bambi's.

But it was still nothing concrete. The cops knew that Fred's gun had to hold the key. But it had already been tested by his partner the night of the murder.

On June 18 – a full three weeks after the murder – Fred, accompanied by Det. James Gauger, picked up his off-duty revolver for test firing at the state crime lab.

Once again, Bambi looked on coolly as her husband and his colleague took away what was to become their most damning piece of evidence.

After stringent tests it was found to have been the gun that killed Christine.

On June 24, 1981, Lawrencia Bembenek was arrested and charged with the murder of Christine Schultz.

At a Milwaukee court in February, 1982, Bambi was sentenced to life for the killing. It took the jury three and a half days of deliberation and circuit judge Michael Skwierawski called it 'the most circumstantial case I have ever seen.'

A campaign was mounted to get the decision overturned but all subsequent appeals failed.

Then, in August 1990, Bambi escaped from the Taycheedah Women's Correctional Institute in Wisconsin. She was helped by the handsome brother of another woman inmate. And the two proclaimed their love for one another before she made her daring escape.

Incredibly, the attractive ex-policewoman was still protesting her innocence when she was arrested in Thunder Bay, Ontario, Canada, three months later. She had got a job as a waitress and was living under a false name with her lover.

Just before her escape, Bambi was asked by a journalist what she would do in her first hour of freedom. She replied: 'Have sex.'

14

THE GREENHOUSE GALLOWS

Everything in Heathway was the same. The houses. The gardens. The street lights. Even the colour of the front doors.

It was one of those typical between the wars roads in a suburb that became a convenient overspill when London's population explosion really began to gain pace. The once neat rows of semi-detached three bedroomed houses had rapidly declined in appearance. Heathway also had other problems – like its location. Dagenham, Essex, is hardly the sort of place to inspire happiness. They say it peaked in the 1960s when the local Ford factory was churning out saloon cars at a rate of 100s per day. Then came the lay offs. Thousands upon thousands of Dagenham residents suddenly found themselves unemployable. It marked a turning point in the town's fortunes. Now, its biggest claim to fame is that it is the birthplace of film star Dudley Moore.

But Dagenham has retained one thing – its reputation as a typical lower middle class London suburb. A place where armed robbers learn how to saw off shotguns. A place where Sharon and Tracey are two of the most popular names. A place where net curtains prevail in virtually every front room window. For behind that petty, finger wagging façade there are a thousand sins being committed.

Marriages come and go in Dagenham these days. The family unit is frequently split in two by divorce. Neighbours are often locked in bitter feuds. But despite all this, the residents of Heathway like to keep up appearances. It might well be a scruffy little street littered with waste in every gutter. But it was still home to hundreds of ordinary, law abiding citizens.

Then there was Barbara Miller. She never really fitted in. Her parents George and Gladys sometimes wondered what they had done to deserve Barbara. She was just not the same as their five other children.

For a start Barbara did not even want to be a girl. Throughout her life she had longed to be one of the boys. She loved to play football, cricket and climb trees. She always kept her dark hair cut short. The longer she could fool the other kids then the longer she would be accepted. Of course the boys always found out eventually – and it broke Barbara's heart.

But that was nothing compared to what had happened to Barbara when she was just four years of age. It was an incident that scarred her for life and helped shape the following years of torment and waste.

She had always been a friendly little girl up until then. And it was no surprise that she befriended a local gardener in her favourite park. She would often accept gifts of sweets from the man. Barbara was just a small child. She did not know any better. But he did. He knew exactly what he was doing when he took little Barbara to an isolated piece of wasteland and ripped down her clothes.

When the terrified youngster was found wandering the streets distraught, a fundamental change had taken place in Barbara's character. The rot had already begun to set in.

The end result was a troubled life as a teenager and then an adult. Barbara, somehow, just didn't seem quite right. Dagenham was a brutal place for a misfit. And all the time in the back of her mind she kept remembering the horror of that attack on her innocent body.

Time and time again she was beaten up by other children. They used to tease her relentlessly about her hair. About her bucked teeth. About her being a girl. She wanted to be a boy to teach them all a lesson. She convinced herself that if she had been a boy then that monster would never have assaulted her. He was the root of all her evil.

Barbara bottled it all up inside herself. She never told her parents what was happening. She did not want to accept the fact – she was a girl. She just let the beatings continue. But they were inevitably affecting her life. They were etching hatred in her soul. Barbara had always hated certain people. Now she hated the world.

Perhaps George and Gladys Miller should have done something. They certainly saw the signs. But, like many parents, they chose not to say anything.

To ignore it, hope it would go away. They were afraid it might push Barbara even further down the road to self-destruction. They were completely unable to put their feelings into words.

She came across to everyone as reckless and uncaring. The truth was that she was eaten up with guilt inside. She felt a failure. She had failed herself by allowing that animal to molest her.

Barbara felt that life had become one big bitch – and she was going to take it for all it was worth. Sexually, physically, morally. By the time Barbara was in her mid-twenties she had long since lost her self esteem. She had waved goodbye to ambition. There were few jobs out there for a girl like her. She knew she had nothing to lose.

Barbara's only pleasure in life was the ultimate act – sex. She craved it day and night. Yet it was that very act at such a frighteningly young age that had damaged her temperament in the first place. What made it worse was that so few men were interested in her. With her closely cropped hair, jeans, T-shirt and hobnail boots she didn't turn many heads. As a teenager, she could only attract the boys by promising them literally anything if they would take her out. Her outlook on life was shaped for ever by that first horrendous experience and the subsequent adolescent sex behind bicycle sheds and in disused railway yards.

Sometimes the boys would line up and take it in turns. She knew it was wrong. But at least they were nice to her before they had their way. The trouble was they were invariably really horrible the moment they were done. But it hurt the most when none of them would even acknowledge her in the school playground the next day. It was as if she did not exist. She couldn't stand that. She would go to the toilets and cry. But she soon learnt to stifle the tears. The world hated her and she hated it back. What was the point of letting them get to her?

By the time Barbara left school at fifteen, she had become a regular visitor to the centre of London. She would skip off school and take the long tube ride up to Piccadilly Circus and wander the streets gazing at the bright lights of the big city. In her regulation uniform of short hair and jeans, she even managed to scare off the pimps that normally home in on young girls like Barbara. Those bucked teeth and cold, dark, staring eyes were like a sign around her neck that said: 'Keep Away. Danger.'

In any case, Barbara wasn't interested in selling her body. She had already been so badly abused by those animals that she did not care if she never slept with another man. If that was the way men behaved she wasn't interested.

But that closely cropped hairstyle and those boyish looks attracted another sort of predator. These intruders in her life did not abuse her and hurt her. They gently seduced her in a loving, caring, sensual manner. They touched her smoothly not roughly. They explored her and gave her pleasure. For the first time in her life Barbara began to discover what it was like to share her body rather than give it outright to some brute who only wanted to satisfy himself. By the time she was eighteen years old, Barbara realised that the soft and caring caress of another woman was far more preferable to sex with a man.

Back in those days, she had always been the one seduced by older women. They would pick her up in clubs and bars. They would hardly make much conversation. They each knew what the other wanted. Barbara was a more than willing participant. She was experiencing something she had never come across in her entire life. A sharing experience. Giving and taking from the same person.

But as she got older those encounters got less and less frequent. It was as if the women were not interested in her because she was no longer a teenager. It seemed that the sort of women Barbara was encountering wanted 'fresh meat' not the old and soiled variety. And Barbara was starting to age rapidly. By the time she was twenty-five she looked almost forty. The toll of life was bearing down on her – and she knew it.

Barbara also realised she had to find a fresh approach if she was to continue finding satisfying female partners. She had let her hair grow during that period in her life. Perhaps that was the mistake? She now looked like an out and out woman for the first time in her life. Maybe that was what scared off her would be lovers?

Barbara decided to return to her old tried and trusted ways – she shaved her hair short, almost into a skinhead style. She wore baggy shirts and those short, masculine windcheater jackets together with loose fitting jeans that did not give away any tell-tale curves. The wardrobe was complete. Now she just had to find the girls.

Barbara was living back with her parents in Heathway by this time. The frustration of being sexually inactive was making her positively withdrawn. Now she had decided a plan of action. She felt good about it. She was going to find girls who were just like her when she was that teenager wandering the streets of London. They were the best. The ones whom she could teach. The ones whom she could love.

'Mum. I'd like you to meet Bobby. He's taking me to the pictures this afternoon.'

Jackie was just sixteen. But she had already had her fill of boys. They only wanted to use you and abuse you. They never tried to caress you and adore you. They only cared about one thing.

Now she was introducing 'Bobby' to her mother. Barbara Miller's guise as a boy was brilliantly convincing just so long as she did not open her mouth.

Barbara – or rather 'Bobby' – just nodded her head in acknowledgement toward Jackie's mother. But she couldn't help herself. She had to inspect the body of her new lover's parent. Her eyes travelled down over her breasts and then down to her crotch, a nestled swollen mound that clearly showed through her skintight jeans.

Jackie's mother caught 'Bobby's' eyes as they stripped her and lusted after her. She felt a tingle of delight. She could read 'his' mind and she felt highly flattered. If only she had known that her daughter's 'boyfriend' was in fact a fully grown woman.

She watched lovingly as Jackie and 'Bobby' walked down the garden path hand in hand at lunchtime on that hot summer's day in 1987. They seemed to be laughing so happily together. They looked such a sweet sight together, she thought. If only …

Jackie and Barbara were laughing. In fact they were in hysterics.

'She fell for it. I can't believe it. She fell for it.' Barbara was holding tightly onto young Jackie's hand now. She was not going to let go … ever.

As they walked up the street towards Heathway, Barbara wanted to make sure that Jackie knew precisely what lay in store for her. Barbara began to tickle the palm of Jackie's hand with two of her fingers. Gently scratching and tickling. Then she pushed her forefinger deep into Jackie's clenched hand. In and out. In and out. In and out. Barbara just wanted to ensure that this pretty, silky skinned young girl got the message. Jackie laughed as she felt Barbara's finger going in and out. She bent over and kissed 'him' there and then.

'I can't wait …'

The television was blaring. But no one was watching it. A cat lay curled up by the gas fire desperate for some loving care and attention. The brass horses on the tiled fireplace looked as if they could do with a good polish. The swirly red patterned carpet had worn thin, tattered at the edges. Suddenly, a lamp stand crashed to the floor.

'Shit.'

Barbara Miller came up for air. She knew her parents would be furious if they found the lamp missing when they got home.

Lying underneath her on the sofa was Jackie. They were both naked.

'Come on Bobby. Come on.'

Barbara's momentary lapse was over. She looked down at the firm young body beneath her and knew she had to have more. She could not help herself.

Their lips locked tight on each other. Barbara opened her mouth as wide as she could and felt Jackie's slithery tongue exploring deep, probing into the walls of her mouth.

'Wider. Wider.'

Barbara commanded her young lover to open her mouth even more. She wanted to feel it's entirety with her tongue. She loved it when she ran it around the inside of her gums and then across her smooth young teeth.

Sex with another female was so much better than with a man, thought Barbara. Little did she know that Jackie was thinking exactly the same thing at that precise moment. They had already climaxed twice earlier together. Now they were going for a third crescendo of lust. Nothing could stop them. Barbara started to run her tongue down Jackie's neck. Every few inches she would stop to kiss and suckle that soft, smooth skin. Then she carried on down towards the teenager's nipples. At first she gently slurped on them. Then she nipped them between her teeth and bit. Jackie let out a small squeal. It could have been a sign of pain or pleasure. Barbara did not care. She bit again. This time harder and longer. Then she lifted her head and watched the agony etched across her lover's face. It gave her even more satisfaction. Now it was Jackie's turn. She was firmly trapped under Barbara's body as they lay locked together on that sofa. However, that did not stop her sliding down past Barbara's breasts and lower. She stopped at her older lover's tummy button and began sucking air in and out of it. Barbara's felt the stabbing sensation from her stomach. It provoked a weird combination of feelings. She did not like it so she pushed her young lover's head further down.

It was not even four p.m. by the time Barbara – or rather 'Bobby' – saw her lover home. Once again, they held hands tightly as they walked slowly and lovingly towards Karen's house.

And there was Jackie's mother waiting at the window for a sighting of her darling daughter. But this time there was no smile on her face. No look of delight at the happy couple wandering along. Instead, there was a look of fury and hatred. Of disgust and shock.

For minutes earlier, Jackie's mother had met neighbour Vivienne Elliot in the street and she had told her about 'Bobby's' secret. Her daughter's 'boyfriend' was a woman. An evil woman who had just seduced her innocent child.

Barbara sensed something was wrong when the front door to Jackie's house flew open.

'You fucking dyke. Don't you ever go near my baby again. Do you hear me?'

Barbara heard her loud and clear. Her heart sank. She did not know what to say. She was going to try and bluff it out but that would hardly work. She knew that once she spoke, her secret would be out. She just had to know who? Who would be so evil as to tell on her? She had to know? She could think of only one person who would stoop so low. It had to be her.

Vivienne Elliot thought Barbara was seeing her first husband and she did not like it one bit. True. She had long since re-married. But that did not matter. He was still her property and she did not want some tomboy like Barbara sniffing around him.

The irony was that Barbara did befriend him. She had tried to 'connect' with him because she was desperate to change her ways. She wanted to give a man – any man – one last chance to prove that they were not really all that bad. They couldn't all be like that monster in the park all those years earlier or those uncaring boys who took it in turns to abuse her body. Surely they could not all be like that?

But now that potential boyfriend's ex-wife had given Barbara all the evidence she needed. Men were just not worth it.

'Don't you ever set foot in this house again. If I see you even talking to Jackie I'll fucking kill you.' Barbara was shattered. She turned around and walked back towards the street. She was dead inside. At last, she had found some real love and lust. Now that was gone. Destroyed by an evil woman who did not care.

But Barbara did not feel any resentment towards Jackie's mother. She understood her reaction. It was perfectly reasonable. After all, she had just seduced her sixteen-year-old daughter.

No. It was Vivienne Elliot whom Barbara felt a rush of hatred for. That woman had just destroyed her love affair. The one thing that kept Barbara going now did not even exist. It was as if those hours of love making were just a dream. They had not actually happened. She had wrecked the one period in Barbara's life where there had been joy.

Barbara raged as she stormed her way back home to Heathway. The world around her was just a blur of distant images. The only world that now existed was inside her head. A throbbing repetitive pain. It seared through her mind, poisoning it with evil thoughts and deeds. She had to do something. She had to destroy her.

Barbara was sitting there in darkness when Karen Miller walked into the house less than half an hour later. 'What's up cuz? You look like death.'

Barbara said nothing at first. Her mind was still firmly entrenched in horrendous thoughts.

'Come on Babs. Tell us what's wrong?'

Karen was probably the only person in Barbara's life who even bothered to listen to her. She had been living at the Miller's house for most of her life because her own parents abandoned her. She called Barbara 'cuz' but in fact she was her niece. But they were more like sisters at times.

Barbara looked up at Karen and wondered. Perhaps this was a rare chance to pour out all her thoughts? It wasn't often that she had that opportunity. It was after all one of her biggest problems in life. She just never had anyone to tell.

'You don't really want to know Karen.'

'Of course I do cuz. Come on! Spill the beans.'

It was then that Barbara decided to change a habit of a lifetime.

'Hello. Vivienne. This is Karen Miller. You couldn't spare me a few minutes for a chat could you?' Barbara and her niece had hatched a plot to destroy Vivienne. This was stage one.

'Great. I'll see you round here in a while then.' Karen beamed as she replaced the telephone receiver. On the sofa – that same sofa where Barbara had made hot passionate love to her girlfriend just a few hours earlier – they discussed the next part of their scheme. By pure chance, Barbara's parents were away for the day. They had all the time in the world to get even with Vivienne.

Now Vivienne Elliot was not exactly a woman who oozed sex appeal. With her wire rimmed specs and penchant for seventies style clothes, she hardly made a sensual impression. But she must have had something going for her because she was never short of a man friend or two – or even three.

At thirty-four years of age and with four children by as many different men, Vivienne certainly knew how to live life to the full.

Her appetite seemed to know no bounds. She had become a virtual legend in Dagenham. She loved to go down to the local pubs and clubs dressed up to the nines in her favourite knee hugging, platform sole leather boots and a micro mini. Somehow, she would nearly always end up with a man in tow by the end of the evening.

Then there were the daytime sex sessions at the tiny two-bedroomed council house she lived in with the kids. She had a particular fondness for schoolboys. Neighbours would look on in wonderment as a stream of teenage lads poured into the house.

Vivienne used to adore the art of seduction. Drawing these nervous, shaking young boys into her bedroom by appearing in the front room dressed just in stocking and suspenders.

Then she would strip them and mother them before teaching them how to do it. Every now and again she would come across an experienced one – they were no good because she did not feel in full control. She hated it when they tried to dominate. Those boys would never be asked back.

She adored the really innocent ones. They were the lads she could mould and seduce. They would do anything she commanded. Sometimes, that might include tying them to the bed – just to ensure they did not escape.

Once, Vivienne bound a boy head and foot and then gagged him before going to the shops. As she bought the week's shopping all she could think about was that young piece of meat back at the house.

By the time she got home she could not wait. She left the shopping in the car outside and burst into the bedroom. She did not care that he had virtually choked to death on that gag. She pulled it out of his mouth and sat on him without even bothering to untie the ropes.

But despite her flamboyance, Vivienne was still very possessive. She still liked to have her first husband under her control. She enjoyed allowing him to seduce her sometimes – even though they had long since divorced. And she was not at all happy that Barbara Miller had come on the scene. However, she would no longer be a threat because Vivienne had just made sure that everyone – including Jackie's mother – knew Barb was a lesbian. That would teach her.

As she walked around to see Karen Miller, she wondered if that was what the teenager wanted to talk to her about. Vivienne knew that Karen was probably Barbara's only friend in the world.

'Hello Vivienne. It's great to see you. Thanks for coming.'

Karen's greeting was as cordial as a meeting of two best friends when Vivienne Elliot arrived around at the Miller household. As she stepped into the front room there was no hint of the horrors that were to follow.

'Like a cuppa?'

The thought of a cup of tea was like music to Vivienne's ears. She'd had a tough day getting the kids off to school. Doing the week's shopping. Cleaning the house. Having sex with that cute fourteen-year-old boy who lived up the road.

'I'd love a cup,' said Vivienne. Little did she realise it would never actually materialise. Karen disappeared into the kitchen while Vivienne sat there on the sofa where a plan for her destruction had just been hatched.

Karen was excited. She had not hesitated when Barbara told her the plan. In fact, she thought Vivienne deserved everything she had coming to her. Karen had her suspicions that Vivienne had been sleeping with her last boyfriend. It was only logical for her and Barbara to decide to finish Vivienne off for good.

'She's here. Just stay in the garden. I'll get her out.' Karen was in the kitchen whispering so Vivienne would not hear. Barbara just stood there. Her glazed eyes said it all. She was shaking with anticipation. The end of Vivienne's life was approaching.

'Come out in the garden with me. I've got something to show you.'

Vivienne never stood a chance as she stepped into that tiny garden in Heathway, Dagenham. Karen was the first one to get a direct hit. She turned and swung a clenched fist right at Vivienne's face. You could hear the crunch as her glasses twisted and fell to the ground.

Vivienne had not even seen Barbara standing behind her with a rolling pin when it crashed down on her head a split second later. The onslaught had begun. But there was a lot more to follow.

Her body slumped to the stone pavement after Barbara's attack. The two women were surprised. They hadn't expected her to be knocked unconscious after just one hit with the rolling pin.

They stood there frozen for a moment. A look of disappointment came over Barbara's face. She had been looking forward to smashing her skull over and over again. She wanted to see the agony contorting Vivienne's face as she literally bashed it to bits.

Instead, her victim lay collapsed in a heap on the ground.

'Come on. Let's take her to the greenhouse.' Barbara was now very much in command. This was her operation. She enjoyed the responsibility. It wasn't often she got to do something useful.

Karen and her aunt did not feel the slightest bit of remorse as they dragged Vivienne's semi-conscious body across the grassy garden. Suddenly, the dog next door barked. Karen and Barbara stopped in their tracks. Vivienne's limp body thumped to the ground. They waited there in complete silence fearing that the neighbour might appear in the garden next door. The fence between their homes was a mere four feet high. He might see them. That would be a disaster.

Barbara and Karen felt a bigger surge of fear run through their bodies at that moment than at any time during the evening. They felt no guilt about

Vivienne. But they did not want to get caught.

Nothing stirred next door. Even the dog did not bark again. Their bloody escapade could continue undisturbed.

Barbara took the arms and pulled. Karen tried with difficulty to carry the legs but they kept dropping to the ground. As they neared the greenhouse, Barbara's strength gave way as well and they dropped Vivienne with an almighty crash.

They both looked down at her now. delighted in the knowledge that she would never again threaten their happiness. Ecstatic by the thought that she would soon be dead.

Just then Barbara looked down at Vivienne's bare thighs, exposed by that rough ride across the garden. For a second, she felt a twinge of lust building up inside herself. Maybe Vivienne could be used for one last moment of sexual satisfaction?

Barbara lent down and ran her hand up Vivienne's cold leg. She stopped at mid-thigh and squeezed it. It felt quite nice. She let her hand slide further up. Vivienne's semi-conscious eyes fluttered. Barbara's touch had stirred her. But she did not try to stop it. Perhaps she thought she might be spared if she let Barbara carry on?

'Bloody hell Babs. Are you a sex maniac or what? Let's just get her into the greenhouse for fuck's sake.' Karen was the more sensible of the two. In any case she wasn't interested in other women. Never had been. Never would. Yet she wasn't shocked by Barbara's brief attempt at a sexual assault. She knew all about Barbara's perversions. She also knew what had caused them.

But she was well aware that this was no time for Barbara's uncontrollable lust to take over. They had things to do.

Inside the greenhouse, they heaved Vivienne's body onto a wooden chair. Then, once more, Barbara took control. First she tied Vivienne's wrists together. Pulling the knot so tight she could feel her victim wince with pain. Then she got down on her knees and began wrapping the rope around Vivienne's ankles. Barbara pulled rigidly on the rope to make sure it really was secure. But she was aware that Vivienne's thighs were parting right in front of her very face. Despite tightly tying those ankles together, Vivienne was showing Barbara what was there. Her thighs were opening wider and wider now. Inviting Barbara to push her hand up there and probe.

Barbara's breathing speeded up. She was having difficulty containing herself. She wanted to let her hand wander up there and explore the soft mound. Vivienne's thighs were on a level with her face as Barbara crouched there on both knees. She looked into Vivienne's eyes. They weren't staring at her as you might expect. There was no fear in them. They were saying: 'Do it. Go on do it!'

Vivienne was fighting for her life the only way she knew how – by acquiescing. This might be her only chance for survival. She would do anything to save herself. She would have opened those thighs to the entire world if it gave her another few minutes longer to fight back.

Barbara was trying to contain herself now. She was trying to resist the urge for self gratification because that is what it would have been. She was just a few inches away from the most sexual part of any woman's body. It was there waiting for her to finger and more. Much more.

'Fucking hell Babs. Let's just finish her off. Forget all that you dirty cow.'

Vivienne had just lost her final battle to live. Barbara and Karen began to construct a make-shift gallows before Vivienne's very eyes. She was forced to watch as they made the method of her murder absolutely clear to her.

Barbara knotted the rope into a large noose and then threaded it through a long metal ladder that was fastened across the roof of the greenhouse. Vivienne struggled desperately. She rocked back and forth on the chair in a bid to fall over. She succeeded just as Barbara stood on another chair to test the effectiveness of their do-it-yourself gallows.

She jumped down and bundled Vivienne back upright. Karen then held her down by the shoulders to make sure it did not happen again. Barbara put her face right up against Vivienne's and told her: 'Your day has come.'

Then she forced the noose roughly over her head, scraping Vivienne's ears in the process. This was worse than any public execution. There were no last rites. No final request. Not even a hood to hide the fear.

Vivienne felt the prickly rope digging into her neck gently at first. Then Barbara yanked hard and the older woman started to choke.

Karen watched it all in a trance. It just did not seem real. It wasn't really happening. Finally, they were getting the revenge they so dearly wanted. But it did not feel the way she expected it to. Karen felt numbed – not excited anymore. Barbara pulled with all her might and tightened the knot holding the noose in place. Then she pulled the chair from right under her love rival and watched as Vivienne's head twisted upwards. The rest of her body crumpled onto the greenhouse floor but her head and neck remained locked to one side. For a few seconds, spasms of life twitched through Vivienne's body. Her head raged from side to side furiously. But that only made her death come quicker. It tightened the grip on her throat.

Barbara and Karen watched quietly as Vivienne gave up her fight to live.

Barbara actually felt elated by the murder. It was as satisfying as the sex she had contemplated with that corpse just a few minutes earlier.

But now there was the matter of the body. It had to be removed.

No one gave Barbara and Karen so much as a second glance as they pushed the wheelbarrow along the crowded streets. They had only covered 200 yards from their house so far, but it felt more like 200 miles to the aunt and her niece.

None of the boys they passed coming home from school that evening could have guessed that underneath a potato sack in the barrow was the randy housewife who had seduced so many of their pals. Vivienne would not be inviting any more of them around again.

As Barbara and Karen reached the corner of Heathway, they turned the barrow slightly to the right to avoid an old lady and the unmentionable almost happened. Vivienne nearly ended up on the pavement. It was a close thing. They felt the corpse shift position as they turned the corner and suddenly the barrow began to wobble. They envisaged scenes of utter horror as the body fell onto the street.

But it never happened. Barbara managed to regain control over the barrow and avoid it turning over. Then Karen noticed Vivienne's hand dragging alongside the barrow. She turned to see if anyone had noticed. There was not a sign of recognition from anyone. They were all in too much of a hurry to get home from school and work to notice two women pushing a corpse through a suburban street.

Karen carefully and discreetly pushed the hand back under the potato sack and they continued their journey. She had not questioned the sense in Barbara's plan to dump the body. It was the right thing to do. What she did not realise was where Barbara was intending to leave it.

'You must be fucking mad Babs.'

Karen Miller was astounded. She could not believe that Barbara would be this stupid. Of all the places in all the towns in all the world, this was the one venue that would bring the police running to their front door within hours if not minutes.

For Barbara had decided to dump the strangled body of Vivienne Elliot in the woman's very own front garden. 'Just fucking do it!'

This was an order not a request from Barbara to her niece. Karen obeyed. Together the two women heaved Vivienne's stiffening body along towards the side entrance of the house. One of them struggled to open the side gate, while the other kept the body slumped upright. With one last shove they threw it onto the ground between the two detached houses. It was still late afternoon. There were lots of people everywhere, but no one saw Barbara and Karen, Vivienne's body or even the wheelbarrow they hurriedly raced back home with.

George and Gladys Miller were in fine spirits when they arrived back at their home in Heathway just half an hour later. They had been visiting another daughter in Norwich and it had turned into a happy family reunion. And, since Barbara had not been invited, it was a peaceful occasion not marred by the usual squabbles that always seemed to follow their wayward daughter wherever she went.

But on their return home even George had to admit he was pleasantly surprised by Barbara that afternoon. She was giving the house a well deserved spring clean.

There was, of course, an ulterior motive. Their little home had seen quite a lot of life, sex and death that day. First there was the love making with Jackie then there was the plotting with niece Karen to kill Vivienne – and that was followed by the murder itself. Barbara would have to do a hell of a lot of scrubbing to clean out that house!

George and Gladys were blissfully unaware of all the horrors that had occurred just a few hours earlier. They were so relieved to see Barbara doing something to help around the house. Usually, she did absolutely nothing.

'Hi mum. Hi dad.'

She seemed like a different person. So cheery. So full of life. So vibrant. This was not the Barbara they knew. But her elderly parents never stopped to ask why she was so happy. They only thought about it later.

Outside the gates of the local primary school at about this time, a little girl was looking distraught. All her friends had been collected but still there was no sign of her mummy.

Veronica may have been just five years of age but she was the spitting image of her mother Vivienne Elliot. It was eerie really – they could have been twins if the 27-year gap had not existed. The little girl even had the same sort of specs as her mum.

'Where do you think your mummy has got to?'

The teacher was very concerned. Vivienne was always very good about being there to pick up her daughter. Some parents were downright uncaring, but not Vivienne. She may have had a racy reputation around town but her parenthood was never in question.

They waited another 15 minutes but still there was no sign of Vivienne. The teacher had no option but to ring Veronica's granny. Something could have happened to her for all they knew.

Iris Ives was puzzled. It just wasn't like her daughter to be unreliable when it came to collecting Veronica. As she picked up the youngster, she felt an odd feeling of impending doom coming upon her. Something was wrong. Something was badly wrong.

There was no answer at the door to Vivienne's house. Iris was confused. She had to be home. Where else could she be. She had to be home.

She tried again but still there was no reply. 'I'll go round the back granny.'

Iris thought nothing of letting little Veronica dash around to the side gate to the semi-detached house. Her eyes followed her little grand-daughter's route and then stopped dead.

There on the ground were a pair of legs sticking through the side gate.

'Mummy. Mummy. Mummy.'

Iris knew it was her the moment Veronica began screaming. She dragged her hysterical granddaughter away from the corpse. It was way too late to save her.

Twenty minutes later police acting on a tip off from Vivienne's relatives knocked on the door of the Miller house and arrested Barbara for murder. Her niece Karen was charged with being an accessory.

Barbara told police: 'She was stirring it between me and my boyfriend. She deserved to die.'

The reality was a far more complex tragedy of life and death.

In July, 1988, at the Old Bailey, Barbara Miller, aged thirty, was jailed for life after pleading guilty to manslaughter on the grounds of diminished responsibility.

Karen Miller, aged nineteen, admitted conspiracy to commit common assault and assisting to remove the body. She was given 3 years probation.

After the case, Barbara's father George said: 'My heart bleeds for both of them. They have had such a raw deal in life. I just hope to goodness they can get the help they need in the future.'

15

DEATH ON A WATERBED

The shrill of a bell ringing loudly in the distance meant only one thing to Judy Benkowski. Her husband was demanding something.

Clarence Benkowski was overweight and overbearing. All his life he had been number one in that miserable household. And, even now, after retiring from his job as a welder, he expected to be waited upon hand and foot.

When his sick and aged mother decided to move in, it got even worse for Judy. Now there were two of them bullying and cursing her. Making her wait on them like a serf.

Often they would sit in the armchairs in the sitting room of Number 508 South Yale Avenue for hours on end without budging. That was when that little bell rang the most. An endless stream of demands came from her husband and mother-in-law.

RING – 'Get me a coffee,' said one.

RING – 'Get me a beer,' said the other.

RING – 'This coffee's cold, get me another.'

RING – 'This beer's bloody warm! Ever heard of a freezer?'

And so it went on. And on and on. Judy did not have time for a job in the outside world. Her full time occupation was looking after two bloated leeches and two ever demanding sons.

Sometimes it would all get too much. She would cry herself to sleep at night. But that was only after Clarence had drunkenly tried to have sex with her. The act itself was totally one sided. He would make her fondle him and then – the moment he was ready – she would just lie there and listen to him grunting. It was always over in minutes if not seconds. But there was so much pain involved. Not love. Just pure and simple pain. The sort of pain that inevitably occurs when an overweight old man forces himself on a slightly built, 5 foot tall woman more than 20 years younger. They might have been husband and wife in law. But they were total strangers in the bedroom.

One day, Clarence had decided he wanted to spice up *his* sex life so he bought a waterbed. But, typically, it was the cheapest one he could find. The result was that Judy just lay there as usual every time he wanted sex – but now she had that awful, overwhelming sensation of rocking up and down as if on a boat bobbing across the ocean. But it did help in one respect: Judy used to feel so sea sick within seconds of Clarence starting, she would insist they stopped having sex before she puked all over him.

But Clarence's attitude towards sex was much the same as his outlook on life: the man ruled the roost. It was her own stupid fault if she didn't like it. She'd said the words: honour *and* obey …

For nearly 20 years, Judy had put up with the insults, the drudgery, the physical pain. What else could she do? She had no career. No existence outside those four walls. She had been trapped for so long she had forgotten what it was like to be free in the fresh air outside.

'You can't let him treat you like this. You've got to do something.'

Debra Santana was incensed. She had heard one story too many from Judy Benkowski. How could a husband treat his wife so badly? More to the point, how could someone put up with it? *She* certainly wouldn't.

'But,' Judy explained in her quiet, reserved way: 'What can I do. I have nowhere to go. No means of support.'

Debra was determined to help her best friend and neighbour. She was a striking blonde, now in her thirties, who had clung fervently to the fun-loving attitude towards life that she'd had as a teenager. She had suffered too. Her marriage had been terrible. But no soldiering on for her. She took the easy, and the sensible, way out – divorce. Now she was enjoying everything that Judy had long since given up hope of ever seeing. That consisted of a black, athletic lover who gave her the ultimate satisfaction and a life with few pressures.

Judy was very jealous of Debra's lifestyle. She so wanted to feel warmth, passion and true love again from a man. She knew Debra was right when she told her to end it. But how? What then?

Clarence would not even discuss divorce. His strict Catholic background meant it was out of the question. He would not even let her get on with her own life. She would have been perfectly happy if they had agreed to lead separate existences. She could have gone out with other men and he could have done as he pleased. But Clarence believed he owned Judy. She was his woman. If he demanded sex he should get it. If he wanted to insult her he could. If he wanted her to be his slave …

Naturally, this was an appalling prospect to Debra. She may have been thirteen years younger than her friend, but she reckoned women should always have fun whatever their age. And Judy was finding herself increasingly influenced by her younger, more outrageous pal. The more they talked about Debra's adventures, the more Judy began to wonder what life would be like without Clarence.

'So tell me brains, what do I do?' pleaded Judy, sarcastic and sad at the same time. 'In fact, what would you do? I'm trapped. There's no way out.'

The desperation in her voice sparked Debra's imagination. She had an idea. An extraordinary notion. But it would solve all Judy's problems if they planned it carefully. Oh, it would work all right.

'This is Eddie,' said Debra. 'Not only is he great in bed but he's also really used to this sort of situation.' Eddie Brown had bestowed upon Debra all the sexual satisfaction she had ever craved. Even fully clothed, his physique was unquestionably beautiful. Biceps filling his sleeves taut, a chest straining his shirt buttons to breaking point. Judy felt a little surge of excitement as she shook his hand. She wondered just what sort of outrageous sex her friend enjoyed with this athletic, dusky lover.

But there was one thing about Eddie that did surprise Judy. He was just 5 foot 3 inches tall. In fact, Debra towered over him by a good 4 inches. But she winked at Judy:

'He more than makes up for it in other ways you know. Anyway enough of that, we've got serious business to discuss.'

Debra had not finally introduced her fantasy-come true lover to Judy to discuss his sexual prowess. Eddie was going to do a job for Judy.

A job that required a certain amount of scheduling.

'Do you really think you can kill him without being caught?'

Judy finally broke the ice with Eddie. The introductions were over. The pleasantries had all been used up. Now she had to confront him with the facts.

And the facts were that he had agreed to murder her husband in exchange for a fee of $5,000. Now they had to sort out the finer details. Where should it be done? What weapon should he 'use? How could they make sure the police did not suspect anything? What if he survived?

For a few moments, Judy wondered if she had gone completely crazy. How could she even contemplate murdering another human being, let alone her husband?

'Maybe we should think about all this,' she said.

There was a brief silence from her two accomplices.

'What?' said Debra. 'After all he's put you through. You're trying to tell me you've changed your mind. We agreed on this Judy. Come on. Let's do it!'

Then Eddie chipped in, 'Yeah. It'll be easy. We can make it look like a random shooting. No trouble.'

The pressure was mounting on Judy. She wasn't a strong willed woman at the best of times. She sensed there was no choice in the matter. He had to die. It was her only escape route from a miserable life. The one way to break the deadlock which trapped her in misery. It might have seemed drastic but then what more did that animal deserve? He had treated her like dirt for too long. Now it was her turn. Revenge would seem sweet.

Before the dreams of a new life, however, there was the small matter of how and where to do it. It was mid-October, 1988, and Halloween was fast approaching. It's a celebration of death and ghouls. Why not do it for real? Judy had a great scheme. Or so she told her two partners in crime.

'Eddie, I'll get you a really scary costume. You're so short you'll look just like a kid out trick or treating. Then you knock on the door, Clarence answers and you blast him away with a gun. A trick on him, a treat for me.'

Debra and Eddie looked stunned. This was a preposterous plan. But they could also tell that Judy was deadly serious. She seemed really attracted to the ghoulish aspects of it. She even laughed excitedly as she described the plot.

'That'll teach him. He never likes to give anything to anyone who comes knocking at the door.'

Judy was really getting into the mood to murder. Her initial nervous approach had suddenly been replaced by a zeal that astounded her two friends. It was as if she had now fully accepted the whole plan as a fait accompli. The risk involved was being outweighed by the fast approaching scenario – the glory of life without Clarence. Judy was feeling happy inside herself for the first time in years.

'But hang on there Judy. Don't you think that might seem a bit suspicious,' said Eddie.

Judy was in no mood for doubters. Her voice rose: 'How? You tell me. How?'

Eager to make his point, Eddie replied calmly, 'Trick or treaters don't tend to gun down their customers. The cops would know it was a contract hit straight off. They'd be down on you immediately.'

Eddie was trying desperately to defuse the situation. Sure, he had agreed to murder this woman's husband. The guy sounded like he deserved it. But the scheme Judy had just described was insane. It was like something out of the mafia. Hardly the sort of low key killing Eddie had in mind. But Judy was having none of it. She reckoned it was the perfect plan.

'The cops will think some crazy trick or treater is out there blasting innocent people to death. They'll never think it was a contract killing.'

Debra and Eddie glanced at each other and shrugged their shoulders. 'You're the boss lady,' said Eddie. Jobless and just out of jail, he needed the money so he wasn't about to lose a contract as valuable as this.

Halloween is a major event in every town in America. Every October, across the country, trick or treat shops open in vacant stores for a few weeks and enjoy hectic business. There's a dollar or two to be made out of tradition. Hundreds of thousands of costumes are sold. Entire schools convert their halls and recreation areas into vast gothic dungeons filled with grisly spectacles like fake bodies in cardboard coffins, headless corpses and other reminders of the pagan rituals that originated the whole event. The schools and youth clubs charge a nominal fee for local people to be scared out of their wits in their home-made dungeon and some well-needed funds are raised for a worthy cause.

Just as popular is the trick or treating. This involves children dressed in witches costumes knocking on the doors of houses in their street and shouting 'trick or treat' when someone comes to the door. Inevitably a liberal helping of sweets are offered to the children and everyone goes home happy.

In the Chicago suburb of Addison, they celebrated Halloween just as fervently as the rest of the country. And South Yale Avenue – where the Benkowskis lived – was as traditional as it was typical. Row upon row of three-bedroomed detached bungalows built to maximize the use of space available. This was middle class suburbia at its most classic.

Down the road at Debra Santana's house, Eddie Brown was for the first time in this entire episode, beginning to wonder what he had got himself into.

As Judy and Debra adjusted the ghoulish face mask they had bought for him at the local Halloween store, he felt more like a kid going out for some fun than a professional killer sent on a deadly mission to seek and destroy someone's elderly husband. To make matters worse, the latex mask was agonising. They had insisted on getting one that covered his entire face so that no one could see what colour he was. But Eddie was starting to think he might never make it to number 508 alive at this rate. It seemed so difficult to breathe. He was already gasping for air and he hadn't even left the house yet!

'This is crazy. I can't even see properly out of the eye slits.'

Eddie's voice was so badly muffled by the mask, the two women did not hear him at first.

So he yelled: 'I SAID, THIS IS CRAZY.'

If Eddie had to shout this loudly to be heard, then he would probably alert the entire street when he went knocking on Clarence's door.

Yet more evidence that this entire plan was doomed. Eddie then struggled to the window to see how active Halloween was looking out there. His face dropped. Well, it would have if he had not had that latex mask on.

There were literally hundreds of kids wandering the nearby streets doing the rounds. It seemed as if the entire population of under fifteens in Addison had decided to hit South Yale that night.

Eddie ripped off the mask in a fit of fury and stood there in his white skeleton costume. He started to jump up and down on the spot.

'I am not doing this. I can't shoot the bastard in front of hundreds of kids. I'd never get away with it.' Eddie had come to his senses just in time. This plan had always had the ring of insanity about it – he had to kill it there and then before it was too late.

Judy was furious. She had woken up that morning with a new outlook on life. She imagined herself just 24 hours away from never having to see that ugly hulk of a husband again. Now Eddie had destroyed her morbid fantasy.

'You made a deal, Eddie,' she said, her voice low and threatening.

'Don't get me wrong Judy. I'll kill him. But not tonight. It would be crazy and we'd all end up in jail.' Eddie was right. Or so Judy reluctantly agreed when she had stopped and thought about that mad scenario. She might have wasted $25 on a ghoul's outfit, but it was nothing compared with the $5,000 she was still determined to pay to waste her husband.

'OK. What do we do then? You've got to go through with it.'

Eddie was as good as his word. 'Right. Let's start all over again.'

Judy agreed to postpone the 'hit' for a week. Eddie had convinced her they would get away with it only if they planned it meticulously. And he had a scheme that he was sure would work.

RING: 'Where's my breakfast? Come on I'm hungry.'
RING. RING. RING.

Clarence Benkowski was about to be served breakfast in precisely the same way he had been for the previous twenty years. In the kitchen, Judy Benkowski muttered quietly under her breath: 'Don't worry. You'll get it in good time.' She snarled a smile to herself. The big moment was fast approaching. Stage One of the 'hit' was about to occur.

But then, if Clarence had not been so incredibly lazy, he might have got up from the breakfast table and lumbered into the kitchen and seen Judy pouring the contents of twenty sachets of sleeping pills into his coffee.

Clarence, however, was not about to change a habit of a lifetime.

RING: 'Come on. I'm starving.'

Clarence was helping Judy to sentence him to death. By ringing that bloody bell yet again he was signalling the beginning of the end of his life. He was guaranteeing that Judy would feel no guilt as she emptied every morsel from those packets and then swilled it around in his coffee. The more he rang that bell, the more she felt good about it. She knew she would never have to hear that noise again. It was a wonderful feeling – just to contemplate the end of such an awful era in her life.

Just keep ringing Clarence. Just keep ringing my fat shit of a husband …

Everything was ready now. Judy had a new spring in her step, a new bounce in her walk. But in her haste to impose a slow, lingering death sentence, she rather clumsily tipped the empty pill packets into the rubbish bin. She did not think about it at the time.

'Here you are darling.'

She hadn't called him that for years. 'Darling' was a term of endearment. How could she even contemplate feeling warmth towards the man she was about to have murdered? But she did for a split second. Judy was only human after all. It was merely a momentary lapse though. Judy felt a tingle of excitement as she put down the tray on the breakfast table. She sat, as she had always done, at the table and sipped gently at her tea. She could not help it – her eyes kept straining upwards and across the table towards Clarence. He hadn't even got anywhere near that coffee yet.

But then Clarence had his priorities. He always liked to gulp down his fried eggs first and stuff some toast in that huge cavern of his. Judy knew his habits only too well. That cup of coffee would soon be lifted to his lips. Be patient. Relax. He's going to drink it. All in good time. All in good time.

The *Chicago-Sun Times* was spread across the table in front of him, as it always was each morning. Something caught his eye. He stopped eating and gasped at the sports results.

'What the fuck? How could they have lost?'

Never over breakfast, had he made conversation with Judy for those 20 long years. Clarence was not about to break the habit of a lifetime. But still that coffee remained untouched. Judy's initial burst of excitement was rapidly changing to desperation. Come on! Come on! Get on with it! She could no longer hold herself back.

'Darling.' (for some weird reason she used *THAT* word again). 'Darling, drink your coffee. It'll get cold if you don't.'

For a split second, Clarence looked at his wife quizzically. She *never* spoke at breakfast. Why the hell was she nagging him to drink his coffee? Never before in more than 20 years. Why now?

But, as with most things in Clarence's life, he gave it only a brief thought. Anything more would have required analysis. Something best left to the football commentators he watched every evening on the television.

Judy was annoyed with her weakness in the face of such adversity. What on earth was she doing trying to make him drink the coffee? It was a sure way to guarantee he'd get suspicious.

She held back for a moment. Looking down at her own cup of tea. Not daring to raise her head in case he caught her eye. Then he might see the signs of guilt. He might even spot the murderous intentions that filled her mind as they sat there at that last fateful breakfast.

Maybe she had blown it? Perhaps he'd sussed her out? She shut her eyes for a split second in the hope all that doubt and anguish would go away.

Then, finally, he did it. The harsh slurping noise came like music to her ears. She opened her eyes once more. Now he was gulping it down at a furious rate. Desperately trying to wash away all the grease down his gullet. It was his favourite way of eating. It was a disgusting spectacle for everyone else. She had never dared suggest he improve his manners. Now he was paying the ultimate price. And for once it was a beautiful sight.

First one whole cup then another followed in quick succession. Judy could feel the rush of relief running through her veins. She sighed quietly to herself. It was, she reflected, the greatest achievement of her life.

'I don't feel so good. I think I'll lie down for a while.'

226

The magic words Judy had been waiting to hear. Eddie had said precisely how many she should feed him. Not too many, he insisted. They should knock him into a deep slumber rather than complete unconsciousness. That way no one would be able to tell he had been drugged.

Now Clarence was struggling towards the bedroom. They had taken effect. So far everything was going according to plan.

He only just managed to get to that wretched waterbed before collapsing in a heap. Judy crept into the room after him — just to make sure he was out. 'He's asleep. You better tell Eddie and get over here.'

Judy slammed down the phone and awaited her two accomplices. Debra was the first to arrive at the house. She hugged Judy warmly. She wanted to make sure her good friend knew that she supported her completely and utterly.

The two women sat side by side on the sofa in the front room and counted the minutes until Eddie arrived. They soon heard the back door opening and their hired killer walked in. With an eerie silence, Judy handed Eddie her husband's World War Two Luger pistol and motioned him towards the master bedroom.

Debra meanwhile put on a pair of stereo headphones and started listening to heavy rock music. It was a bizarre reaction. Maybe she was trying to blot out the noise of the gunfire that was about to occur?

The two women were once more sat down on that same sofa. Eddie had said he would use a pillow to muffle the sound but that did not stop Judy from hearing the exact moment when her husband died. It was a strange kind of thudding noise. Nothing like what she had expected. But she knew that was it. A feeling on immense relief flowed over her. It was over. At last it was over.

But there was more work to be done. Judy and her two friends had to make it look like a burglary that had gone wrong. The two women and Brown began tearing the house apart to make it look convincing.

They pulled drawers of clothes out and spread them all over the bed where Clarence lay under the covers. The waterbed was still intact. No leaks despite the hail of bullets. Judy wasn't sure if that was a good thing or not. She really did hate that waterbed. But then it would have caused such a mess if it had leaked everywhere.

Then she gasped with anguish. Eddie was about to start making the place look turned over downstairs. But there were limits to such authenticity.

'No. Not the china.' Judy was insistent. There was no way Eddie was going to be allowed to destroy her vast collection of china memorabilia. She had lovingly collected it over years and years. It was the one possession in that house she cared about.

'But this is supposed to look like a burglary.'

Eddie was only trying to be a thorough professional. He wanted to make sure the cops were convinced. Judy would have none of it.

'Just leave it. We can still make it look good without ruining everything.'

Eddie just shrugged his shoulders. She was paying him so it was up to her. But he certainly would have done things a lot differently.

Within a few more minutes, it was time for Eddie to make his escape out of the back door. But first he wanted his down payment for the job. Judy handed over $1,000 and let him take two rings from a jewellery drawer. The rest would be delivered to him within a week.

Seconds later Eddie was gone. Now the whole scenario was starting to dawn on Judy. Debra could clearly see the relief on her friend's face. The two women embraced once more. They had done it. They had got rid of the animal. There was a big wide world out there waiting to be conquered. They were on their way. They had right, if not exactly God, on their side.

But before they could leave the ransacked house, they needed to make sure the coast was clear. First Judy checked down the street. It was mid-morning: husbands at work, mothers out shopping. Deadly quiet. Debra glanced out of the back door just in case. But there was no one around. Time to celebrate.

The Italian restaurant was so crowded that Judy and Debra were hardly noticeable. The only unusual thing about them was that they ordered a bottle of expensive white wine. Few people drink alcohol at lunchtime in middle America. But then Judy and Debra had good reason to propose a toast.

'To us. Long may we live.'

It sounded innocuous enough. But if only some of the other customers realised what those two women were so happy about. If only they had known that just one hour earlier they had witnessed a brutal killing that they had organised. Perhaps it was entirely apt they should celebrate in an Italian restaurant. After all, they were acting like a pair of Mafia contract killers.

But it wasn't just a new life that Judy was looking forward to. She reckoned Clarence's life insurance would be worth at least $100,000 and then there was the $150,000 mortgage paid house.

Mrs Benkowski was going to be a very merry widow indeed.

'He's been murdered! He's been murdered!'

Judy's screeching tones sounded truly horrific to Addison cop Det. Sgt

Tom Gorniak. He had been patched through to the Benkowski home after the nearby police station had received an emergency call from Debra and Judy, who had discovered Clarence shot dead on their return from a shopping trip.

In a three-way conference call between his patrol car, the police station switchboard and Judy, he was trying to ascertain what had happened as he rushed around to South Yale Avenue.

Gorniak had no doubts this was a genuine call. He was facing his first murder enquiry in a month. Within minutes he was on the scene.

An ambulance had already arrived when he got to the tidy, white painted house. Gorniak immediately consoled the two women and got a uniformed officer to escort them from the house.

Then he began a detailed inspection of the property. Gorniak knew he could not disturb anything until the crime scene technicians arrived, but he was well aware that this was the best time to look around. To get a feel for what must have happened.

Within minutes, he found himself puzzled by certain aspects of the crime. At first, he couldn't quite work it out. Then he realised what was bothering him.

The victim's body was laid slumped in bed as if he had been taking an afternoon nap. How could he have slept through the noise of an intruder who then leant over him and fired three bullets into his head at close range?

Gorniak knew that few burglars would do that. In fact, few would even carry a gun and even if they had, they would have been reluctant to use it. A good burglar gets the hell out of a house if he is disturbed. All he wants is the goods as fast as possible. If someone stumbles upon him, his first response is to run – not shoot. No, thought Gorniak, this victim was asleep when he was shot. He did not even have time to turn around and see who his killer was.

Then the policeman noticed the clothes thrown from the drawers over the body. That meant the killer had ransacked the room *after* the shooting. It just did not make sense. This guy would have got out of there as fast as possible following the shooting.

Gorniak had been a policeman for 10 years. He knew how dangerous it was to draw any conclusions at such an early stage in a murder enquiry. But this most definitely looked like a contract killing.

'Did your husband have any enemies Mrs Benkowski?' Det. Sgt Gorniak was trying to be as gentle as possible. After all, this was the widow he was talking to and she seemed really cut up badly.

No. He had no enemies.

Gorniak had a hunch, nothing more than that. But it was enough to make him persuade Judy to stay on at the police station for a little longer that evening. He explained to her that he knew how awful she must be feeling but it really would be in everyone's interests if she stayed behind. Judy agreed. She did not want to appear to be hindering the police enquiries in any way.

Gorniak and his colleague Det. Mike Tierney began to gently probe the widow for clues. They were convinced there was still a lot more to tell about this case. Judy, meanwhile, was getting edgy. She knew she had to tell them something. Maybe a half truth would solve her problems. Then they would leave her alone and go after the murderer?

'I did see someone outside the house this morning,' she recalled.

Gorniak and Tierney raised their eyebrows. Why didn't she mention this before? How could she have forgotten to tell us this earlier?

Judy then described how she had returned from her shopping trip with her friend and they had seen this rather short, stocky black man.

'Now I come to think of it, he did seem to be running away from our house,' said Judy.

The two officers were astonished. They started to pull in the reins a little bit. They sensed that Judy knew more than she was letting on.

The next step was to haul Debra Santana in for questioning. As the detectives waited with Judy for her friend to arrive, they tried an old and trusted technique.

'It would help us if you could tell us everything you know,' said Gorniak.

Judy waited for a moment. It was just like a weightlifter pausing before lifting a barbell over his head. She had a lot of weight on her mind and those officers knew it.

'I know the black man who was running from my house. His name is Eddie Brown. He is Debra's boyfriend.'

Tom Gorniak and Mike Tierney were about to hear a full confession to murder.

In September, 1989, Judy Benkowski cried when she was sentenced to 100 years in prison for hiring a hitman to murder her husband.

Du Page County prosecutor Michael Fleming had argued that Benkowski should receive the death penalty.

But Judge Brian Telander ruled that there were mitigating factors that 'precluded the imposition of the death penalty.'

These included no prior criminal record, numerous health problems and several character witnesses who testified on her behalf.

Fleming described the sentence — which means Benkowski will not be eligible for parole until she is ninety-seven — as 'fair and appropriate. She claimed she wanted a divorce and he wouldn't go along, but she never even talked to a lawyer about it.'

On August 31, 1991, Benkowski married sweetheart Clarence Jeske at the Dwight Correctional Institute, in Illinois. The couple had first met before her husband was murdered but they both insist their relationship did not begin until after the killing.

By a strange twist of fate, Jeske now lives in that same 'house of death' in South Yale Avenue. He has been made legal guardian of Judy's two children by her marriage to Benkowski.

16

THE CHILDREN SLEPT ON

She had an affinity for light. Her skin was luminous. Her dark hair glistened. But it was the brown of her eyes, like jewels on velvet under a storekeeper's spotlight, that were the source.

He looked into them, felt their warmth, oblivious of the darkness to come. For somewhere, within her stunning beauty there lay a twisted mind. A mind warped by time. A mind that wanted him all to herself. A determination to get what she wanted — no matter what the cost. How dearly the innocent would have to pay.

But for the moment, Lydia Galladan just wanted her lover Augusto Pineda. She wished to obey his every command. She wanted him to be her master.

Augusto could barely endure her presence without feeling an overwhelming lust for her. Every time he looked at her, he thought of the passion, the unashamed love making that knew no bounds. He knew she would do anything for him. It was an extraordinary sensation — knowing that your lover would obey any request, however bizarre. Lydia just could not refuse. She was obsessed and infatuated with Augusto. He had made her perform sex acts she never even realised existed. But she did not hesitate in her quest to satisfy. If he wanted it that way — then she would do it. Her own enjoyment was a bonus. If she felt a surge of excitement as well then that was good. But if it did not happen, then there was always another time, another place. It was far more important to Lydia to serve her master. To please him in every way possible.

On this day in September, 1982, the red flames of passion were burning brightly between the two lovers. It was mid-afternoon but it could have been midnight for all they cared. The curtains in the bedroom of the tiny apartment were closed. But the lights were on. Augusto always insisted on the lights being on. He wanted Lydia to see as well as hear everything – in graphic detail.

They had arranged the rendezvous the previous day in a coded phone call.

'Ok Mr Galladan I will see you at three.' Augusto wanted to make sure that no one knew where he was really going.

Now they were about to seal their lust for one another yet again. Within seconds of getting through the front door of that modest flat in Philbeach Gardens, Earls Court, South West London, they started.

Lydia took his coat slowly off his shoulders, stroked his neck, kissed him full on the lips. There was no point in making conversation. They both knew what was about to occur. But Augusto liked Lydia to do everything for him. It was sort of traditional in his family. The female would honour and obey the man's every command. In any case he was sure she enjoyed it.

No sooner had she removed his coat than she knelt down in front of him and ran her hands from the top of his thighs down to his knees. She kept both hands spread so that her nails dug slightly into his skin through the flannel material of his trousers. She knew he could feel a tingle. A subtle sensation as her thumbs rode up and down the inside of his thighs. So near and yet so far.

Augusto's only response was to spread his hands through her thick, luscious hair. Then he held her scalp firmly, almost roughly for a moment. Excitement surged through his body. His breathing quickened. He looked down at the crown of her head, covered in those dark, silky locks.

Lydia was still on her knees. Probing him with thin fingers. She wanted it to last for ever between them. She would not rush the act – unless he wanted to. Augusto appreciated her gentle touch but he wanted more. She was there to serve his every whim.

He stopped stroking her hair, and grabbed at it more roughly, pushing her face towards his groin. She did not mind the slight pain of her hair being pulled. She knew he was giving her a sign. He wanted her to take him all the way. She could feel the stiffness through his trousers. Throbbing against her cheek. Then she kissed him through the material. Not enough, he wanted more; he wanted it now. He dug nails into scalp and pushed. It was time for her to unzip his trousers.

The first time Augusto climaxed, she felt nothing. No satisfaction for her. He made no attempt, no move to turn her on. But that did not matter to Lydia. She had already consumed the evidence of his own lust. Now, they were about to start again.

But first, she had to remove her clothes. She knew he would never even attempt that for her. In any case, he liked to watch her undress herself. He enjoyed the pleasure of watching her perform a private striptease just for him. And Lydia was happy to oblige. She was obsessed. She would do anything for him. Absolutely anything.

He could not resist the way she looked at him while she slowly and sensuously removed each garment. Her hair fell forward, across slightly slanted eyes. Each time it covered her face she would flick it back and look straight at him. Then her tongue would push out from between her full, pouting lips and lick the rim of her mouth from one side to the other. Just thinking about where that tongue had been made Augusto rise to the occasion.

The strip was important to Lydia as well. For it marked the only moment in their sessions when she was in charge. When she could provoke him. When she could control his lust. In many ways, it was the most exciting moment for Lydia. Maybe if she had stopped to think about that then she would have realised just how dangerous her obsession was becoming. But Lydia did not consider it. She was built to serve her master.

Now she was down to her red bra, red stockings and matching suspender belt. Slowly and provocatively she unhooked the bra, leaving it hanging there for a few moments. There was just a hint of her shapely breasts below the line of the bra. She ran her hands up her stomach — slowly, ever so slowly. She watched him watching her. Once again running her own tongue around the rim of that pouting mouth. Then she pushed her hands up and under the bra and squeezed her breasts hard. She knew he liked it when she did that. But Lydia had not yet finished. She held both bosoms out towards her lover. Pointing them, invitingly, towards him. Then she knelt on the double bed and began rubbing her nipples between thumb and forefinger. She squeezed them fairly tightly to ensure they would grow quickly. Within seconds they had become bullets, hard and aimed at him. Lydia closed her eyes for a moment and soaked up the pleasure she was giving herself. If only he would do it to her sometimes.

She removed the bra completely, crammed her breasts together and lent over her lover's face, smothering him with the fullness of her body.

Lydia was in ecstasy. At last she was close to climaxing. They had been making hot passionate love for almost 3 hours but this was the nearest she had been to satisfaction all afternoon. Augusto might have come three or four times already but then he was not really interested in Lydia's contentment.

Suddenly, as if by some cruel stroke of fate, the doorbell sounded. Lydia was so close and yet so far. She tried to keep going. She wanted Augusto to carry on. Don't stop now! Not now! But the bell rang continuously. Mocking her. As though there were some deliberate plan to stop Lydia climaxing, to ruin her one and only moment of sheer enjoyment. She tried to keep going but the noise was too much.

'Please Lydia. It might be an emergency. You must answer it.'

Augusto was quite relieved the doorbell had interrupted them. He had long since passed the point of satisfaction. It was actually becoming a bit tedious now – in any case it was almost time to go to work. The bar where he served was expecting him there at seven p.m.

The bell was still shrilling away as Lydia pulled herself off her lover and wrapped a pink silk dressing gown around her naked, burning body. Who could it be? What was happening? Lydia unhooked the latch and opened the door. She could not believe her eyes.

Bella Pineda was shaking with rage as she rang the bell, her mind scarred by the knowledge that her own husband – the father of their two children – was in this flat having sex with that slut. It was just a few days before she was due to give birth to a beautiful bouncing baby boy.

She knew what was happening because she had followed him all the way there. She did not want to believe it. In fact, she had sat there – hot and uncomfortable – in her car outside the flat for nearly 3 hours before she decided to confront them. She knew they could not have spent all that time just talking. They had to have been screwing together. There was no doubt in her mind. She just felt so betrayed.

'You bitch. Where's my husband?'

Lydia was stunned. For a split second she stood there in silence. She just did not know what to say. She tried to wrap the silky nightgown more tightly around her lithe body. It was a strange reaction to the situation – almost as if she did not want her lover's wife to see what he had just devoured.

'I don't know what you're talking about.' Not exactly convincing and she knew it.

At that moment, Augusto appeared. When Bella saw him, it really was the ultimate insult. Her husband and his lover standing there almost naked while she stood by, heavily pregnant with their baby.

'If you are not home in one hour then I never want to see you again.'

Despite the situation, Bella was still prepared to forgive. She did not mean what she was saying. She just wanted to make sure he returned. She loved her husband very very much. She would do anything to make him happy. She was there to serve and obey. But then both women were originally from the Philippines. Their subservience had been ingrained deep within them from an early age. They had a lot more in common than they ever realised. Both existed solely for his pleasure.

Now, even as she stared at the evidence of her husband's adultery before her very eyes, Bella thought only of how to hold on to him. She wanted to make sure that other woman could never have him all to herself. She wobbled away from the apartment feeling a strange mixture of sadness and satisfaction. She had suspected Augusto was seeing another woman. Now it was out in the open and he would have to end it. Bella would never return to that flat ever again.

'Look Lydia. I don't think I can see you for a bit. It's better if we don't meet.'

Augusto was struggling to get his clothes on as he tried to explain to his mistress why they would not be making love ever again. But Lydia was not going to accept it all that easily.

'But I want you. I want to be your wife.'

Augusto cringed. What had he done? This was supposed to be an innocent love affair. But then how can any illicit sex be innocent?

He said little but decided a lot. He was not going to see Lydia again. It was not worth it. In any case, all this talk of marriage was really worrying him. He wanted sex not love. Couldn't she understand that?

'I'll be in touch.'

Augusto did not sound very sincere as he left the flat that day. But what else could he say? For her part, Lydia read the blank spaces between the words all right. But she could not contain her love for Augusto. She had to have him. He was her salvation. Without him, she was just a lonely nurse living in a big, unfriendly city.

'Hello Augusto. I must talk to you ...' CLICK.

Lydia's heart sank when the phone line went dead. She dialed the number once again.

'You must talk to me. Come round tonight ...' CLICK. It happened yet again.

Lydia could' feel the resentment building up inside her. She had to see him. He could not just discard her like this. 'He said he loved me ... He said he loved me ... He said he loved me.'

The words kept ringing through her head. She picked up the phone once more and dialled the number.

'I love you Augusto. How can you do this to me?' CLICK.

The phone went dead for the last time. Lydia thought about Augusto. Lucky Augusto. Happy Augusto. The man who had everything. A wife, two children and a pretty lover. He had it all and she had nothing. She could not stand to even contemplate him getting into bed later that night with his wife after having kissed his two children goodnight. He had what she wanted. She could not bear it. It had to change. She would not give him up that easily. There had to be a way to win him back.

Lydia sat and thought for hours and hours. Every time a plan came to her she dismissed it from her mind because it was too outrageous. But she could not get him out of her head. She thought back to all the passionate love making. The things he used to say to her.

It was then she decided. She had devised a scheme. She reckoned it could work if she planned it carefully. She was obsessed. She had to have him.

The underground train was virtually empty on that early morning of September 6, 1982. It was travelling out of the centre of London to the suburbs when millions of commuters were going the other way. In one carriage, there was a solitary figure staring demurely out into the blackness of the tube. She seemed to be in a trance. Even when the train stopped at a station her eyes did not waver, did not follow the people getting on and off. She was just looking into a huge nothing. A cavity of emptiness. She felt no emotion. Just steely determination. She often thought this way when she about to perform some unpleasant task during her work as a nurse. It helped to divorce herself from the reality. It made the most distressing moments much more tolerable. But this time, Lydia Galladan was about to perform a special duty – one just for her own, tiny, insignificant little self.

She got off at Balham Underground Station. The sun shone brilliantly, market stalls lined the nearby streets, crammed with bustling crowds. But she walked in a vacuum. The grey, tatty cheap shop fronts might as well not have existed as far as Lydia was concerned. She opened the A to Z street directory and marched up Tooting High Road. It wasn't far. In any case, she would have walked a 100 miles to find this particular house. It could have been a war zone anywhere in the world – it would have made no difference to Lydia. She was going to get to that house and perform her duty. Her only wish was to love and obey him and she was about to make the ultimate sacrifice. Soon she would have him all to herself. She neared the house in College Gardens,

Tooting. But there were a lot of people in the street and she did not want them to notice her.

She waited at a corner discreetly. Watching and hoping. Then it happened. She saw Augusto leaving the house. Again, she held back just to make sure he had not forgotten anything. She knew he had an early shift at the bar that day. He would not be back for hours.

Lydia walked casually towards the small terraced, red brick house. She passed it without a glance. There were three builders opposite. She did not want them to notice her at the front door. She did not want them to see her break in. She returned to the street corner in frustration. It was no use while the builders were there. And she could not exactly hang around on the street corner much longer without attracting attention.

So what? she thought. I'll go through with it regardless. She walked back to the house and stopped at the front garden.

'Hello darling.'

The builder's wolf whistle was a form of flattery to Lydia. She returned the compliment with a soft smile. But she knew it was no good. She had been seen. What could she do?

Then it came to her.

Lydia started to pick some of the beautiful array of late summer blooms in the front garden. She would make sure those builders thought she was tending to the garden. For twenty painstaking minutes, she pretended to clear the weeds and other bits and pieces from the flowerbeds. The builder's wolf whistles had long since subsided.

Inside the house, Bella Pineda was blissfully unaware that she had hired a new gardener. Across the street, the builders were getting thirsty. It was almost nine and they'd been on the job for more than 2 hours. Perhaps it was time for a good old fashioned British tea break.

As the four burly men walked off up the road to a nearby cafe, Lydia saw the opportunity to fulfil her duty to Augusto. She knew what she was doing was right, was just. She felt safe behind that knowledge. It gave her the resolve she needed.

It would not be difficult to get into the house. While she had been pretending to do the gardening, Lydia had spotted a ground floor window with an insecure catch. Ever so quietly she slipped the catch on the bay window and silently pushed it up just far enough to allow her the space to climb in. It was a typical front reception room of a modestly sized Victorian terraced house. Toys were spread across the floor. A TV set on a badly made shelving unit in the corner. Beige carpet – perfect to hide a multitude of sins. Two very plain sofas.

No one around. Lydia was pleased. This was perfect. The element of surprise was all important.

Slowly, deliberately, she crept through the room towards the door at the far end. Then she heard a whingeing, whining sound. It seemed like a hell of a loud noise to Lydia in that silent and tense atmosphere. She stopped in her tracks. Sounded as if it was in that very room but there was no one around. She continued walking but there it was again. This time it was slightly quieter but just as disturbing to the soul.

Lydia looked down at her feet. She had kicked a teddy bear with her foot. It had grunted the first time she connected with it. Then it had rolled over and grunted again. This was the nearest she had ever been to his children – the children she wished she could have by him. For the first time that day, Lydia felt a twinge of fear. Somehow that teddy bear's grunt had scared her. Maybe it was the first evidence of what was to come? Or perhaps it reminded her of the task she was about to face?

Lydia reached the door. She opened it ever so gently just in case there was someone in the hallway. The door creaked painfully. She stopped for a second – afraid she would be heard. There was no one around.

Then she heard it – the unmistakeable cry of a tiny baby coming from an upstairs room. She had heard the same sounds so many times before in the Cromwell Hospital where she worked. But this was different. This was *his* baby. The child he had by her – the woman who would not let go of Augusto.

'There. There. There Michael.'

Another unmistakeable voice. Her lover's wife. The woman who had wrecked Lydia's happiness. She was invigorated by that voice. It inspired her to continue. The time was approaching.

But first, a suitable weapon. Lydia went to kitchen. It did not take long to find the drawer with the biggest knives in it. The sounds of the new born baby upstairs and his attentive mother carried on throughout. They gave Lydia strength. They motivated her. They also covered the racket she was making.

Now she was on the stairs. Clenched in her right hand was a huge 12-inch long carving knife. As she slowly climbed the steps, it glistened slightly in the midmorning sun. Lydia stopped on the landing. The cries of the baby had subsided. The mother had obviously got him to sleep. She had better move fast before he awoke. She hoped her lover's other son Donkelly was resting. It would make it all the more easy. She had to get Bella, before she left the bedroom.

She leapt up the last few stairs. There was a spring in her step now. It would be so wonderful. Just him and me, just him and me, she thought.

She burst through the door in a frenzy. In front of her lay tiny ten-day-old

Michael in a cot and his elder brother in another cot next to him. They were both asleep. Bella, however, was very much awake.

'Get out of here. Get out.'

Bella showed no fear. Just hatred. Pure and unadulterated hatred. She saw the knife clearly enough but she would never be afraid of Lydia. Her only emotions towards her were seething anger and resentment. This was the woman who tried to steal her husband. This was the illicit lover who tried so hard to ruin her life. And she had the audacity to threaten her with a knife she didn't have the guts to use?

The moment Lydia heard Bella speak it purely affirmed her determination to get him back from her. This was it. There was no going back.

Bella stepped towards her. She might as well have committed suicide there and then. The knife plunged into her left breast, tearing at the flesh, grating metal hard against bone.

The children slept on unaware of the life and death struggle between the two women in their father's life. Lydia twisted the handle of the knife to cause maximum damage. Her rival crumpled to the floor as she pulled the blade out.

But Lydia wasn't finished yet. For a moment, she stood above Bella's contorted body and stared down at her. It was a satisfying stare. A look of contentment. But there was more to come.

The children slept on.

Lydia leant down and held the knife in front of Bella's face. She wanted to see that defiance turn to fear. She longed to watch those eyes fill with the dread of impending death. And they were. The self-assurance was gone. Brave Bella was no more. Just a quivering wreck with a gaze locked on the knife. Too scared to blink. Too weak to move.

Calmly, sweetly, Lydia stabbed her in the throat. As the prick of the blade jutted into the windpipe she felt the handle quiver slightly, slicing through the gristle. Then she pushed doubly hard and the knife pitched in through the throat and came out at the back of the neck. It was a fast, furious movement. There was no resistance from the victim. She was already going to another, safer, world.

And still the children slept on. And still Lydia was not finished.

She had to be sure. She had to know that he was now all hers. She craved for the security he could offer her. She had to make sure. She stabbed at Bella's other breast. It felt like one of those sacks soldiers pierce with their bayonets. Lydia wanted to mutilate her, destroy the beauty of her rival. To make sure that if he ever saw her body then he would be so repulsed he would have to turn away. That was how she wanted Augusto to remember his wife. A mess of bloodied garbage ...

She twisted and turned the handle each time just to ensure the maximum damage. Blood gushed out of Bella's breasts and throat in torrents. But no atrocity would deter Lydia. For her, it was quite beautiful. Natural justice.

And still the children slept on, unaware.

It was around the twentieth stab that Lydia stopped for a second to examine her handiwork. The body in front of her was clearly drained of life and much blood. But something inside drove her forward. She had to destroy the body in such a way he would never look at her again.

She lowered the dripping blade and pulled up her victim's skirt. Once again, she started to plunge the knife in. Twenty-one, twenty-two, twenty-three, twenty-four, twenty-five, twenty-six, twenty-seven. There was little or nothing recognisable left.

Then ten-day-old Michael stirred. At last one of the two other human beings in that room had been disturbed by the murder that had been committed just a couple of feet from them. He began to cry. It served one important purpose. It stopped Lydia from continuing her dance of death. The sound was unbearable. Shrill and piercing. Lydia looked down at the tiny infant. She could not stand the noise. It had made her regain her senses but she had wanted to remain in that insane frenzy. She would have carried on butchering that body if he had not cried.

But now she had to do something about it. There was only one answer — little Michael needed a bottle. Lydia was a nurse after all. She knew how to cope in trying times.

Leaving the baby crying there in a room filled with bloody carnage, she calmly walked down the stairs to the kitchen. In the sink she soaped her bloodied hands and arms in much the same way she had done at the hospital a thousand times before. Some of it had turned into a maroon crust on her skin. She had to scrape hard to remove it. But the sight of blood had never bothered her.

Then, having scrubbed herself clean, she carefully simmered the infant's milk before filling a bottle. It was extraordinary — almost as if she were the mother of that child rather than the murderer of his mother.

After pouring the contents into the bottle, she even tested the milk on the outside of her hand — just in case it was too hot. No. It was perfect.

Who said she was not a caring person?

'There you go little chap.'

It was just like being at the hospital for Lydia as she leant into that cot and lifted her lover's infant out and put him on her lap. She had frequently bottle fed newly born children when their mothers wanted some rest. On this occasion the mother would be at rest for ever.

And baby Michael took to the bottle as if it was being given to him by his very own mother. She could feel and hear the sucking noise of the teat being strained by the hungry infant. It did not take long for him to settle once more. She placed him back in his cot gently and carefully. Making sure he was on his tummy not his back — she did not want him to choke after that feed.

On the floor beside the two cots lay the bloodied remains of their mother. Puddles of red had appeared around the corpse where the blood had gushed out so ferociously only a few minutes earlier. Lydia glanced at the body casually. She felt no emotion. Only satisfaction that at last he would be hers. She could not stand in their way anymore.

Even so, her duty was not quite yet complete.

Lydia walked over to the wardrobe and looked through the many brightly coloured dresses hanging in neat rows. Her eye was caught by one very pretty and expensive looking flowery cotton garment. She took it out and felt the material. It was thin, almost papery in texture. Perfect for what she required.

She crumpled the dress up and dropped it next to the partly clothed remains of Bella Pineda. She stopped and glanced at the two children sleeping so peacefully in their cots. They would never know, she thought to herself. They would never know.

Lydia lit the match and dropped it onto the dress. Instantly it caught fire. A look of total satisfaction came over her face. Now she had done her duty finally and completely. They would start a new life together. He would have no past to tempt him back. She had destroyed that for good. Or for worse ...

The flames swept slowly through the room, as Lydia walked down the stairs and let herself out of the front door. No one in College Gardens that day even noticed her leaving. Not even the builders who had admired her so much just a few hours earlier.

Lydia quickened her pace to try and get away from that street before the alarm was raised. She need not have worried. The flames devoured those two little children and the corpse of their young mother before anyone even realised there was a fire.

Inside that dreadful room, the stench of death would remain forever. Those children never stood a chance. They choked in their sleep, still blissfully unaware of what had occurred. Perhaps that was some small blessing at least.

Lydia Galladan, aged twenty-six, would never have been caught if police had not at first suspected Augusto Pineda of that horrendous mass murder.

After days of interrogation, he told police of her existence. She confessed within minutes of their arrival on her doorstep. It had taken the murder of Bella and her two small children to make Lydia realise she would never win back the love of Augusto.

At the Old Bailey on May 9, 1983, Lydia Galladan was found guilty of murdering Bella Pineda, aged thirty-five. She was cleared of murdering the two children, but found guilty of their manslaughter.

Galladan told the court: 'I am sincerely sorry for the harm I have caused and I deeply regret the shame I have brought my parents and my vocation.'

Judge David Tudor Price told her: 'I believe the deaths of the children will hang very heavily on your conscience.' But she showed little remorse for her murder of Bella Pineda.

Augusto Pineda, aged thirty-five, returned to the Philippines shortly after the case to try and start his life all over again. 'It started off as an innocent love affair. I know it was wrong but in my wildest dreams I never imagined it would end like this,' he said after the case.

17

RIVALS IN LoVE

Bill Buss felt as if all the worries of the world were heaped on his broad shoulders. He had worked incredibly hard over the last 3 years to build up the farm into a going concern.

But there were always problems. Then more problems. And then even more problems. As sole owner of a 50-acre farm, he had to absorb all those pressures single handedly. When should the harvest be picked? How many times a day did the cows need milking? How could he afford to maintain all that equipment? It was a never ending task. But farming was his life. He was good at it, and he had no other choice.

At twenty-six years of age, Bill Buss's one remaining ambition was to find the perfect girl and start the family he so desperately wanted ... and needed. What was the point of flogging your guts out on the land if there was nothing to come home to? The 18-hour days were gruelling but even they would all seem worthwhile if he could start a family. Then the never ending list of problems would not seem as bad. A homesteading woman, and perhaps even some healthy bouncing babies. That was the answer for Bill Buss.

Meanwhile, he had to continue grafting away. And the most important task on his agenda that evening was to organize the midnight milking of the cows.

For this was Eland, Wisconsin. And in middle America they take their farming very seriously. Bill was under great pressure to have a full quota of milk ready for the early morning pick-up by the dairy company tanker. It was

245

a vital part of his income from the farm. It did not matter whether it was twelve midnight or twelve midday, the job had to be done and Bill was the only one there to do it. It was his responsibility to have that milk ready for a dawn pick up. It was also his income that would suffer if the dairy company did not get every drop he could supply.

But the worst part of it was the waiting. He could not milk the cows any earlier because they would not yield the maximum quantities. That meant Bill had to literally force himself to stay awake for the midnight session. Sometimes, he would be so tired after a full day's work that he would go to bed at around nine, set his alarm for 11.45 and try to get a few hours shut-eye before heading for the cow sheds.

But on this particular evening, he struggled to stay awake in front of the television. Flicking channels continually as a way to eliminate the boredom, he sat there with a glazed expression. Bill was not a great TV fan. He found it difficult to concentrate on the banal ingredients that make up much of American television. But it kept him awake and that was the most important thing.

As midnight approached, Bill made himself a hot coffee. It was mid-September in Eland and the nights already had a certain bite to them. The dew came early in those parts and that always brought a slight chill to the air. In any case, a hot drink might help snap Bill out of his sleepiness.

On the stroke of twelve, Bill wandered into the vast cow shed to connect the FILL IN to each of the dozens of cows that stood there, resigned to their regular fate. Bill never really gave it much thought – did these animals mind having their udders emptied in such a mechanical fashion? They certainly never seemed too upset but then no one had really bothered to ask them their opinion. And they wouldn't have got much of an answer if they had.

Within 30 minutes, Bill's familiar task was complete. He unhooked the FILL IN and shuffled back to the farm house for that desperately needed four or five hours sleep. He had to be up by 5.30 at the latest. A farmer's work was never complete.

'Bill. Bill. Open up.'

Bill thought he heard something. But then again he might have been dreaming. He stirred ever so slightly but then fell back into that richly deserved slumber.

It seemed like he had only been asleep a few minutes anyway. He needed every second of sleep he could get. But then why did a dream wake him up? Maybe there was someone outside? He grappled for his watch on the bedside table. It was 12.45. He had only got into bed ten minutes earlier.

But now everything was once again silent. It was that eerie silence that fills the air with its presence. Perhaps it was something particular to the open countryside. There were no roads nearby, no gentle buzz of a car engine or the siren of an emergency vehicle. Bill's farm might have been close to town, but there were wide open spaces for miles around.

Bill fell back to sleep. He had obviously been dreaming. What about he was not sure. But his exhaustion was such that it would take a hell of lot more to stop him sleeping.

'Bill. Bill. Open up. I must talk to you.'

Now the high-pitched voice was accompanied by a steady banging on the door. The way Bill heard it, it sounded almost muffled but then that often happens when you are asleep.

'Bill. I know you're in there.'

Bill had no choice. If he was going to get any sleep at all, he had to answer the door. He knew who it was and it annoyed him. He just wanted to stay snuggled up in bed. He certainly did not want to lose another few precious minutes answering the door to *her*.

He wrapped his dressing gown around his aching body and shuffled to the front door.

'All right. All right. I'm coming.'

Now, under normal circumstances, Bill might have rushed to the door to find out what all the commotion was about. Perhaps there had been an accident nearby? Or maybe some of the farm animals had escaped?

But he knew who it was at the door that night. And he was fed up to the back teeth with *her*. Why couldn't she just leave him in peace? It wouldn't be so bad if it were the middle of the afternoon but this was just *too* late.

Lori Esker had no such qualms. She wanted to see Bill and she did not care what time it was. Her love for him was so strong that she felt he should have been happy to see her at any time of the day or night.

Lori just could not get Bill out of her mind. She found herself eating, sleeping and fantasising about him every moment of her day at university in River Falls Wisconsin.

She could not hold herself back any longer. She had to see him. She thought nothing of getting in her car and driving the 125 miles from college to Bill's farm. It was a small sacrifice for love.

However, Bill was not inclined to feel the same way about Lori. She might well have been an attractive, curvaceous blonde twenty-year-old. She might even have been the 1989 Dairy Queen in Marathon County. And she was certainly a girl whom many men would die for the chance to love.

But none of that meant anything to Bill. Sure, he had had a love affair with

Lori after he and yet another dairy princess, Lisa Cihaski, had split up. In fact, Bill had found Lori extremely attractive at first, but he was a cautious sort of guy and she was, well, just a bit too much for him to handle. But he did not regret his passion for Lori. They had a great time together while it lasted. And Bill certainly had Lori to thank for something very dear to him – his on-off-on again romance with Lisa.

You see, all Lori's sexiness had taught Bill that Lisa was the right girl for him. Basically, he could now see what a fantastic girl Lisa was – compared with Lori. It was what you might call the classic rebound.

But Lori had not taken her rebuff that lightly. She interpreted all that passion with Bill as a sure sign that they were meant for each other. Sex meant love to Lori. She had given her all to Bill and then he had turned around and rejected her. In the tightly knit farming communities of rural Wisconsin that was easier said than done.

Now she had come around to Bill's home to lay claim to what she rightly saw as hers. He was not going to get off that lightly.

As Bill unbolted the front door, he knew exactly what to expect. After all, in the 3 weeks since he had ended his affair with Lori she had been virtually haunting him. This was obviously going to be the price he would have to pay if he was to revive his love for Lisa.

But Lori refused to even acknowledge the existence of Lisa. As far as she was concerned, Bill was her property. She had given herself to him in every sense of the word. 'Oh Bill. I'm sorry if I woke you.'

Lori was not sorry at all and Bill knew it. What he did not realise was the extent to which he was becoming the sole object of her fantasies.

Before leaving college that night for the long drive to Bill's home, Lori had found herself swamped with desire for Bill. She had been planning to leave directly from the campus classroom to drive to Eland but as she sat in the lecture hall her mind wandered to the last time she had made love to Bill. She remembered every detail of their passion.

When class ended, Lori decided she had to make a quick diversion to her digs at the other end of the campus. It would only hold her journey up by a few minutes, she thought. She could feel her breath getting uneven with the expectation that she would soon be with Bill once more.

As she burst into her college room, she was relieved to see that her room-mate was not around. Lori ripped open the wardrobe. She wanted to find something very special to wear for Bill.

For a few moments she panicked. Where was it? Maybe she had left it at home? She had to find it. She wanted to use it to convince Bill there was still a great physical need between them.

At last, she saw it hanging there. Just finding it had aroused her. She laid the silk all-in-one teddy on her bed and pulled out a small suitcase to pack a few other overnight belongings. The teddy was really a skintight negligee – the same shape as a swimming costume but with an even more extreme, plunging neckline. Around where a woman's breasts would snugly fit were edged see through lace. Lori was about to put the teddy into the bag when she stopped momentarily. She sat on the edge of the bed and tried to picture the scene later that night. The scene she hoped would seal her love for Bill.

She recalled how shy Bill always was as she thought about those first few inevitably awkward moments whenever they began kissing. She always had to lead the way to the bedroom, undo his trousers, fondle him and then show him where she wanted to be stroked and caressed. He would always want to immediately push his hand between her legs. She had to teach him that there was more, much more, to a woman's desires. Bill would also often lose interest if Lori decided to dart into the bathroom to quickly change into something sexy for bed. By the time she reappeared, he would often have drifted off to sleep

That made Lori decide to take some defensive action. I'll put it on now, she thought to herself. So, she peeled off her tight fitting jeans and blouse and bra and slipped on that slinky, sexy feeling negligee. Lori could already begin to feel a certain warmth running through her body.

As she pulled it up over her milky white thighs, she momentarily closed her eyes and thought of what she hoped was to come later that evening. She was standing in the middle of the room pulling the straps of the teddy up and over her shoulders. It was a really snug fit. That smooth, silky material felt warm against her cold nipples. She could feel them going erect. She began to wonder if she could hold herself back for the next few hours.

For a few moments she stood there in the room and looked at herself in the full-length mirror. Her left hand moved up to touch the blue silk where her nipple was pressing against the material. She could feel a tingle running through her body down to between her thighs.

She sat down once more on the edge of the bed and let her right hand travel slowly down across her flat stomach to the tops of her legs. She was trying desperately to resist the urge to push her hand down between those thighs. Her legs opened just enough for a noticeable gap to appear. Her fingers were pressing and stroking the flesh just inside the tops of those thighs. She was only half an inch away from the mound she so desperately felt the urge to stimulate.

But she thought better of it. I have to save myself for Bill. It will be much better that way. It was a real dilemma for someone as sexually keyed up as Lori, but she wanted it to be something really special with Bill that night. She was going to do everything imaginable to win him back. If she satisfied herself now, it might detract from that eventual, all-consuming pleasure.

Hurriedly, Lori pulled on a figure hugging skirt and a loosely fitting blouse. Making sure it was open just enough to reveal a glimpse of the see-through edging of the teddy where it covered her breasts.

Then, as a final touch, she put on her highest, newest, white stiletto heels. The seduction uniform was complete. Back at Bill's farmhouse at that ungodly hour, Lori neither knew nor cared about her ex-lover's exhaustion from a hard day at work. She just wanted a guarantee that her unashamed seduction techniques would lead to the long term love she was convinced she deserved.

Bill blinked through his sleepy, weary eyes at Lori. He really did not need this one bit.

'Lori. Why don't you just go home. It's so late and I'm exhausted. Please. Let's talk in the morning.'

But Lori could not hear him. She was stripping his body with her eyes. His hair may have been ruffled. He might have looked unkempt with a full day's stubble, but she loved him all the more for it. She pushed into the house and shut the door firmly behind her.

'I want you Bill. I cannot stand it. I have to have you. I want every part of you. Make love to me now. Here. You have to.'

Now, many men might have succumbed there and then to Lori's advances. But not Bill. He had made a commitment to Lisa. He had even asked her to marry him. In any case, he was dog tired from his exhausting work schedule. Sex was the last thing on his mind at that moment.

'Go home Lori. Just leave me alone. It's over.'

Once again, Lori was not listening. She wanted what she wanted and nothing was going to get in her way. Bill did not know what to do. Lori had called around late at night before but she had always eventually accepted his pleas and turned around and left him. But this time she seemed like a woman possessed. Her eyes were fiery and alive with lust and obsession all rolled into one.

Usually, by this stage in the proceedings, Lori would have just walked out of the house. But on this occasion she was not budging. For a moment, Bill looked at her. He had to confess she looked gorgeous. The high white stilettos had somehow given her more poise. By adding those extra inches to her height, it seemed to accentuate her curves. The tightness of that pencil thin skirt where it covered her shapely bottom and the fullness of her firm breasts pressing hard against the silk blouse. He remembered how much Lori loved the feel of silk against her bare skin ...

Bill snapped out of his trance. He had to get Lori out of that house somehow. He was not prepared to risk losing Lisa for a silly one-night stand. In any case, that was not the way Bill Buss ran his life. He was an honest, decent citizen who just wanted to lead a perfectly normal, trouble-free existence.

'I am going to bed Lori. You can stand here all night if you like. But I've got to get up early.'

Bill stomped away towards his bedroom. He was seriously pissed off but he could not think of any other way of handling the situation other than physically throwing her out of the house. And Bill was far too much of a gentleman to even consider that option.

Maybe now I can get some peace, he thought as he slipped back into bed. He was convinced she would let herself out of the front door and leave him in peace for a few hours. Lori Esker had no such intention.

She had been thinking through every moment of her great seduction scene for the 3 hours it took to get to Bill's home. She had her own masterplan and she was about to put it into action.

She had to act swiftly. She did not want Bill to fall asleep – then he would be useless. She craved for physical satisfaction as well as that long term aim to be his wife and mother to his children.

Standing there in the hallway of the tidy bachelor house there was only one thing for it. A plan that no man would be able to resist.

Lori hastily unbuttoned her blouse. It dropped to the floor. Then she wriggled out of her tight fitting skirt. Anticipation flooded through her veins. It was just like earlier when she changed her outfit at college, but this time the object of her desires was just a few feet away.

Wearing just that dark blue silk teddy and those high white heels, Lori walked slowly through the darkness towards the bedroom she had once got to know as well as her own.

She opened the door silently. It was as if she was a burglar desperate not to be heard. The truth was that she was an intruder and she had plans to steal Bill's body. Not surprisingly, Bill was already drifting off to sleep and did not hear a sound as his seductress crept into the bedroom.

Lori stopped momentarily and looked at Bill's broad, naked shoulders as he lay curled up like a young child in the double bed. She had to have him. Still ever so quietly, she lifted the sheet that covered him from the waist downwards and knelt over his body.

Both his legs were caught between her thighs now. She had him trapped. She could even feel the points of her stilettos sticking into her own buttocks. It was a pleasant, if slightly painful, sensation.

Bill was shocked. He knew exactly what was happening. But he could not actually comprehend what Lori was trying to do. She must be crazy, he thought to himself. He lay there too stunned to move. In any case, she had him firmly trapped between her thighs. There was no escape. But then how many men would want to get away from this?

'I am going to have you Bill. Nothing will stop me.' Lori's hand darted down between Bill's legs and grabbed at his penis. She started to stroke him. It was virtually impossible – even for Bill – not to start getting an erection.

'I cannot stop wanting you Bill. You have to satisfy me.'

Bill was wriggling now. Trying to loosen her vice like grip on him. While one of her hands continued caressing him, she began to stroke her own nipple through the midnight blue silk teddy.

Lori was telling Bill in her own inimitable way that if he did not return her passion she would still satisfy herself. And there was another, almost as strange, aspect to this as well. For she started to talk in fantasies – to tell him about her innermost thoughts.

'I love watching you on the tractor. It makes me excited to watch you with that thing between your legs.' Bill was astounded. He had never heard a woman talk like this. Lori wasn't shocked though. This time she was the one driving that tractor, in a sense. And the sexual excitement was going through her body like a rush of adrenalin.

She closed her eyes and remembered how months earlier she had watched Bill on his tractor. She recalled how she would focus in on his buttocks as they jigged up and down slightly in motion with the movement of the vehicle.

She watched transfixed for ages. She kept speculating that maybe he had an erection as he drove the tractor. But then Bill was not really the type of guy you asked those sort of questions. Instead, Lori kept it stored in her memory bank for those lonely moments when she was lying on her own in her little single bed at college.

There was something about the tractor and the way Bill would sit astride it. She kept imagining she was that seat. She would fantasise that he was sitting on her, dominating their lovemaking. The reality of the situation was that she was always the one on top.

And, as she sat firmly on his naked body that night, she was reminded yet again of those sexual preferences. Bill, meanwhile, was dumbstruck. He did not know how to handle the situation.

A beautiful blonde, dressed in a silk, partly see-through teddy complete with white stilettos was trying to force him to have sex against his will – and better judgement. And Lori's enthusiasm knew no bounds. She was gently rubbing her body against his chest in a desperate attempt to get him aroused. Her left hand was still stroking his groin. Squeezing and then pulling at it. Never letting up. She would not let go. She wanted him to keep a full erection.

Then Bill snapped. He could not stand it a moment longer.

'Get out. Just get out and leave me alone. I don't love you. I love Lisa.'

Lori ignored Bill for a few moments still. She continued her desperate efforts to arouse him.

'Get off me. Just get off me.'

Bill's final outburst actually worked. Lori stopped in mid-stream. She clambered awkwardly off her former lover and walked out of the bedroom without saying another word.

Minutes later, he felt a great surge of relief when the front door slammed shut.

Bill hoped he had finally got Lori permanently out of his life.

'I'll pay cash. It's just that my grandma needs me to help her move house.'

Lori sounded desperate to the rent-a-car woman at Wolf's Auto Centre, in River Falls. She was really one year too young to qualify for a hire car but Kassandra Hotchkiss felt sorry for this well-mannered, attractive young girl. After all, she was going to help her granny.

'Just this time, we'll make an exception. But you make sure you don't get in any trouble.'

It was typical of Lori really. She had that sweetness and charm that almost always got her precisely what she wanted. She used to love twisting her mom and pa around her little finger. At the family's 450-acre farm in Hatley, Wisconsin, it was no surprise she ended up being crowned Marathon County Dairy Queen in 1989. She wanted that title badly, so she went out there and got it. Butter wouldn't melt in Lori Esker's mouth, they all used to say. And all the boys at Wittenberg-Birnamwood High School used to worship the very ground she walked on.

Back at the car rental office, Lori was delighted and relieved that she had managed to hire a vehicle. She had got a very important errand to run that evening. It was something that she was sure would change the whole course of her life. Lori wanted to be certain the lady in the rent-a-car office knew precisely why she was hiring a car. It was all part of one of those masterplans that Lori was so fond of having.

She also wanted a car that would definitely get her the 125 miles from college back to Birnamwood, where she aimed to make a very important rendezvous. The journey between River Falls and Lori's home area was mainly one long quiet interstate freeway much like many of the motorway routes that dominate the United States.

There was never much traffic on the road and that meant it was not the sort of place a young single girl should drive alone in a less than reliable car. Hence her decision to hire a vehicle.

The drive was fairly monotonous. The car had a radio but no cassette deck. Lori had to make do with some less than endearing radio stations blaring out rather dated seventies hits like the Eagles and Steve Miller. Next time, she thought to herself, I must make sure I ask for a car with a cassette machine.

But the easy drive did give her an opportunity to think about Bill. Even the way he had rejected her seduction attempt did not put her off. She convinced herself he was just a shy kind of guy and, in any case, it was Lisa's influence that was making him less responsive towards her. But Lori was going to do something about that.

Then Lori began thinking about the good times – the moments she was determined to re-live when he became her husband. Her mind began to drift once more towards her own private fantasy – his tractor driving.

Now she was nearing the moment when she could really influence their future together. That determination was in itself a pleasant sensation for Lori. She liked to be in control. She did not like losing at anything. She nearly lost Bill. Now she was going to win him back – whatever it took.

Lori's rented Dodge saloon car hardly stuck out amongst the other vehicles parked outside the Rib Mountain Howard Johnson Motel in Birnamwood. This was the sort of place where traveling salesmen make overnight stops during their high mileage trips from town to town in middle America. And the majority of them drove cars very similar to Lori's Dodge.

Lisa Cihaski had just finished her late shift at the motel and was walking towards her own car parked just near the Dodge.

'Hey Lori what you doing here? I thought you were at college?'

Lisa was surprised and edgy. There was only one possible reason for Lori to be there.

'I must talk to you Lisa. Now.'

Lori's voice was cold and unemotional. She was virtually barking an order at Lisa.

The two girls got into Lisa's car. There was no one else anywhere in the car park that night. No witnesses to the horrors that were about to occur.

'You've got to stop seeing him,' said Lori. 'He's mine you know.'

Lisa was astounded. She had always known about the existence of Lori. After all, her love affair with Bill the first time around had long fizzled out when he met and fell for Lori. There was no suggestion of Bill two-timing one girl for the other. But Lisa was also painfully aware that Lori had been very upset when Bill had broken off that romance to go back to his former love.

There had been incidents in the previous few weeks. Like the time Lori had called her a 'bitch' and a 'slut' when their paths had crossed in a local bar. It was humiliating in public but Lisa did not really think twice about it. She put it down to a bit of old fashioned jealousy. She could not believe that Lori would take things any further.

Bill had not dared tell her about the midnight visits. The silky teddies. The high heels. The demands for sex. He probably knew she would find it difficult to believe that nothing had happened on those fateful nights.

Now Lisa was facing Lori alone. It could end in trouble but nothing she couldn't handle. Or so she must have thought at the time.

Lori had one great advantage over Lisa: she had been planning this moment for quite a while. She knew exactly how she was going to handle the situation. She wanted Bill back. She believed he was rightfully hers.

'You know, I may be pregnant by Bill don't you?' Lori's outburst was deliberately timed for maximum damage. She had caught her rival off guard. Lisa was stunned. She did not believe Lori. She knew how obsessed she was. She was not going to give up her husband-to-be that easily.

It was a shock for Lori. She had calculated that Lisa would be knocked sideways by this revelation. She had convinced herself that it would destroy any love Lisa might have for Bill. But she could not have been further from the truth.

'I don't believe you. You're lying because you want him back.'

This was not all going according to Lori's carefully staged plan by any means. Lisa was showing the one characteristic that Lori did not know how to handle – unswerving loyalty.

Lisa believed in Bill. She had also known him for much longer than Lori. She knew he would have told her first. He was an honourable, simple kind of guy. He just did not deceive girls. That's why she wanted to marry him so badly. In Lisa's mind, that was precisely the reason why she would end up being Mrs Bill Buss not her.

'I tell you it's true,' said Lori.

It was a last desperate bid and it was falling on deaf ears. Lisa knew it wasn't true. Lori's plan had backfired. Now she had to think fast. She had no intention of just letting Lisa walk off with her man. She had thought she could warn her off with the pregnancy story. It was not enough.

'Get out of my car,' said Lisa. 'I never want to see you again as long as I live.'

She never would.

Lori looked around her inside that car. She wanted to do something to Lisa. She wanted to punish her for stealing her man. She wanted to leave Lisa with something she would never ever forget.

In the back seat of the car, Lori saw a blue belt. If she could somehow get to that belt then she could teach Lisa a real lesson.

Lisa, meanwhile, was getting impatient. She wanted Lori out of her car … and out of her life.

Something snapped at that moment. Lori leant over and grabbed at the belt.

Lisa could not fully comprehend what was happening. She looked quizzically at Lori at first. Unsure what the other girl was doing by taking that belt from the back seat. Within seconds, Lori had wrapped that it around Lisa's neck. Now she had the upper hand. Now she could make her rival squirm, apologize for muscling in on her man.

The shock and surprise of what was occurring combined with the sheer brute strength of the heavier-set Lori was too much for Lisa to contend with. With a soft cry of terror, she tried desperately to pull the belt away from her neck. But she could not even get her fingers around it. The inside of that car felt icy cool as the belt dug deeply into her windpipe. She tried to grab at it but she could not summon the energy. Already, all that life was being drained away from her lithe young body. Her heart felt swollen by the sheer terror of what was happening. It was pumping furiously. She could feel it hitting her chest each time.

All she could see out of the corner of her eyes was the belt. It seemed to have a mind of its own. She could feel the heavy breath of her assailant but she could not see any part of her face. Then nothing but bars of light and darkness. Stars floating in front. The soft felt of the interior lining of the roof of her car went out of focus, merged with the light, closed in around her.

Pathetic whimpers squeaked out from between her lips. Little gasps that would have been screams but for the tightness of the belt. She tried one last desperate claw at her assailant. In the process she managed to draw blood from her own neck where her finger nail had pierced her skin as she tried to shake free.

Her head felt like it was coming away from the rest of her body. Her arms went limp.

'Bitch. Fucking Bitch.'

The venomous words spat from behind her echoed large and loud in Lisa's head. They were the last things she ever heard.

Lori quickly realised Lisa was either dead or unconscious. She snapped out of her murderous trance and found herself facing the slumped body of her rival in love. But she had no time to consider the enormity of what she had just done. She had to know one thing – was Lisa alive or dead?

With the cold calculating calm of a professional hitman, she leant over and opened her rival's handbag and scrabbled through the contents of the bag until she found Lisa's make-up kit. She took out the tiny vanity mirror and held it up to Lisa's mouth for a few moments. No mist. Nothing. Then Lori pulled the engagement ring off Lisa's limp finger and put it in her pocket …

On August 24, 1990, Lori Esker was sentenced to life in prison for the murder of Lisa Cihaski. The judge at the court in Marathon County, Wisconsin recommended she serve at least 14 years.

Lisa's father Vilas Cihaski – referring to the first-degree murder charge – said after the verdict: 'Lori always wanted to be number one and she got number one.'

18

THE SHE DEVIL OF NANCY

The sun had not yet risen above the fields of the picturesque village of Rosieres-aux-Salines. But the birds were already singing in the trees and the cattle were grazing peacefully on the green pastures that surrounded the sleepy hamlet.

The fruit trees in the garden of the white-washed cottage were carrying plentiful supplies of apples and pears that summer. Every now and again, a sparrow nestled its beak into a ripe piece of fruit, prompting it to drop to the ground where the insects feasted upon it.

A cock crowed from the distant farm across the fields, near the road where the cottage and a row of charming houses nestled neatly into the scenery.

That narrow route had the rather unnerving name of Ruelle de L'Abattoir – Slaughterhouse Lane. Livestock from miles around were taken there to be chopped up into slabs of meat for a hungry public.

But now the slaughterhouse was no more. Only the name remained. The smell of rotting carcasses was just a distant memory to some of the village's older residents.

When the sun rose above the vast plains on clear dune mornings like this, the white-washed houses gave off a wonderful warm orange glow before shimmering brightly as the day wore on.

The orchard that belonged to the cottage was flanked by well kept gardens filled with blue pine, dwarf juniper and beds of hydrangeas and zinnias.

Inside the house, Madame Simone Weber was stirred by the shrill of her alarm. It was 4.15 a.m. and she had a vital appointment to keep.

In fact she never really needed to bother with an alarm clock. For there had not been a day in her entire life when she did not wake up before it actually went off.

It was hardly surprising really. Madame Weber was a tense, highly strung woman of fifty-six. She had seen much suffering during her life. Perhaps her soul wanted to make sure she never failed to rise each morning? At least that's what she told herself.

Madame Weber was a small, lumpy woman with watery eyes that stuck out from a gaunt face. Her mouth was tight and hard with lips that looked like they hadn't received, or given, much love. A demeanour that did little to endear her to others. And yet, as the early morning puffiness around Madame Weber's eyes subsided, there was a hint of attractiveness about her. Something she used to her great advantage whenever she came across a possible suitor.

By 4.30 a.m. she was up and dressed in a white blouse and tweed skirt. It was an image that cut a respectable figure among the other residents of the village.

She looked out of the window at her garden. A beautiful sight in the low, golden sun.

But the splendour of the scene made no impression on Madame Weber. Her only concern was that appointment. It was a vital liaison. More important than any meeting she had ever planned in her entire life. She could not be late – no matter what.

As she got into her tiny green Citroën and started the engine, she didn't even notice the farmer from up the road waving good morning. He thought nothing of her rudeness. He was used to her strange behaviour and had come to accept it. In fact, he and the other locals preferred it that way. Most of them had refused to even acknowledge her existence after she inherited the house from her husband in 1980.

That might have seemed a heartless response – until you learned that she had only been married to eighty-year-old former gendarme Marcel Fixart for 3 weeks.

The marriage had scandalised the district. Local gossip had it that Madame Weber forced Fixart into a marriage he did not even realise had occurred.

The couple met through the lonely hearts column of a local newspaper. Madame Weber had once run a dating agency herself and knew just how vulnerable the people were who used their services.

Broke and virtually destitute, she decided that a brief relationship with an elderly man could be the answer to her problems.

She was only too well aware that her job at that time, as a washer woman, would hardly impress any prospective partner. So, before her first meeting with the old man, she bought herself a grey wig and renamed herself Monique Thuot – a retired professor of philosophy.

The relationship went slowly – far too slowly for Madame Weber's liking. She needed to marry Fixart to survive and he was reacting to her affections about as fast as a tortoise trying to climb the Alps.

There was only one answer.

At the registry office in Strasbourg, it seemed like the fairy tale wedding of the elderly widower and the retired philosophy lecturer. But Fixart was back in Nancy – completely unaware of what was going on.

His place had been taken by aged retired actor Georges Hesling – paid a nominal sum by Madame Weber to act the part of Fixart.

It worked like a dream. To make matters even better both men died within weeks. No witnesses to the deception.

Fixart's family were outraged when they heard about the marriage after the old man's death. But there was nothing they could do about it.

Madame Weber's survival plan had worked. She inherited £10,000 and a beautiful cottage. It was only years later that the truth emerged.

Her mind was still only on one thing – that appointment.

Madame Weber's car slammed to a halt outside the gates of the battered looking factory on the edge of Nancy, none of the workers trouping in for the start of a hard day's work even looked up.

They were used to seeing the car. Madame Weber was a familiar face and they nearly all knew exactly what she was waiting for.

As the minutes passed by, she sat, looking more and more irritated in her car.

Just 3 yards away forty-eight-year-old factory foreman Bernard Hettier cowered behind a wall wondering what he should do.

He could see the Citroën in the distance. But luckily Madame Weber hadn't spotted him.

Bernard was a good looking guy in a very French, older man sort of way. He still had a good head of sandy coloured hair and he was slim with craggy, almost rock-like features.

In recent months, he had been studiously trying to avoid Madame Weber. It was all his fault really. He should never have encouraged her into his bed in the first place. He should have known better. But his insatiable appetite for the opposite sex frequently led him into trouble.

Throughout two marriages, Bernard had found the lure of the flesh impossible to resist. He would often pick up vagrant women and seduce them before sending them packing. He loved them all; alcoholics, drifters, lost souls.

Like the time, only a few weeks earlier, when he met a dark haired woman in a bar in Nancy. Bernard was sitting quietly sipping a beer when he caught her eye. At first she just looked away, slightly embarrassed by the attention. But he persisted and eventually swaggered over to her table. Few words passed between them. But Bernard was determined to get his way. Fifteen minutes later, he walked out of the bar with the woman, who was in her late forties. He always preferred them a bit older. They were far less complicated than the young ones. In his experience, the older women were more carefree – less obsessed with actual love. More interested in lust.

Less than one hour later the pair emerged from the tiny pension and waved coldly goodbye to one another having just made love.

He had an astonishing record of success. It seemed the Bernard Hettier school of charm really did work. And it was based on one simple theory: all women want to make love, whatever they might say at first. It was this principle that had attracted him to the distinctly unattractive Simone Weber in December, 1983.

She had called him after her lawn mower had broken down. A friend had recommended him highly. Madame Weber should have known how to fix it herself after her many years of experience as a car mechanic and restorer of old motors. But despite spending many hours tinkering with the engine, this lawn mower had her beaten – until Bernard appeared on the scene. Within minutes he got it going and was cutting the grass under the fruit trees in front of her cottage for the last time that winter.

For more than 30 minutes he trundled around the vast garden. She watched him fondly from a ground floor window as he did his job meticulously. Eternally grateful, she asked him in for a drink after all his efforts. It seemed only polite.

As she poured the bottle of beer for him, she felt a slight quiver in her stomach. Her hands shook with excitement. She couldn't take her eyes off him. He seemed so beautiful. Bernard sensed with his ever delicate nose that sex was in the air.

As the drink begun to work inhibitions and altering perspectives, he studied her bulbous features and they began to look beautiful in their own unusual way. He could feel himself beginning to fall for this plump, matronly creature. Fatter women are always more sexy, he thought. They've got more to offer. He felt sure she was thinking along the same lines.

Just one hour later Bernard and Madame Weber were making hot, passionate love in her bedroom upstairs. The relationship had begun.

Now, he was cowering behind a wall in the factory, watching and waiting. Unsure whether to face the woman, whose obsessive love became so unbearable that he broke the rule of a lifetime and ended an affair acrimoniously.

Bernard had always used his easy going nature and superb sense of humour to survive the onslaught of discarded women that littered his life.

He had such a relaxed attitude that it tended to rub off on his lovers. He was proud of the fact that even when he split with his lovers, it was always deemed by mutual agreement. Never acrimonious. Never nasty. Just civilised.

But then a lot of his women did not even know his full name, so it was not that difficult. Madame Weber was an exception to that rule – and it made Bernard feel uneasy. She also happened to know there was no other exit to that factory on that day. She was quite content to pass the time. Her lover was going to have to come through those gates – no matter what.

She seemed blissfully unaware that Bernard was a less than willing participant in this game of romance. He might have told her in no uncertain terms that it was over because he was seeing another woman, but she had steadfastly refused to accept the notion. She needed Bernard desperately. She longed for his body and his company. He made her feel young in a way no other man had ever done.

She was desperate for that physical contact. The emotion. The touching. The sex.

It's no good. I am going to have to face her, thought Bernard to himself that morning.

He could not cower there for the rest of the day. He was exhausted from a gruelling 10-hour night shift at the factory. And now this.

Bernard braced himself, took a deep breath walked towards the factory gate. He knew that Madame Weber would spot him within seconds but he steeled himself to look only dead ahead. She'll get the message if I don't look her in the eyes, he thought. He couldn't have been more wrong.

Madame Weber was elated. There was Bernard. He looked tired but what did that matter? All she saw were his handsome features. There was a sensuous, warm feeling in her stomach. Like getting butterflies but far more forceful. She knew at that point she loved Bernard. Those were the vital signs.

Bernard sneaked a glance to his right to try and make out whether she had stirred from the Citroën. He didn't want to look her in the face.

He hesitated for a moment, taken aback with surprise. The car was empty. Where was she? Perhaps it wasn't her car? Relief flooded back into his body.

Suddenly, a hand grasped his from behind. 'Bernard. It's so good to see you. We must talk.' His heart sank.

The tension returned instantly. Why couldn't she just leave him alone? How could he get away from her? He was her emotional prisoner.

The worst part of it for Bernard was the temptation. Months ago, he had wanted to get rid of this woman from his life forever. But now he was near her, he knew it would be virtually impossible to resist her. The physical need was always in him. Lurking. Just waiting for an opportunity. No matter how much he told himself he hated her, he wouldn't be able to stop himself.

But he truly wished she was not there in the first place.

So far, Bernard had responded with nothing more than a cursory 'Oh hello.'

But that was enough. He had caved in. He had accepted her presence.

He was her captive. Emotionally and physically sometimes he would black out in her living room for no apparent reason. It would always happen just as he was about to leave after giving her the promised dose of passion she so actively pursued.

Bernard always wanted to get out of that house the moment they had completed the act. The feeling of guilt and disgust would sweep over him as she lay there in her layers of middle-aged fat, looking longingly into his eyes. He would turn away in horror and promise himself, 'Never. Never again.' But he always came back for more.

After fainting, he would wake up in her bed and she would be nursing him back to health. Tending to him so lovingly. Spoon feeding him medicine she said would make, him feel better. And he would be eternally in her debt. He couldn't just get up and walk out. It would be so rude so he'd stay there a little longer, duty bound to perform once more.

As if his dizzy spells weren't enough, he'd recently been plagued by regular lapses of memory. On a number of occasions he would completely forget arrangements that had been made after going out with Madame Weber.

Sometimes he would make love with her and find himself slipping into a trance-like state. Losing track of time and staying far too long in her company. His friends began to complain about his unreliability. Why was he always late after he had been with her?

He began to wonder whether she was doing something to him to ensure that he became her prisoner, whenever she wanted him. But it seemed a ludicrous notion. However, it got really serious when he started falling asleep at his desk in the factory. On one occasion, he was almost fired by his boss when he was discovered slumped over the bureau.

He went for tests at the local hospital and the doctors suggested he was perhaps being drugged by someone. At the time he hadn't really clicked. Who would want to do that? And why?

Now, as he stood outside the factory gates with the one women in the world he had no wish to ever see again, he reckoned he knew the answer.

'Let's go to your home. We must talk,' insisted Madame Weber.

Once again. Bernard didn't need to bother replying. This was an order not a request. There was no point in arguing.

As they drove the 3 miles to his modest home along twisting hedged-line lanes, he thought about the last time she had caught him outside the factory gates. How he had sworn he wouldn't let her cast her spell on him ever again.

That was a few weeks ago. And here he was, weak as ever.

As the couple pulled their cars up alongside the flat fronted house, all was still deadly quiet in the neighbourhood. It was still only 6.30 in the morning but in *preparation for the long day ahead* Bernard Hettler felt as if his day was over.

Inside the house, Madame Weber's warmness returned the feeling she had enjoyed so many times when they had been regular lovers. Before she had had to become much more forceful.

She remembered the love they had shared inside the slightly tatty bedroom with its worn, cream coloured walls. At first he had been so energetic, so innovative. He'd brought her to unbelievable peaks of ecstasy.

She made them both a cup of coffee while Bernard wondered to himself how he ever got himself into this messy affair. What on earth drove him to seduce this roly-poly shaped woman? And then expect to just walk away from the relationship. It was obvious she would come after him. How could she – the plain ex-nurse turned motor mechanic – accept that it was all over? She had nothing else. No one to love her. *He* was all right. There were always women around for *him*. But she had no prospects of companionship other than him.

He should have thought of that when they met in her garden on that very first occasion.

Now, as they sat making difficult, almost stiff conversation, it finally dawned on Madame Weber that he was trying to get away from her for good.

There was a certain deadness about his responses towards her. That wouldn't do. It wouldn't do at all. She must make sure there was no escape for him. He wasn't going to discard her like some used car. Not this time. It had happened to her so many times before.

She had put up with his philandering. The constant flow of other women. She even recalled the day she arrived at his house unexpectedly only to find him performing an unspeakable act. What hurt so much was that this with some waif and stray, another woman who was even older than her.

Then again, it excited her to realise what a sexual animal he was.

Bernard was starting to feel slightly queasy. He presumed it was the fact he had been working all night was taking its toll.

He watched Madame Weber sitting opposite him at the coffee table but she was gradually slipping out of focus.

Then he blinked and his vision of her was cruelly sharp once more.

Her mouth spouted words that jabbed in the air. 'How's work going. Holiday. Holiday. You, really.' They seemed like solid objects so that every time they entered his head they bounced around him.

Then his brain awaiting recognition began to drop. Sleep gorgeous, welcoming sleep was all he need. He jerked it up again and just managed to recover consciousness.

He never woke up again.

Madame Weber had a lot of strength in her fat-enclosed muscles. She'd acquired it through her work restoring and fixing vintage cars in her Nancy garage.

She needed every tiny bit of that power to help Bernard from her car to her sister's tiny apartment in the noisy Avenue de Strasbourg in the heart of the bustling city.

He wasn't conscious but somehow she managed to make him look like just another late afternoon drunk as she struggled up the stairs to their floor flat in the four-story Victorian house.

She was driven by a hard determination to settle her love for this suburban style Don Juan once and for all. This was the ultimate test that she had to pass. It would be a true insight into how much she really cared for him.

Jean Haag and his wife Marie were both in their eighties and had been residents on the ground floor of that very same building for 40 years. They knew Madame Weber and her sister Madeleine reasonably well in a neighbourly sort of way.

The Haags were very steeped in their own ways. They couldn't cope with new-fangled contraptions like television. But the pre-occupation that kept them alive more than anything else was a healthy inquisitiveness for all that went on around them. There wasn't a thing that went on in that house or the street outside, they didn't know about.

Frequently they would view the comings and goings from their front window, just by the only steps into the building, or peep through the spy-hole in their door if they heard anyone coming up or down the hallway.

They didn't need television. They had a round-the-clock live show featuring real people instead.

One of their favourite subjects was Madame Weber and her activities. She really intrigued them. Sometimes she would burst through the hallway doors late at night to stay the evening at the apartment. On other occasions she would spend entire days entertaining men friends above them and the Haags would listen, puzzled to the bumps and the squealings, it was a long time since they'd used a bed in that way.

They couldn't help noticing Madame Weber on that afternoon. After all, she did seem to be helping a rather drunken male friend into the house.

Madame Haag watched intently at the window while Weber struggled to find the key. Then her husband spied through the peephole in their door as the couple slumped through the hallway.

They never saw him come down again.

Upstairs, Madame Weber was making a hell of a racket. Bernard now flat out on the floor of the living room. She felt his pulse. It was weak. She began tearing up black plastic bin liners and spreading them flat next to Bernard, tucking them under his back every now and then.

In the corner of the room lay a huge concrete cutter. It was a mean, unforgiving piece of hardware in every sense of the word. It seemed oddly out of place. In the room next door lay two .22 rifles, a silencer and three sticks of dynamite. She grimaced gleefully at the same.

This was the sweet climactic moment. Ever since he had broken off what she saw as their engagement, she had been building up to it. She always hoped they could get together again. But she knew that it was not to be.

She kept thinking of how happy she had been when they were true lovers. Much happier than she had ever been before.

How she survived a first marriage that produced five children God only knows. Her husband had been a quiet, stoic man called Jaques Thuot. But his calmness was soon countered by the sheer dominance of Madame Weber.

It was a marriage that M. Thuot described as 'living hell'.

Not exactly helped by the fact that she got him committed to a mental hospital after pretending he had tried to kill her.

It was the ultimate revenge on a husband whose only sin was to seek a quiet life without the emotional upheaval that was a part of Madame Weber's staple diet.

When M. Thuot was committed to a real straitjacket environment it was, as he later explained, 'like going from one version of hell to another'.

And what of those five children? The unstable nature of her own life rubbed off on them with heartbreaking consequences. One daughter committed suicide in her teens. The reasons were never really uncovered. The son she so doted on was sent away to Germany on national service. He also took his own life – because he could not bear to be parted from the mother he so desperately loved.

That was before the farcical second marriage that was never consummated. Then along came Bernard. But he proved to be as bad as all the others. Actually, in many ways, he was even worse.

At least the others were faithful, if somewhat unlikely creatures.

Now she was planning a future where he would always be in her thoughts. If she could not have him then no one else would get him.

She always knew she had it in her to kill. She had to prove it.

The saw turned slowly at first when she switched it on. But it rapidly gained such speed that it was impossible to make out the serrated edge of the blade.

The man in the equipment hire shop the previous morning had warned Madame Weber that the saw was really built for men to handle.

She was outraged. She had handled much larger bits of equipment over the years. How dare he suggest she wasn't fit for the job. She would show him.

Women are just as strong as men when they really want to be. Men always think they are supreme. They need to be taught a lesson.

But all the same she heeded his advice when he warned: 'It's very dangerous. Handle it with care, or it'll slice your finger off just like that.'

It sounded perfect.

Back in the flat, Madame Weber heaved up the heavy saw.

Protected by a brand new plastic fronted apron and wearing skintight black rubber gloves, she knelt down and tweaked the whirring blade against Bernard's flesh. It was surprising how little resistance it met.

The incision was sharp and precise. Her hand trembled with excitement before she swept the cutter across his chest. It was so easy, the blood burned as it met the hot metal while sealing the flesh as she went along. Soon he would be in nice square slabs. She'd be able to handle him quite easily then.

Oh yes indeed …

Downstairs, the Haags could not help but notice the sound of what they presumed was one of those vacuum cleaners. It seemed a slightly strange noise for a vacuum cleaner to make. But what did they know?

Madame Weber was now beginning to appreciate why concrete block carving was considered by some to be an art form.

Every time she sliced into another portion of Bernard's body she felt an exquisite rush of adrenalin to her brain. The patterns she could make were so pretty. It was so *nice* of Bernard to continue to provide her with so much pleasure.

She had severed all his arms and legs from the torso with ease. It had been a bit like cutting up a chicken after it had been cooked. Now, she had to remove the head. That might be a little difficult? With the blade still whirring furiously she knelt down and held the throbbing machine over his jugular vein.

It had to be neat and tidy. Putting the body on plastic bin liners had worked perfectly. It had prevented the blood from seeping through to the floor below.

As the blade sliced through the throat, she waited for the blood to spurt, but it just came out in a steady, manageable stream.

Within a minute the entire head had been decapitated. Her pudgy fingers grasped the head by its hair. It was remarkably heavy. For a second she feared she might drop it. But soon it was wrapped up safely in a heavy-duty plastic bag. She had bought thirty of them at the same time as hiring the saw.

It was to hide the head from view. It was the one aspect of the dissection she had found faintly distasteful. But there was still work to do – a massive spring clean. She couldn't leave her sister's apartment in a mess. It would be so inconsiderate …

'You have got to help. We know he's in danger. This woman was very strange. He told us she always had a pistol with her, day and night.'

Bernard's sister Monique Goetz was frantic with concern for her missing brother as she stood in Nancy Police Station, pleading for help. Her appeal was falling on deaf ears. The police had heard it all before.

A self-confessed Romeo goes missing, leaving behind a long list of women he has loved and left.

'So what's new?' asked the cynical policemen behind the desk at the station. Here was a man known for his sexual liaisons with hundreds of women and the police are supposed to sit up and take immediate action? He *knew* what had happened. Good old honking Bernard Hettier had arranged his own disappearance to start a new life somewhere else, probably with a new lover.

Back at the tiny flat, Madame Weber was struggling out of the house with plastic bag after plastic bag. The Haags were fascinated. They had never seen so many bags left out for the rubbish collection in one go.

On the fifth load, Madame Weber felt a pang of panic when she noticed a gaping hole opening in the side of one bag. His head might fall out! She rushed to the bin just in time.

By the time the seventeenth and very last bag had been disposed of, Madame Weber felt a weird mixture of relief and exhaustion.

Inside the flat she opened up a suitcase Bernard had left at the flat many months previously, after one of their romantic interludes. It seemed the perfect place to put his torso. In the end, in Madam Weber's eyes at least, he had brought about his own downfall. Now his own suitcase was going to carry his remains to their last resting place at the bottom of the River Marne. His remains would be weighted to the river bed by a slab of concrete from the garden he so lovingly mowed all that time ago. She wanted him to feel the full weight of her fury dragging him down, even after death.

Her sister Madeleine and her nephew had virtually volunteered their assistance in covering up his disappearance. They felt duty bound to help this poor, much maligned woman.

'He's gone away for a while. He doesn't want to be bothered. He'll get in touch when' he feels the time is right,' the male voice on the phone was hesitant, nervous.

On the other end of the line was Bernard's latest lover — the woman who had ultimately lured him away from Madame Weber. She was stunned. How could Bernard just get up and run away? They hadn't argued. There had been no hints of discord.

She felt angry and betrayed. His behaviour was outrageous. But, her friends told her, that was the sort of man she was dealing with.

The blurred voice, who described himself as Bernard's friend, was adamant. He would not be back for a long time. A very long time.

At the factory where he worked, the boss was hardly surprised to receive a Paris doctor's medical certificate stating that Bernard was too ill to work. Madame Weber's loyal nephew took care of that by posing as Bernard in the

French capital city – a long way from Nancy. His stomach pains were so realistic, the doctor warned him to go to hospital if they persisted.

It might be some time before Bernard would be returning to work again.

At the equipment hire shop, the attendant was in a dismissive mood. Muttering to himself 'Typical woman. She goes and gets that concrete cutter stolen. She should never have hired it in the first place. It's a man's machine.'

Just moments earlier, Madame Weber had bitten her lip and held her temper after the man had mocked her when she returned to the shop to pay for the stolen item. She knew she shouldn't create a scene. She wanted her visit to that shop to be as low key as possible.

Madame Weber parked outside a row of garages near her sister's Villa in Cannes. This was where they would hide Bernard's rickety old car. Her sister, a dark haired version of herself in almost every way, pulled open the garage doors and Madame Weber drove the car straight into the opening.

As she slammed the garage doors shut she was overcome with relief. Yet another part of that man's life had been locked away. Soon there would be nothing left of him in the entire world. The two sisters walked away and Madame Weber turned and warned Madeleine, 'We must be careful. People will be watching us. Listening to our every word.'

It proved to be a chillingly correct statement.

Back in Nancy, Bernard's family were very persistent. They wouldn't rest until an investigation was launched.

'He may have been a lady's man. But he wouldn't just disappear off the face of this earth. Something has happened to him. You have to help.'

Eventually, the police accepted that this was no everyday disappearance.

There was only one person the gendarmes could turn to – Judge Gilbert Thiel.

The bearded, bespectacled former lawyer was, under French law, the man who would have to head the investigation – and find out if there were any suspicious sides to the enquiry. His correct, formal title was Juge d'Instruction, or examining magistrate, a position with no equivalent in the British system of justice.

In principle, his duty was to gather all possible facts relating to the matter in hand, weigh them with the proper objectivity and deploy his powers accordingly in deciding whether or not a case can proceed.

The appeals from the family were growing and Judge Thiel knew something had to be done – and quickly Bernard's sister Monique was adamant that Madame Weber was involved.

'It is completely within her powers. She is a strange woman. Mad enough to do it. I *know* she's involved.' Judge Gilbert had a hunch she might be right. Whatever the situation, he had little else to go on, so he launched the investigation by ordering a phone tape on Weber and her sister Madeleine.

'Do you think we should find a new school for Bernadette?' Madame Weber was talking on the phone from her cottage to her sister in Cannes.

They weren't discussing a child as one might presume. They were talking about the car. It was their cryptic code word for it. The 'school' was the garage.

Madame Weber was worried. She had heard strange clicking sounds on her phones for weeks.

She was pretty sure she was under surveillance but she had no hard and fast evidence.

Then she got a phone call from the estate agent who rented her the garage.

'Mme Chevalier. Do you wish to renew this monthly agreement,' he asked.

The officers listening to this were intrigued. Suddenly, some of those missing pieces of the jigsaw were starting to come together.

Judge Thiel and his officers soon traced the garage to Mme Chevalier. Weber had been using a false name and they were on to something. Anybody who uses a false name has something to hide.

The garage door was not difficult to force. The Cannes police were somewhat bewildered by the request of their colleagues in Nancy, but they understood it was a murder investigation so they cooperated.

Inside the tatty lock-up they found Bernard's Renault 4. Now Thiel was beginning to understand Weber's cryptic telephone conversations.

But the car in itself was not enough to prove Madame Weber was involved in the murder of Bernard. They needed more evidence. Much more.

For she had a left an intricate trail of deception across France in a desperate bid to avoid implication.

Judge Thiel was stunned. He had just burst into the tiny apartment on the Avenue De Strasbourg hoping to find some traces of human flesh or maybe even some blood on the floor. Instead he had found nothing to connect Madame Weber with Bernard Hettier's mysterious disappearance.

Then, as the officers casually looked in the room next door, they uncovered an arson that more befitted the safe house of an international terrorist than a grandmotherly widow. He was staring straight into the barrels of two .22 rifles, a silencer, three sticks of dynamite in an old handbag and in a casserole pot in the kitchen, forty rubber stamps stolen from town halls, local government offices and chemists' shops.

It was an astounding haul – and it put matters in a completely different perspective.

But he still had found no trace of a body.

The children playing on the edge of the River Marne, just south of Paris, thought it was their lucky day. They had spotted a suitcase washed up on the bank and were trying to open it.

They didn't bother to think why a breeze block was attached to the handle in order to make it sink without trace. And they wouldn't have known that the blue dab of paint on the stone was the same colour and brand as the freshly painted blue gable of that cottage in Slaughterhouse Lane.

As they grappled with the lock to try and force it open, a man walking on the river bank waved them away. He instantly knew that this was not hidden treasure.

The policeman who eventually forced open the case vomited on the spot. Inside was a torso without head, arms, or legs. In Nancy, Judge Thiel reckoned he had the body of Bernard Hettler.

On November 8, 1985, he and three officers turned up at the white-washed cottage in Rosieres-aux-Salines and arrested Simone Weber.

For more than 5 years – the longest period of remand ever instituted – Madame Weber was kept in custody without facing her accusers as Judge Thiel continued, some said obsessively, to gather evidence that would conclusively prove the crimes she had committed.

On March 1, 1991, Simone Weber, by now aged sixty, was found guilty of the brutal murder of her lover Bernard Hettier and sentenced to 20 years in prison.

In one of the most sensational trials in French legal history she was also acquitted of the murder of her second husband Marcel Fixard for lack of evidence.

The newspapers labelled her 'The She-Devil of Nancy' and it stuck.

19

HELP ME SOMEBODY...
PLEASE?

Shopping malls are a virtual institution throughout the United States of America. They are vast spreads of stores all in one place with just one car park. Very convenient. Very cosy. Very safe.

The idea behind them is that shoppers can get everything they want in one place. It saves time – and time is money.

The Puente Hills Mall, in California's San Gabriel Valley was a typical example. Despite being just 25 miles from the centre of sprawling, glamorous Los Angeles it could have been one of a thousand such malls stretched across the nation.

At any one moment there would be hundreds of vehicles parked in the vast car park in front of the main entrance to the Puente Hills Mall. Mothers with their children. Husbands with their wives. Grandparents with their grandchildren. Every cross section of the local population. The rich. The not so rich. The poor. The not so poor. They all had one thing in common – a need to shop, a need to buy – and Puente Hills was the perfect location.

Besides every type of store, there were banks, estate agents, restaurants and, naturally, a MacDonalds. Basically, shopping malls like the one at Puente Hills were the classic example of the American Dream. Stores competed with each other to keep prices rock bottom. Huge advertising hoardings blared out at you the moment you drove into the car park. It was a place where you could spend all your hard earned cash, but still feel you were getting good value for money.

Robbin Machuca, Eileen Huber and John Lewis looked every inch the products of that American Dream as they sat in Eileen's brown Mercury car at the Mall on August 27, 1991.

Robbin and John were half-brother and sister. Her darker skin contrasting with the lighter brown features of Lewis. Eileen was caucasian – the product of a one-parent middle class family in a cosy nearby suburb. But the racial mix of the group hardly raised an eyebrow in the mall on that day. This was not the Deep South in the 1930s. This was California in 1991 – blacks and whites had long since learned to befriend each other without fear of retribution.

But then you wouldn't think so if you met Eileen's father Gary. He was known as 'John Wayne' in the neighbourhood where they lived because of his vast collection of guns. But, other less kind souls, called him 'White Trash' or 'Redneck' because he still hinted at believing in white supremacy.

Though overpowering, his attitudes had not rubbed off on twenty-year-old Eileen. Her fiancé John was black and she was proud of it. Maybe she was also secretly quite pleased that her father so disapproved.

Eileen loved being in the company of John and Robbin. They had such a laid back attitude towards life. 'Live for the day for tomorrow may never come.' They worshipped that famous line written by Jimi Hendrix. It encompassed their feelings about the world.

You see, so many tragedies had already befallen John, aged twenty-one, and Robbin, aged twenty-six. Their lives were a like web of endless disasters. One outrage leading to the next. Long ago, their American Dream had turned into an American Nightmare. John's mother was an alcoholic. His father a pimp shot to death on the mean streets of South Central Los Angeles when he was a baby.

As a small boy he would throw rocks at the family's German Shepherd dog until one day the dog broke its chain and mauled him viciously. At just eight years of age, he was arrested for armed robbery. By the time he was ten, he was in a juvenile detention centre. Then he joined one of the city's most notorious gangs – the Westside Bloods. It was his escape from anonymity. Now he was a person in his own right. He had an identity at last. A reputation as a cruel, violent gang member. But at least they knew who he was.

Then he met Eileen Huber.

John's half sister Robbin could give a pretty similar account of her background. Her father was an American Indian in jail for armed robbery when she was born. At twelve years of age, she became pregnant by her stepfather. Confused and afraid she denied it at first. Even as the doctor delivered the baby, she told her stepfather: 'You're lyin. You cannot be the father.' But he knew it was true.

A few months later, Robbin's stepfather confessed his evil deed to his wife. He handed her mother a gun and ordered her to shoot them all. Her mother refused. But, to her daughter's eyes, she committed the ultimate act of betrayal by refusing to kick her husband out of that house. Bitter and hysterical, Robbin grabbed the baby and jumped out of the back window of their home. She never came back. She joined the gangs. She did hundreds of burglaries. At fifteen she got jailed. It was a blessing in disguise. At last, Robbin had a place to rest her head. A place to learn. She was taught secretarial skills. On her release she got a job in a mortgage company. Her probation officer was convinced she had escaped her tragic background and could start afresh. Robbin seemed happy. But then there came a turning point. Her apartment was wrecked by burglars in just the same sort of crime she used to commit. She could not cope with the losses. Robbin quickly returned to her old, familiar ways.

It all made Eileen's family history pale into insignificance. Until very recently she had lived in the same house all her life. Even her freckle-faced strawberry blonde looks had hardly altered since early childhood. She was so skinny they used to call her Olive Oyl, after Popeye's girlfriend.

All the other kids used to love going around to her house because it was like an Aladdin's cave of film star fantasy. On the lounge walls were posters of John Wayne, her father's hero. But Eileen's room was like a shrine to her favourite idol Lucille Ball. When people walked in, they felt they were entering a time warp back to the fifties. Pictures of the blonde comedian adorned every inch of wall space. She'd always loved Lucy. They used to say she was just like her. And that made Eileen feel good. On the book shelves were videos of every movie Lucille Ball ever made. They were crammed between countless novels with titles like *Miss Teen Sweet Valley*.

But Eileen started to question her life just a year earlier. She had begun to wonder what future lay ahead. The outlook was bleak. It felt empty and meaningless. Written in red felt tip pen on the wall above the headboard of her bed was a nagging piece of graffiti dated July 25, 1990. 'What's come over you?' The adolescent scrawl begged. 'Help me somebody ... please.'

Eileen's father Gary never even bothered to read it.

Now these three desperate people seemed to be putting on a brave face as they laughed and smiled whilst chatting between mouthfuls of tasty Chinese food in the Puente Hills Mall on that day in August, 1991.

'Don't you care about anything?'

Eileen was laughing as she uttered those words. But there was a serious undercurrent to what she was asking her friend Robbin.

'I'd rather not care than care 'cuz then you get hurt.' Robbin's reply summed it all up really. She was dead inside. She had felt like that for so long she reckoned there was nothing left to lose. Life had dealt far too many blows in her direction. What could she possibly owe to anyone? No one had given her anything but pain. To care would be like paying back a debt that she didn't owe …

Just a mile away at the Lynx Golf Company, fifty-six-year-old Shirley Denogean was leaving her firm's offices for her lunch break. She usually bought a sandwich at one of the nearby cafes but on this particular day she had to buy a birthday card for a relative.

The easiest place to find one was at the Puente Hills Shopping Mall. And Shirley was a regular at the Mall – it was her favourite place to hunt for bargains. In any case, it was a beautiful hot sunny day in the San Gabriel Valley. Perfect for a short drive.

As Shirley turned on the ignition of her silver 1980 Mercedes, her only thoughts were on buying that card and getting back to work on time. She did not want, to upset her bosses by taking an extra long lunch break.

At first the car did not start. But then it was always doing that. Shirley tried again. This time the vast V-8 engine came to life. If only it hadn't.

'She's perfect.'

John Lewis spat out the words between heaps of Chinese food stuffed in his mouth. All three of them were watching Shirley Denogean driving her Mercedes into the parking lot at the Puente Hills Shopping Mall. 'Let's wait until she comes back.'

The two women giggled nervously in anticipation as Lewis barked his order at them. They all knew what was about to happen. This wasn't the first time.

Inside the greetings card shop, Shirley looked at her watch slightly anxiously. The drive had taken longer than she expected. She had to be back at the office in a few minutes. After paying the cashier, she walked briskly back to her gleaming, spotless car. There was no time to waste. In her haste, she did not see Lewis and the two women approach. There were so many people around that day. There was nothing unusual about a black couple and a white girl. Why should she notice them?

'Get in the fucking car – now!'

Shirley Denogean felt a sharp stabbing pain as the barrel of Lewis' gun prodded deep into her back. For a split second she felt annoyed that anyone should come anywhere near her. How dare they? They must have made a mistake. This could not be happening to her surely?

But the reality of the situation rapidly dawned on Shirley when she turned around and saw the blank, emotionless faces of her assailants and then looked down and saw the gun pointing towards her.

'I said, in the car bitch!'

This time Shirley did exactly what she was told. She felt her stomach tighten inside, like somebody had grabbed it then twisted. She wanted to heave through fear, but there was absolutely nothing she could do. To anyone walking by, it would have seemed like a perfectly ordinary scene. Four people sitting in a saloon car about to drive off. If they had looked more closely, they would have seen the horror on the face of Shirley Denogean. They would have sensed the robber's adrenalin pumping, seen the pupils in the eyes dilating through nervous excitement.

'What do you want? Have anything.'

Shirley began ripping open her purse. Cash and credit cards cascaded onto the floor of the Mercedes. She looked at the faces of those two women. She wondered how they could do this. She understood a man but not the women? Surely they must feel some empathy for another female? But there was nothing there for Shirley to grasp at. Robbin and Eileen had done this before. This was just another 'job' – they would not have even known what the word empathy meant. She had money and that was all that mattered.

'Give me the fucking number NOW! Or we'll kill you mother fucker.'

Lewis grasped hold of the bank cash card and yelled at Shirley. He seemed out of control. Almost on a terror trip. His head felt filled with blank spaces. There was no feeling. There was no sorrow. There was no pity. He just wanted the password for that card so he could steal her money.

Shirley watched helplessly as Eileen Huber walked off towards the ATM machine just a few yards from where they were parked. Beside her in the back seat of her own Mercedes was Robbin Manchuca. In front, Lewis. She wanted to scream her head off to alert one of the hundreds of people walking nearby. But she feared they might use that gun if she so much as uttered a word out of place.

This was a battle for survival for Shirley. And pride. Your dignity is the first thing that goes when fear grips you and won't let go. She tried to remain calm but the tears of terror were welling up in her eyes. She felt close to bursting

279

point. But she wasn't going to let them get her. She had to be hard. She did not want to show them her emotions. That would give them instant victory. She did not want them to win.

Shirley looked closely at Robbin. She had an attractive, almost soft face. How could this woman even contemplate the crimes they were participating in? Surely they would not kill her? Not two women? There had to be some mercy there. There had to be some understanding.

By the time Eileen returned from the cash dispenser, the atmosphere had relaxed somewhat. Few words had been exchanged between any of those people in that car.

But something was about to happen. She could sense it. Her hands were sticky with sweat. She felt the silence on them and the air was so thick she could hardly breath.

Robbin stepped out of the Mercedes after Eileen got back in. What was happening? Perhaps they were going to leave her now? Shirley prayed that this was the end of her nightmare. Tragically, it had only just begun.

Lewis started up the car. Just like earlier it did not turn over first time. For the first time in her life Shirley wished her car would conk out completely. Behind them, Robbin had started Eileen's Mercury first time. She waited for her stepbrother and his fiancée to get going. After a few agonising seconds, the Mercedes roared into life.

Then followed a bizarre trip around all the cash dispensers that existed in Puente Hills Shopping Mall. Each time Lewis spotted one he would carefully pull the car to a halt in a parking space and prod the barrel of his revolver into Shirley's side.

'What's the number for this fucking card? What is it?' Shirley had a lot of cash cards in her purse that day – it was like a windfall to Lewis and the two women.

Robbin's boyfriend Vincent Hubbard had been absolutely right when they had discussed a good way of making fast bucks.

'Hit the cash dispensers man,' he'd said. 'It's fucking easier than holding up liquor stores. Fewer witnesses. Less problems.'

Hubbard would have been there with them that day if he hadn't volunteered to stay home with Robbin's five-year-old daughter. But then Hubbard should have known. He had just got out of jail after serving time for everything from robbery to drugs. Cash card dispenser hold-ups were the talk of the cells in the LA County Prison.

Now Lewis, Robbin and Eileen were cleaning up as much cash as they could from Shirley Denogean's credit cards. It was a horrific ride for her. The longer it went on the more certain she was that they were going to kill her. The more money they got the more brazen they became. By the time, they had taken cash out of a sixth machine, Lewis and the two women were positively oozing excitement.

'This is fucking great. We won't have to do another job for weeks.'

Lewis was ecstatic. All this cash was like a gift from God.

'Hey John. We're goin' to have ourselves a real good time.'

Eileen was looking forward to a few weeks without the usual money problems. Robbin – following behind in the Mercury – was happy too. None of them gave a moment's thought to the terrified middle-aged woman they had just kidnapped on a ride to Hell.

They had run out of cash dispensing machines. Now this horrible convoy of death was about to begin its final journey.

'Let's head for the freeway.'

Lewis knew that the nearby motorway was the best route out of the Puente Hills Shopping Mall. If anything did go wrong then they could be away and on the main road in seconds. Shirley Denogean knew what it meant as well. She was convinced it meant the beginning of the end of her life.

'Go ahead. Kill me now.'

Lewis looked around the moment he heard Shirley utter those words.

'What the fuck ...? Shut the fuck up will ya?' Eileen looked away almost embarrassed by their captive's outburst and her lover's reply. But it was only a momentary lapse – she worshipped the very ground John Lewis walked on. She could see no evil in his ways. She did not even stop to think that anything he had done was wrong. He was the man she loved. The man she was going to marry. The man whose baby she thought she might be expecting. The man with so many bloody victims. The man who did not care about anything other than her. She remembered how – just a few days earlier – Lewis had given her a beautiful sapphire ring to celebrate their engagement.

'There you go sugar. Now we are one.'

It was the first time Eileen had ever been given anything in the name of love. She looked at the well-crafted ring and ran her finger tips across the smooth stone. She did not ask where he got it from. She already knew. But she did not care. She did not care that he had taken it from the corpse of one of his victims. She had been a woman very much like Shirley Denogean. Same sort of age. Same sort of dress. In fact they had robbed and killed her after kidnapping her at the Puente Hills Mall as well. That Mall was supposed to be the prime example of safe shopping for a safe society. John Lewis, Robbin

Machuca, Eileen Huber and Vincent Hubbard had made sure that all those illusions had been well and truly shattered.

'I said go ahead and kill me now.'

Shirley Denogean shouted the last word at the top of her voice and smashed her fist down on Lewis' neck and tried to grab the gun out of his lap.

For a few wild moments, he lost control of the car and it skidded across two lanes of the Pomona Freeway. Luckily there was no traffic nearby. Shirley must have wished there had been. Then, at least she might have stood a chance of surviving this living nightmare.

Lewis was furious. His empty emotionless behaviour had been replaced by a fit of temper that was truly terrifying.

He swung his fist across Shirley's face. 'Shut up you fucking bitch.'

The atmosphere inside the Mercedes was now unbelievable. But Shirley was not sobbing. She was angry. Angrier than she had ever been before in her entire life. She was not going to die easily. If they wanted to kill her they had better get a move on because she was going to fight them all the way. Behind the Mercedes, Robbin was apprehensive. She did not care about that woman. But she did worry about her brother and Eileen. They had almost got themselves killed a few seconds earlier. They had to get rid of that piece of trash. Robbin considered Shirley to be just another victim – nothing more or less. She had no feelings about her. But then people she had been much closer to during her own painful life had not cared about her. She thought about her stepfather. The so called, loving father figure who crept into her bed at nights and raped her. She thought about her mother. The one person in the world who should have loved and protected her. Instead, she allowed that animal to carry on his attacks unhindered. Never once did she step in and stop those brutal sex attacks. Not once.

Robbin didn't care about Shirley Denogean. Why should she? Human decency had long ago ceased to exist in her life.

'Go on. Go ahead and kill me.'

Lewis couldn't stand this woman a moment longer. Why didn't she just shut up? Why was she making it all so fucking painful? Shirley knew this was her only opportunity. She had to harass and hinder them as much as possible. Then she might stand a chance. Her instincts would not allow her to give up the fight. She wanted to live.

But all she was actually doing was forcing Lewis and Eileen to face a situation they had already dealt with on at least three previous occasions. They saw themselves as latter day Bonny and Clydes. Rightfully taking what they felt was theirs. Shirley was making a nuisance of herself. Her time had come. Lewis pulled the Mercedes over onto the hard shoulder of the freeway. Just a few yards behind, Robbin came to a halt in Eileen's Mercury.

'I am not getting out. You'll have to kill me first.'

Shirley just would not give in. She knew they would never shoot her there in front of all those passing motorists. If she refused to budge maybe, just maybe, she still stood a chance.

But Lewis was not going to let Shirley stand in his way. He lent into the back of the car and pulled the grandmother out of the seat of her own Mercedes. This was just another one to Lewis. Another face. Another day. Another victim. When Shirley Denogean looked into Lewis' eyes at that moment she knew he did not care. She knew that her death sentence was already confirmed.

At gunpoint, he made her walk along the side of the freeway towards an embankment. Just behind, Eileen and Robbin followed. They knew what was about to happen. They had seen it all before. But Robbin did not flinch when Eileen stopped walking and hung back so as not to see what was about to happen.

'Lie down.'

Shirley did not flinch despite the order from Lewis. 'I said fucking lie down – bitch.'

Shirley Denogean was not about to lose her dignity after all this time. She turned and looked into Lewis' eyes. He tried to avert her gaze. He felt uncomfortable. He hated the way she was looking at him. He felt challenged. But he also felt uneasy. She would not lie down and let him shoot her in the back. She was still looking straight at him. He couldn't handle it. This was not the way it was with the others. He could not shoot into her face and look at those eyes staring at him.

He aimed the revolver at her stomach and pulled the trigger. Whether he hoped to kill her or just injure her we will never know. Shirley fell to the ground instantly. She clutched her stomach but she was still very much alive. Lewis turned and walked away. He could not stand to look at her a moment longer. He did not care if she lived or died but he could not bear to see those eyes again.

'Bastard. You bastard.'

Shirley wanted him to know. She wanted him to realise what he had actually just done. Lewis could not stand the noise of her screaming.

He turned around, walked back towards her and lifted his gun. This time he pulled the trigger again and again and again. Each time a shot rang out he saw her body jerk with the force of the bullet as it entered.

The first shot entered her shoulder and split open a gaping wound. Bits of flesh flew upwards.

The next bullet ripped into the side of her body. But still Shirley fought back.

'Bastard. Bastard. Bastard.'

'Why don't you shut the fuck up bitch?'

Lewis aimed at the head this time. That shut her yapping. He hated the noise. He hated the screaming. It reminded him of reform school when the kids yelled so loudly in the playground before they beat him up. But worst of all, it reminded him of his perverted stepfather and how he would shout at him in fury before forcing him onto the bed.

'SHUT UP! SHUT UP! SHUT UP! SHUT UP!'

With each word he fired again and again. John Lewis had to get all those dreadful memories out of his mind for ever.

Peppering a twitching, innocent human being was a therapeutic way of cleansing his soul. When it was all over he looked up and saw his half sister Robbin looking down at him. She smiled. She approved. They had nothing to lose.

Lewis, Machuca, Hubbard and Huber were arrested in September 1991 after detectives identified them from security photographs taken by one of the cash dispenser machines. An alert shop keeper also took the registration number of Eileen's Mercury when they tried to use some of their stolen credit cards in a clothes store.

All four are accused of at least four similar random killings that terrorised the residents of the San Gabriel Valley in August 1991.

If found guilty they all face the death penalty.

20

THE SCAPEGOAT

Sara Thornton threw the newspaper on the bed of her cell in a fury. She could not believe what she had just read. How could they? How could they? How could they free a man who admitted killing his wife?

She was serving a life sentence for an identical crime. The only difference was that she was a woman and her victim was a man.

Sara had been locked up inside Her Majesty's Prison Bullwood Hall, in Essex, for almost 18 months. Her appeal against her sentence had just been turned down. Yet Joseph McGrail had kicked his frail wife to death and been allowed his liberty. It all seemed so unjust. So unfair. So inconsistent.

Sara faced a near lifetime in prison while Joseph McGrail had walked to freedom from the very same Birmingham Crown Court where she had received her sentence. That made it even worse somehow. The inconsistency of the law was one thing, but when the same court handed out two such entirely different punishments for basically the same crime it was a cruel double blow.

As she walked the jail corridors towards the refectory that afternoon she could not see or feel anything. Her mind was asking over and over again. Why? Why? Why?

'Hello Sara.'

Her fellow inmates might as well not have existed. She did not hear them when they greeted her. They knew something must be wrong but they did not like to ask. The killers often got depressed. Who wouldn't if they faced half their life behind bars?

Sara took a small bowl from the pile of plates at the beginning of the food counter in the prison kitchen. She glanced past the hot, steaming overcooked meat. The broiled vegetables. The stinking fish. She stopped at the salad bar and picked at the lettuce, tomatoes and cucumbers on offer. They hardly looked appetising, but then Sara Thornton did not feel particularly hungry.

She looked at the rows of inmates sitting at the long refectory tables and realised she could not face a conversation with any of them. The strain of prison small talk was bad enough at the best of times, but she could not get her mind off Joseph McGrail. She did not even know the man. Not even what he looked like. But her thoughts were consumed by him. Why did he get freed when she was rotting in jail for an identical crime? Maybe he bribed the judge? Perhaps he begged for mercy? No. None of those reasons seemed entirely plausible. There was only one answer. It was because he was a man. That had to be the reason. What else could it possibly be?

Sara found herself just standing there with the salad bowl in her hand staring into oblivion.

'Are you sitting down or what?'

She snapped out of her self-induced trance the moment she heard that voice. It helped her decide. There was little pity between the four walls of a prison. Sara made up her mind there and then to do something about it. She wanted the world to know how unfair her sentence was. She walked back to her cell with that bowl of salad still gripped in one hand.

A few minutes later, she heard the ominous clank of her cell door locking. It was the beginning of the end of yet another horrible day.

As Sara lay on the wafer thin mattress of her cast iron bed, she started to cry. It was controllable at first. But then she just let the emotion take over. The earlier tension was being replaced by floods of fear and anxiety. There was now no light at the end of her tunnel. No hope for an early release from this hell on earth.

No one else did anything to try and console Sara that night as she sobbed into her pillow. She had no one to turn to except herself, inside that grim, soul-less place. Now she had run out of giving herself reassurance. There was nothing left.

On her bedside table, that bowl of salad lay untouched. Sara's appetite for all things had disappeared. She looked at the bowl for a moment and then sent it crashing to the cold stone floor. She decided there was one last way to force them to, change their minds.

'It's your life Sara.'

The prison officer in charge of her block was not unsympathetic to Sara's plight. But when she announced she would be going on hunger strike in protest against her sentence it merely provoked a sigh of acceptance from prison staff members. After all, they had seen it all before.

Their main aim was to keep the inmates alive and healthy with the minimum of fuss. This was just another problem as far as they were concerned. And it was a problem they could have done without.

Back in her cell, Sara felt a fresh surge of energy. She had inspired herself by deciding to refuse food from then on. Now she had an aim in life – even though it could lead to her death.

A few days later, sitting at the tiny desk in her 8-foot by 8-foot cell, she started to write a letter to her twelve-year-old daughter. The daughter she had been forced apart from 18 months earlier. The daughter she loved and cherished like no other human being. The daughter she so desperately wanted to see again.

Hello Darling,

It is Sunday morning. I feel fine, a little weak I guess. You do make me laugh when I tell you I am going on hunger strike, you tell me to take care of myself. Perhaps you don't quite understand. Either they let me free, or I will die. It is that simple, there are no alternatives.

I think I am forcing people to examine their own commitments to their lives. Just how many people know that things are wrong yet always find excuses not to do anything simply because it is the easier thing to go with the flow?

I feel weak, tired and bone cold but my spirit is strong. My skin is drying out. I'm going to end up just as one big wrinkle.

Sara Thornton put the pen down to rest a while. Her wrist ached from the pain of those words. She stretched and rolled her fingers to warm them against the cold. Then she shut her eyes and thought back to life in the outside world. Was it really that good?

Sara had felt something special toward Malcolm Thornton the first moment she had met him. He was such a nice bloke. Nothing was too much trouble for him. He'd been a policeman once. An upholder of the law. Sara was convinced that made him a fine, upstanding person. A man who could be trusted.

Malcolm was such a contrast from her earlier disastrous relationships. She was ecstatic when he asked her to marry him. She did not hesitate.

Their home in the picture postcard town of Atherstone, Warwickshire, looked like the perfect place for peace and harmony. But then appearances can be deceptive.

'You've got to come quickly doctor. I think he's going to kill me.'

Sara Thornton had been married to Malcolm for just a few weeks. Now she was at her wit's end. Her fine, upstanding husband was not just drunk. He was absolutely paralytic. As she put the phone down she turned to face the mounting fury of her beast of a husband. The very same man who had just a few weeks earlier promised to love and cherish her for the rest of his life was now smashing furniture to pieces. His eyes flared up in an alcoholic blurt when he spotted Sara. He had finished with the furniture. Now it was her turn.

When Dr Kenneth Farn got to the Thornton house on that hot summer's day in July, 1988, he was shocked. Sara was shaking with fear as the drunken lout who called himself her husband lay on the floor of their lounge gurgling and slurping uncontrollably. He looked like a beached whale. His time would come. His time would come.

'You have to sort yourself out Malcolm. You need treatment.'

Malcolm Thornton knew the doctor was right. But then he was sober now. You see, there were two Malcolm Thorntons. One was a funny, bright, witty man who would bowl people over with his generosity. The other Malcolm was like a raging wild animal destroying everything and everyone in his path. Sara Thornton knew both of them. She wished she did not.

But now the charming, reasonable Malcolm was facing up to the facts like a true man. He was an alcoholic and he accepted the fact. Dr Farn wanted to help his patient. Malcolm took his advice and headed for a specialist in London. Sara sighed with relief. He was doing something about it. He was a good man. He would sort himself out. She really wanted the loving, sweet Malcolm back forever.

By Christmas, 1988, Sara really thought she had got him back. 'Mr Hyde' had been beaten back into a shadowy past. And there, she was. The treatment had worked wonders. He was like a different man. She was so happy. So was her daughter Louise, aged ten. She wanted her mother to have the best in life. She deserved it.

Sara really felt true love for him. She had a reason to get up in the mornings. It felt so good to be so content. But it didn't last. It never does when you are dealing with the Malcolms of this world. There is always something lurking beneath the surface. That's why he had taken to the drink in the first place. There was a hidden motive behind his madness. Somewhere in there was a tortured soul desperate to get out. Alcohol was the only way it could manifest itself. It was his release from endless emotional torture. He could not hold it back for ever. Malcolm Thornton was the only person who really understood that.

'He's trying to kill me doctor. You've got to do something.'

Dr Farn was not surprised when he picked up the phone and Sara Thornton was on the line once more. In more than 40 years as a GP, Malcolm Thornton was not the only alcoholic he had come across. Nevertheless, Dr Farn was still very concerned. His priority was the health and safety of Sara and Louise. He did not want to have a battered family on his conscience. Now he had a duty to protect his patients.

At the other end of the line, all hell was breaking loose in that pretty little house in the pretty little street in that pretty little town.

'Bitch. Uhm gunnuh kill you.'

Malcolm Thornton could barely speak the words coherently. But she knew exactly what he was saying. He was raving drunk. Completely out of control. He could have done anything to her. He didn't care.

But she still did not see his right hand clenching into a fist as his fury mounted. The first Sara knew about it was when she felt the knuckles crunch into her ribs. It was agonising. He had put his full, drunken force behind the punch and hit whatever he could focus on. It was easier than trying to aim at her face.

Thornton stumbled as he threw the punch into her stomach. It just made it worse. His full weight was behind it. There was no way to stop the double impact as his fist connected.

Sara doubled up in pain and collapsed to the floor of their lounge, clutching her stomach. It felt as if she had been turned inside out. She tried to push her stomach muscles outwards. The pain was appalling. The internal bruises had already begun.

He stood over her glaring, ready to follow up his assault with a flurry of punches. But there was no need. Sara would never recover.

'I want to kill him. I hate him.'

Sara Thornton knew she shouldn't have said it the moment she saw the reaction on her friend's face. She had spoken her mind once too often. Now was not the time to tell someone her feelings about her husband. It was better to keep everything bottled up inside herself. That way the hatred could fester and fester until she reached a point of no return. Pouring your problems out was too easy an answer to Sara's anguish. If she could rid herself of the hatred and fear just by telling a friend her innermost thoughts then life would be simple wouldn't it?

No. Society much preferred you to keep it all locked inside your brain. Never let it out to anyone. That way we might never know what awful thoughts you have. Basically, most people do not want to know what their friends are really thinking. It might be embarrassing. It might be shocking. It might be the truth.

As Sara quickly changed the subject following her candid disclosure, she realised that Malcolm Thornton was a problem she was going to have to sort out on her own. No one was going to help her. She would have to do it alone.

Malcolm Thornton's life was already falling apart without any assistance from his wife. He had lost his job after being breathalised. He had gone on a drinking spree following his release by the police. He had assaulted his wife. He had battered himself into submission.

What else did he have left in his life other than alcohol? It was his easiest form of escape. When the drink began to take effect he felt a surge of relief. He knew he could forget all his problems for a few hours and just soak himself in the dull throb of alcohol. The mortgage payments. The wife. No job. No future. Who gave a fuck? All those thoughts were left behind while he lapped up the beers and spirits that had become his staple diet in life.

The pubs were like a separate world for Malcolm Thornton. No one bothered him. He could talk to who he liked when he liked. If he wanted to sit in the corner and sup silently he could. If he wanted to talk to his drinking partners about football and women he could. It was his choice. It was his way out.

Meanwhile at home, Sara was at the end of her tether. Her husband – the man whom she so adored when they married just a few months earlier – had now become an out and out failure. No job. No income. No love. No life. And no future for them.

He had put paid to that and she hated him for it. How could he destroy everything around him?

It was all such a waste.

She sat and watched the television but she did not know what was on the screen. Her mind was a million light years away from that programme. She was contemplating the future and it looked bleak.

She had to talk to someone about it all. But who? Her friend had not been interested. Her daughter was too young. Who could she turn to? But Sara already knew the answer: No one. She had to deal with this herself. If she did not then no one else would.

She went up to bed alone as usual that night. He would appear eventually. Too drunk to take off his clothes let alone give her the love and attention she so craved. Sara took out her lipstick and sat looking into the bedroom mirror for a few moments. She rocked back and forth gently yet tensely and shut her eyes and let her, mind wander.

At first they were good thoughts. Louise playing in the garden, wide-eyed, face smiling. Other children looking happy and so contented. Then *HE* came on the scene. She could see his face angrily close up against her own. He was shouting abuse at her. Then he threw a punch.

She snapped out of her day dream and looked in the mirror once more. All she could see was a desperately unhappy face, lined with fear and misery. Sara twisted the bottom of the canister of lipstick so that the red tip slowly grew longer. She studied it for a second. Then she put it between her fingers like a pen and began to write on the mirror in front of their bed:

'Bastard Thornton. I hate you.'

Sara did not go to bed that night after all. It was still early. She was not going to give him the pleasure of knowing she would be waiting obediently in bed for his return. That had happened on too many occasions in the past.

This time she was going to surprise him. Sara tidied herself in front of that same mirror where she had just scrawled her desperate message of hate and walked out of the front door.

This time she was going to have a drink. She had been through enough. Why couldn't she enjoy herself for once. But Sara did not like being out for long. Within an hour she was back at the neatly kept house. He wasn't there. She felt so disappointed: She had hoped that perhaps he would get back and find her gone and start to think about the consequences of his actions.

But he had gone past the point of no return. He did not care. As she sat there downstairs in the tiny living room, she heard him scraping the front door lock with his key. She did not need to even see him to know he was drunk. Probably so inebriated he could not get that key in the lock at the first, second or even third attempt.

It must have taken ten goes before the key connected and the drunken mess stumbled through the doorway. He stood there for a moment and just stared at her. She wondered if perhaps he felt a twinge of guilt. Maybe even a little shame?

But Malcolm Thornton did not feel anything of the kind. His only thoughts were filled with hate. She seemed to be smirking at him. Making fun of him. Trying to make him feel guilty.

'What's your problem?'

He did not really care. He just did not like being made to feel bad. But he would get his own back on her.

'Just come to bed Malcolm.'

Sara had given up on her husband. The message written on the mirror upstairs said it all. She wanted him to know how much hatred she felt towards him. He had made her life a misery. He had destroyed her future. What more could he do? Now he lay slumped on their sofa. A drunken hulk of a man once again incapacitated by the alcohol he craved for. Malcolm Thornton wanted to escape. Soon he would escape for good.

'Well. I'm going to bed.'

Sara did not really know why she bothered saying the words. He was still collapsed on the sofa. He mumbled some obscenity at her but his lips could not keep pace with his brain. He was out of sync. When he spoke it was like an actor in one of those badly dubbed foreign films. His mind was filled with evil thoughts but he was having immense difficulties making his mouth work accordingly.

Then she heard the unmistakable words. The utterance that was totally unforgivable in her terms. The threat that shook her into action. So vicious that it convinced her utterly that he was no better than scum.

'Keep that daughter of yours out of my way or else she'll be dead meat.'

There was no mistaking his words. He had paused long and hard before saying it. No doubt he wanted to make sure he did not suffer his usual lip synch problems. He was determined to ensure that she heard it all.

'Keep that daughter of yours out of my way or else she'll be dead meat.'

Sara sat there in silence. She absorbed the words slowly. She could not comprehend it at first. What did her ten-year-old daughter have to do with their problems? Why was he dragging her into this?

When it dawned on her, she was barely able to contain herself. She clenched both her hands into tight fists, struggling to stop her finger nails digging too deeply into the palms of her hands.

How dare he threaten my daughter. My only reason for living. My only happiness. My only joy.

Now she really understood him for the first time. Through all his dozens of drinking sessions and abuse he had never tried to involve Louise. Now he had crossed that final barrier. This was worse than all-out war. This was a warning about the safety of her only piece of true flesh and blood. He was putting her life at risk. He was daring to suggest that Louise could be in danger from him – the only other person living in that tiny house. Malcolm Thornton made it sound like he was pronouncing a death sentence on Louise. Actually, he was helping to guarantee his own.

'You fucking whore.'

Sara's drunken slob of a husband had just got a second wind. The tirade of insults that followed were far more audible than his earlier words. He had seen the look of shock and horror on her face after he made that threat to her daughter. Now he was going in for the kill with a flurry of blue obscenities that turned the atmosphere real.

Sara still sat there totally stunned by his bullying tactics. She wasn't really listening to the tirade of verbal abuse. Her mind was on one person – her darling little daughter who lay asleep just a few feet away. What if he meant it? What if he really did intend to do her harm? How could they live under the same roof with that threat hanging over? He was calling her little baby 'dead meat'. Sara was not going to risk it. She had to do something.

'Whore! Whore! Whore!'

Sara's silence seemed to inspire Malcolm Thornton to even nastier language. He was shouting at the top of his voice now. But the only words she heard were: 'Keep that daughter of yours out of my way or else she'll be dead meat.' This bastard was going to kill her daughter unless she did something. He was going to butcher her beautiful little girl. One day, when she was out he would creep up on Louise and murder her. But he would only be doing it to get at his wife. Louise would end up being the innocent victim of her mother's hatred for her husband.

Sara hated the feeling that she was responsible. It made her realise she had to act – fast!

She got up without saying a word and walked into the kitchen. The drunken lump was still continuing his stream of obscenities. He was oblivious to the fact she had left the room. He did not care. He just wanted to hurt her and Louise.

In the kitchen, she opened a drawer and found what she was looking for.

It was one of their very best steak knives. Malcolm always wanted the best. Now he was going to get it. First she had to make sure it was going to do the job properly. Sara pulled out the knife sharpener and began, almost lovingly to scrape the knife over the rough edged metal. Each time, she would gently rub her thumb across the edge to see if it was definitely sharp enough. Finally, it was ready. In the lounge, Thornton was still shouting. But Sara had heard it all before. She was not going to hear it much longer.

She looked down at him one last time. She glanced at his bloated beer-filled stomach with disdain. He had dared to threaten the life of her daughter. Now he would pay the price.

But did she really want to kill him? Did she honestly want to take another person's life? Sara Thornton did not really know the answer to that herself. She stood with the specially sharpened knife waiting. Perhaps he would grab it off her? At least he would ward her off surely?

It was possible that for one strange moment she hoped he would stop her. After all, killing is not an easy task for anyone. It takes a lot of courage, fear and hatred.

She could not wait a moment longer. She plunged the knife into his soft protruding stomach and dug the six-inch blade in as far as it would go.

Suddenly a frenzy took over. She started to stab and stab and stab. Nothing could stop her now. The killing was done. Little Louise could live safely. He wouldn't get to her. He was not going to harm her.

'I've just killed my husband. I've stuck a 6-inch carving knife in his belly.'

It was a matter-of-fact statement, with no emotion except, perhaps for a faint air of resignation.

Sara did not bother to wait until the emergency services arrived to make her confession. She told the operator after she had dialed 999. She had nothing to hide. She felt no shame. In fact she felt relief from the awful burden of living with a bullying brute who had plagued every working moment of her existence.

Still she felt as if she needed further re-assurance. She went to a cupboard and took out a camera. She wanted to record her husband's final dying moments. She wanted to have a record of the terror she had inflicted on him after years of being on the receiving end.

Sara looked at the bloody corpse of her forty-four-year-old husband through the view-finder of the camera and pressed the shutter tight.

Click. She captured his dying moments.